"Honest and raw and he[artbreaking and funny and] fracks! There's not one sentence here that takes the easy route and goes for a quick gag and an easy out. This is the hardest of things, this is writing."
— RUSSELL T. DAVIES, AWARD-WINNING WRITER AND CREATOR OF *QUEER AS FOLK* AND *DOCTOR WHO*

"A deft blend of tragedy and comedy, these striking lyric essays are essential reading."
— ROLLI, AWARD-WINNING CARTOONIST AND AUTHOR OF *PLUMSTUFF*

"Lezza's debut memoir is a riot. Lezza has turned chaos into insight, anger into testimony. *I'm Never Fine* is a tender, hysterical, sharply-rendered and often surprising portrait of love and grief from a talented new voice. Joseph Lezza is a writer to watch."
— EDGAR GOMEZ, AUTHOR OF *HIGH RISK HOMOSEXUAL*

"Lezza captures the ruthlessness of losing a loved one with such lyrical finesse. Adeptly managing to weave humor and banality into nearly every page, the reader is immersed into a world that feels so familiar. He captures what it is to love and what it is to lose that love. The result is a beautiful tribute, full of raw and honest humanity, that makes the reader feel a little less alone."
— STEPHANIE WITTELS WACHS, AUTHOR OF *EVERYTHING IS HORRIBLE AND WONDERFUL: A TRAGICOMIC MEMOIR OF GENIUS, HEROIN, LOVE AND LOSS*

"An at once gorgeous and gut-wrenching memoir about the loss of his extraordinary father. Relentlessly honest, vulnerable, and brave. His prose sparkles and swirls in time and emotions, never shying away from the cruel realities of cancer or death, but also reminding us of 'weird little joys that make waking up exciting.' I highly recommend this startling and stylish book to anyone who has lost someone they've loved so massively. With beauty, wisdom, and dark humor, he also gives us a blueprint for life, love, and loss."
— LIZ SCHEID, AUTHOR OF *THE SHAPE OF BLUE*

"In his debut memoir, Joseph Lezza weaves a bold, fearless, and highly innovative account of a deeply personal story, the kind that can only be rendered by someone who has lived inside the dark contours of a life, and never blinked once to shield himself from the impact, but rather, stared it down long enough to take note."
TIM Z. HERNANDEZ, AUTHOR OF *ALL THEY WILL CALL YOU*

"Lezza makes his grief corporeal by molding the loss of his father in sickness and in death into profound and poignant essays. We mourn alongside him while acknowledging that grief is a shapeshifter that never leaves. There is a uniqueness and levity that only Lezza can bring to the page—where humor and calamity go hand-in-hand in a seemingly effortless way. *I'm Never Fine* is a stunning—and necessary—debut."
VICTORIA BUITRON, AUTHOR OF *A BODY ACROSS TWO HEMISPHERES*

"Joseph Lezza weaves a necessary tapestry of family relationships, loss, anticipatory grief and the brief moments of joy that flash when we show up for ourselves as we show up for those who hover in the in-between of life-in-transit and death. Lezza narrates the various states of waiting and witnessing from the vantage point of a queer caretaker—these insights are vital as they are voluminous. Lezza's voice is hearty and full-throated; a voice that helps navigate the trembling waters of grief any of us have ever endured or have yet to explore."
RAQUEL GUTIÉRREZ, AUTHOR OF *BROWN NEON*

About the Author

Joseph Lezza is a writer and proud son of Italian immigrants and a decorated war veteran. He currently resides on the East Coast where he bides his time between autumns sporting a pair of white Chucks and drinking obscene amounts of coffee. Holding an MFA in creative writing from The University of Texas at El Paso, his work has been nominated for the *Best of the Net Anthology* and has seen publication in, among others, *Variant Literature, The Hopper, Occulum Journal, Unstamatic, West Trade Review,* and *Santa Fe Writers Project.* When he's not writing, he spends his time worrying about why he's not writing.

His website is *josephlezza.com* and you can find him on the socials *@lezzdoothis*.

I'M NEVER FINE

SCENES & SPASMS ON LOSS

JOSEPH LEZZA

www.vineleavespress.com

I'm Never Fine
Copyright © 2023 Joseph Lezza
All rights reserved.

Print Edition
ISBN: 978-618-5728-00-7
Published by Vine Leaves Press in Greece 2023

Losing My Religion
Words and Music by William Berry, Peter Buck, Michael Mills and Michael Stipe
Copyright (c) 1991 NIGHT GARDEN MUSIC
All Rights Administered by SONGS OF UNIVERSAL, INC.
All Rights Reserved Used by Permission
Reprinted by Permission of Hal Leonard LLC

No parts of this publication may be reproduced, stored in a retrieval system, or transmitted in any form or by any means, electronic, mechanical, photocopying, recording, or otherwise, without the prior written permission of the copyright owner.

This book is sold subject to the condition that it shall not, by way of trade or otherwise, be lent, resold, hired out, or otherwise circulated without the publisher's prior consent in any form of binding or cover other than that in which it is published and without a similar condition including this condition being imposed on the subsequent purchaser. Under no circumstances may any part of this book be photocopied for resale.

Cover design by Jessica Bell
Interior design by Amie McCracken

A catalogue record of this work is available from The National Library of Greece.

*For anyone and everyone barebacking their grief
without a compass.*

Author's Note

This book is a work of nonfiction. However, inasmuch as I have relied on observer testimonials, medical research, available records, and personal journals to assemble the most factual account possible, this is—and always will be—a representation of moments and events as I experienced them.

Our recollections, of both the remarkable and unremarkable, are recalled in as many unique iterations as there were individuals who bore witness. These are mine.

Names of the living have been changed. Except for mine. Not much point in that.

Preface

Dear Friend,

I find it dangerous to begin any piece of writing with the objective of crafting the words to deliver a particular message or impart a specific lesson. To the observer, such intentions would seem important but, in reality, are ill-informed for two reasons: firstly, it forces the writer to course-correct any time they feel the narrative shifting away from their predetermined endpoint. This is often perceived by writers as a diversion when, in reality, it's the story attempting to reveal itself. By continually reigning ourselves in, we inevitably strangle the language and wind up producing a flat and predictable story with zero stakes; all purpose, no payoff. Secondly—and I ask this with all due deference—what the hell do any of us know about what it is we have to say? In all honesty, any time I put pen to paper, I am armed with nothing more than a vague idea, a feeling that there is something to be divined if I can manage to sit myself down long enough to explore it. It's only along the way that we come to realize our true, and usually unattractive, feelings on a subject or personal experience. We're then left to confront those realizations on our own from a distance while allowing you, the reader, the same measure of distance to analyze and draw your own conclusions. Yet, despite all that I've just laid out and the apparent conviction with which I speak to it, I am going to defy my own logic, here and now, at the outset, and show you my hand. If you are to understand one thing—the most vital thing, the skeleton key to unlocking anything worthwhile from the sojourn upon which you are about to commence—let it be this: you are not special.

On first glance, I understand that these words read as harsh. I wouldn't be at all surprised if your initial response were something like, "This asshole clearly doesn't know I hold the Midwest regional record for clog dancing on Lake Minnetonka in subzero weather," or "The nerve of this guy. Just wait 'til he sees pictures from the time I constructed a scale model of Tenochtitlan made entirely out of Boo Berry and snot." Minus proper context, your reflex reactions to my assertion are perfectly valid. To be frank, it is not even my assertion. This darling little nugget was actually passed along to me by a book agent who, upon reading my manuscript, deigned to descend from the workbench where she polishes her gems of wisdom to impart, ever so eloquently, that "everyone's father dies." Imagine that. After all that time, work, and pain spent recounting what I thought was a wholly individual experience, this angel of mercy sought to unburden me of my gross misperception. I tell you, I nearly tore up the pages and built a church in her honor. Someone had to spread the good word, to all the scribblers in every Starbucks far and wide. There I would mount my soapbox and beseech my laptoped brethren huddled in corners. *Hey, you! Fledgling screenwriter! Hey, you! Budding romance novelist! What? You think you're the first person to ever hop an express to Bonetown? Wipe the latte off your face, delete that twenty-seventh revision, and do something that contributes to society. And you, there, high-school girls, chattering over the melted carcasses of your pink drinks. Don't you know everyone talks out of his or her mouth? If you want to be original, learn to babble out of your own behinds. Then you can be as remarkable as a certain book agent I know.*

But I did not do that thing. Rather, I stewed and rankled and dug in my heels for several months until it began to dawn on me just how important her words were. The more I thought about it the more it became clear that what was intended as a dismissal was, in fact, a three-word defense of my book's right to exist. So, before I go any further, let me say again: you are not special. "This must be distinctly understood, or nothing wonderful can come of the story I am going to relate." (See, even that sentence isn't special. That was lifted from chapter one of Charles Dickens' *A Christmas Carol*. But, insofar as none of us writers have an original word to say, I suppose even Charlie himself wasn't the first person to string those particular words in that particular order).

See, after spending fifteen months watching an unrelenting swarm of pancreatic cancer cells make a blue-plate special of my father (you know, that old chestnut), I was left, upon his passing, overwhelmed by a single nagging emotion: anger. Anger not so much at the act of being robbed of my father—although, to be sure, some element of selfishness surely contributed—but, rather, anger over my father having been knocked out of the game by what could only be seen as a sucker punch. At sixty-seven, my father, a man who loved the sea, a good meal, and most of all, his family, was poised to begin the second phase of his life in a house by the bay where he could enjoy the sun-sweet days for which he'd so earnestly labored. What he received instead was a sentence under that new roof with each morning more constrained than the one before by an illness hell-bent on turning his dream home into a prison. And this undoing, so pointed and meticulous in its manner and succession, made it difficult—if not impossible—to see it as anything other than a personal attack against one of the best and most decent men to tread upon this planet. To this, I argue anger is a rational reaction. When an outside force comes for one of our own, our reflex is to shift into fight mode. But, when that outside force is a higher power, a conflagration of the fates with their flames lapping at your fuse, it becomes all too easy to feel as if everyone and everything is suddenly out to get you. All this considered, it's fair to say my dander was up.

Even still, I was confident in those early days that, like anything else, the anger would run its course and eventually pass. This confidence was not informed by any historical or personal experience, but, alternatively, it was informed by the system. It was informed by the tropes, those "stages of grief" we're all somehow aware of to varying degrees irrespective of whether or not we've actively researched or read about them. To spare you the trip down the rabbit hole, here's a reminder. They number in five: denial, anger, bargaining, depression, and acceptance. That's it; your simple-step, easy-bake, trauma-to-tranquility turnover recipe with no prep and no cleanup. Neat, isn't it?

Now, you'll notice some rather crucial information is absent, the most glaringly being order and duration. However, you can write that off as an allowance for variations in the individual journey. Nevertheless, progression and subsequent resolution are advertised and promised. In my case, I either zipped past denial or missed it entirely. Nothing about it really made sense. During my father's illness, not a soul could have accused me of denying its existence. In fact, my focus on it could best be described as obsessive. Whereas, postmortem, there seemed to be nothing of value in denying his absence. Anger I had in spades, as we've established. That left bargaining, which, to be frank, never made much sense to me. Perhaps it was (is) my penchant toward terminal realism, but I never quite understood for what I was meant to bargain. Short of waking up one morning to find my father shimmying down the street to "Thriller," there was no satisfactory consolation prize, certainly none worth having to endure some other indeterminate sacrifice. I wanted my dad back, and I would accept nothing less.

My inability or unwillingness to transition to the next stage left me with no other option than to remain parked at anger. I'd hoped I might be able to bypass it and move straight on to the fourth stage, but when that never happened, I could only interpret it as ineptitude on my part, some fundamental flaw. Somehow, I'd figured out a way to fail at grief. From failure, it's not a long jump to self-hatred and a shorter one still from self-hatred to—you guessed it—more anger. Thus birthed a perpetual feedback loop. I became a walking, talking rage factory. Let me tell you something about anger. She's a monster. She's hungry.

The more you give her, the more she wants. She sneaks up on you. She starts off small with a huff and a puff when the person in the self-checkout lane appears to have never seen a computer before in their life and all you want to do is buy your damn Tide blobs. Then, before you know it, you're snapping at friends for having the gall to ask you where you want to have dinner that night. Anger took my legs, it took my lungs, it took my brain, and it left me having screaming matches with railroad crossings, a conspiracy of them all working in concert to add five minutes to my drive home. It wasn't until I put my fist through the faceplate of my bathroom light switch that I began to suspect something was amiss. The light was too harsh. Yes, subbing in a lower-watt bulb might also have fixed the problem. But, when Hulk angry, Hulk want smash. Sometimes it takes the cartoonish to illustrate our own absurdity. If I didn't confront this mounting ugliness, it would swallow me up and spit out my bones.

Therapy helped. As a longtime believer in mental healthcare, I understood the innumerable benefits that can come from seeking counsel. The unfortunate realization, though, was that the results didn't amount to much more than a patch job. I did all the work in the room. I was introspective, I sought clarity, I confessed my sins. I would leave feeling lighter, feeling as if I had a sense of direction. Trouble is, I gave in too easily to my old instincts and it wasn't long before I was once again giving Regan MacNeil a run for her money. Then I thought I could run it out, that by eating better and ramping up my exercise I could mitigate my own volatility by introducing structure and regular releases of pressure. I wound up losing so much weight that the head rush from standing up too quickly would just about send me to the floor. To add insult to near-injury, the anger remained, just packed into a smaller frame. An angry, woozy, stickman.

So, I did what readers do: I sought advice from books. Nothing from the self-help section, mind you. The prescriptive approach to grief had already done a fine enough job of making me feel broken. No, instead I hoped I might find comfort and feel less alone by sharing in the journey of someone who'd tread down a similar path, someone who might allow me some measure of hope that, no matter how long it took, there was another side to this valley. To a great extent, they did. With unflinching transparency and candor, these writers reflected their odysseys, paying just as much mind to the pitfalls as they did the progress, in ways that I could see my own journey reflected. They let me into dark corners and swept me to far-off landscapes. I was stalked by foxes on the Pacific Crest Trail with Cheryl Strayed. I watched the neighborhood fireworks all over Honolulu with Joan Didion. I ate and prayed and loved my way through Italy, India, and Indonesia with Elizabeth Gilbert. Then I saw the movies. And as much as these great women—all writers far better than me—helped me, I couldn't help but step away from their work feeling all the more alienated.

To be clear, these writers didn't intend for me to have this newfound sense of alienation. Its invention was the sole byproduct of the knee-jerk comparison of my own journey against theirs—an act that, as we all know, mugs the self-esteem and leaves it for dead in an alleyway. I mean, we're talking about individuals so wracked with grief that the only viable solution involved shedding all of their worldly possessions and embarking on messiah-esque quests for self-discovery across the Judean Desert. Sagas so epic they warranted immortalization in both print and on film. Huddled over a Yoplait in my office cantina, I found it a bit difficult to measure up, despite the mug of coffee that promised to transport me to Jamaica's Blue Mountains but only took me as far as the toilets. Somehow, in the shadow of these stories, I'd convinced myself that as long as I remained either afraid or unwilling to mortgage my whole existence to meander the map in search for meaning, I alone was responsible for my own stagnation. As an added bonus, I also managed to interpret timidity as an assessment of my loss. That, because I was not intrinsically inclined to such life-altering undertakings, it stood to reason that my trauma was unremarkable; my claim to grief was an invalid one.

Some years later, I found myself in the writing program at The University of Texas working up an essay topic around which to craft the final for my course in creative nonfiction. Writing about my life hadn't even occurred to me when I'd decided to go back to school. However, I had a clear directive, and at that point, a three-year-old elephant I'd been carrying around, so it seemed there was nothing to lose in trying to nudge off the pachyderm from my chest and onto the page. To that end, I made my peace with the vanity of it all and began to write, revisiting some of the most painful haunts of my life and stringing together what seemed to be a disparate collection of vignettes that, when fashioned in such an order, somehow made sense. Not only did there appear to be narrative unity, but the years that had elapsed between their occurrence and my reexamination had created enough distance wherein I could see the picture more clearly and more completely than I ever had. This clarity came only as the result of a decision to frame the experience against the light instead of the dark. That light raised from the shadows; things that, in the moment, I had missed, things that I'd been either too close to or too blinded by rage to notice. While I'd love to say that such brilliance facilitated a swift come-to-Jesus revelation, I cannot. It did provide for one crucial thing: it allowed me to develop a cogent counter-argument to the long-held notions that had fed my anger, and by extension, it presented a more even-tempered thought alternative where before none had existed.

The writing had forced me to do the work I couldn't seem to do outside the confines of a therapist's office. It allowed me to loosen the grip on things that had been toiling for years to drag me underwater. Through it, I found the release I'd spent so much time pounding the pavement in search of. Once I began, there was no stopping it. From then on, every exercise in fiction, poetry, or essay would be influenced by some vision or sense memory tracing back to that point in my life. When the time came around to choose a topic and genre for my manuscript, I'd amassed a body of work substantial enough that it rendered the luxury of any other pursuit unavailable. The only way I could ever hope to write myself outside of this was to first write my way into the mouth and through the guts of it.

That's what I did. Across the months, the years, the doubts, and the questions. Not because I thought I had some revolutionary idea. Not because I thought I was a prophet. Certainly not because I thought what I'd produce would warrant some big book deal and big-screen Hollywood adaptation. Let's be real, the vistas aren't that sexy and Julia Roberts would have no problem fitting into my jeans. So, really, where's the drama? No, inasmuch as it was a self-serving exercise, I did it because I had a nagging suspicion that, for each Strayed who strayed, there were hundreds if not thousands of us who took our paltry, corporate-issued minutes to mourn and then went right back to our status reports and memoranda. Thousands who return to their workspaces or work pods or work amniotic sacs and say they are fine because it is easier than telling the truth, it is easier than trying to relate that which we feel is not relatable.

How helpful it would have been, I wonder, to have shared in a journey that more closely mirrored my own. How validating to see myself reflected in the mistakes, the hopes, and the uncertainties of another bloke who, for one reason or another, remained in the maze. How freeing to know that I was not an exception, that I was not special, that there are, indeed, batches of us in here, all skirting around one another, all sniffing out the same cheese. So again, reader, let me say this: You are not special. The anger tells you that you are. The stages reinforce it. But consider this for a moment: what if the stages are bullshit? I know by saying that I've thrown a great disturbance into the force. I can feel the hordes of gurus and life coaches whittling their wall plaques into shivs and lofting their paperweight flails—all gunning for me, the heretic. Still, tally it up. What if there aren't five stages but two? Or one? What if there are twelve? Or none?

Consider that there might not be a recipe for this. I offer that anyone trying to convince you otherwise is trying to sell you something. (Not a book, though. Not like this one. This is a cool book. This book'll let you smoke then take the rap when your mom asks about the smell in the car. This book ain't no rat.). There is a very real possibility that I'm wrong in this assertion, and that I accept. But it's been my experience that you cannot just stick a toothpick in your abdomen, and if it pulls out clean, you're done grieving. It's going to take time, often longer than we thought, longer than we want, and longer, still, because our tendency to fixate on getting past something delays the realization that we must first get through it.

What's the big lesson in all of this, then? What wisdom do I have to impart? Not a lot, to be frank. As I stated at the outset, to force one all-encompassing principle upon you would do nothing more than rob you of the ability to appreciate the text in your own way, free from influence. I won't do that. Furthermore, it would be the height of egomania for me to pretend, for any duration of time, that I am an authority on any matter other than my own. Even there, it's a toss-up. And, yes, I quite agree with your initial impulse to accuse me of taking the easy way out, offering that no prophecy is just as worthless as false prophecy. To that I suggest we meet in the middle, whereabouts I can—in lieu of crystal-gazing—submit a theory. Here it is: love and anger may, very possibly, be one and the same. I surmise that love, like all good and natural things, has a shelf life, a sell-by date. Love is perishable. Just as our bodies produce it, they must expend it. In the immediate aftermath of trauma, our impulse may be to hoard it, to keep it from the world as an act of cosmic retribution. But left on the shelf, perishable things will do what they do best—perish. That love, squirreled away in the dark, will wilt and wrinkle and spoil until the process of putrefaction renders it a gangrenous anger that, if given the opportunity, will rot us from the inside out.

But, friend, hope is not lost! We can cut it out. That necrotized tissue can be removed and the underlying malignancy kept at bay by simply denying it the good tissue it needs to gnash between its tartary chomps. By this, I mean dispense with your love. Give it away, indiscriminately if you're so able. Give it freely and without expectation. Of course, there is nothing wrong with being discerning about with whom we share our light. There are, indeed, thieves of joy. However, discernment can get the better of us. To that end, I do my best to identify the places where love would be most valued—or, better yet—where it is most needed. Put into practice, I've found I'm never happier than in those moments when I'm driven purely by my desire to bring love into someone's life, to show them that they matter, especially in those instances wherein we are not obliged by the calendar or by ceremony. I wish I could say it was the easier choice. Anger is so much easier. I also wish I could say I'm a fundamentally changed person who spends his days shoving daises down gun barrels and giving the world a Coke. I'm not. The anger remains. Some days it gets the better of me. It won't have me whole, though. Because, while I shudder to think of some of rage-fueled things I've done, I've never once regretted anything done out of love. As the son of a man who supplied more "I love yous" than carbon dioxide, I know I'm never closer to being him than when I'm acting in kind. Perhaps that, really, is the cosmic retribution. By allowing those we lost to live through us, death will never really have them. Not completely. Not all the way.

Before I let you get on with it, let me just say that whether or not you stumbled upon or sought out this book because you find yourself smacked by a circumstance that has since caused an unraveling, and whether the threads from that unraveling bear a remarkable resemblance to those of my own or you have to squint really hard to find the commonality, I am not sorry. I am not sorry for what has happened to you. I don't know how or where this practice began wherein we apologize for the unfortunate turns in the lives of our brethren. An apology implies blame. I didn't kill or harm or cause your distress. If we are to believe all that comes to pass is a part of God's grand plan, then He is the architect of your predicament and your beef is with Him. If we are to believe that being made in His image allows Him to communicate His sorrow by proxy then, many pardons, but that's just all too convenient. He can do it Himself. I've grown tired of being His mouthpiece. What I will say is this: you are going to be ok. Of that, I am certain. It will take work; it may take years. You may find yourself needing to melt the face off a street sign with your hot, wet screams. But you will find the other side of this chasm.

And, to whomever this copy inevitably gets thrifted, regifted, or White Elephant'd, I do hope your table is now much sturdier. Season's Greetings!

Part One
Prognosis

Death, the Moon, & Dry-Rubbed Steak

I have seen death in the moon's many faces. Each one an absinthial blend of color and light. Each one both an absence and a presence.

I have seen death in the new moon; in a pervasive and suffocating blackness. It siphons the complexion from your world, leaving you bloodless and breathless. Arms extended and wildly splayed, you work your way through the pitch, grasping for walls, and patting the floor in search of a feeling.

The new moon rose the morning I heard my mother screaming my name. I woke in a blind fury and tumbled from my sleepy perch on the living-room couch. Hitting the floor and wriggling myself free from a tangled web of blankets, I saw Mom crouched over the hospice bed. The bed we'd rolled next to the transom window during Dad's final days so that he could still take in that marvelous view of the water. This place was his vision, the home by the sea he'd coveted his whole life.

I recalled the hot summer nights he'd spend sitting on the porch of our old house; the house that sat on your normal, everyday cul-de-sac in your normal, everyday suburb. The humid, East Coast air carried the scent of his freshly lit Romeo y Julieta as I played under the weeping cherry in our front yard and felt the rhapsodic harmonies of "Sloop John B" slip through its billowy branches. Night after night, he'd sit there staring out at the black pavement, wishing for it to melt into saltwater. A wish so fervent at times you could hear the tide lapping at the shoreline. Night after night, he'd sit until the light drained from the sky and a man dissolved into an orange circle of tobaccoey cinders.

Finally, at sixty-seven, his harbor-front palace became a reality. But the long-awaited dream home would only know nightmares. For, just as quickly as the closing papers were signed, cancer made a comfortable home out of his endocrine system. And, as I ran to his bedside that clear July morning, my hand reached for his chest as the cresting whitecaps glistened in his still-open eyes. And there, palming his ribs for signs of life, is where I found death, the new moon; nothingness where something once was.

> ***I have seen death in the crescent moon,*** *the flame that struggles and dances and gasps for air at the end of its wick. An incandescent, carbon-particled, bluish burn living just on the outskirts of darkness, demanding to be light where all other light dare not go.*

The crescent moon hung, waxing blithely as my Mustang hugged the corner of Route 35 that bent past the old Arbor Terrace Senior Home. For years, I'd made a point of avoiding eye contact with that place, having spent most of my high-school career volunteering at all manner of convalescent homes. Even now, years later, the sight of one triggered a bitter sense memory of stale, sterile sadness; a cocktail I'd never acquired a taste for. Turning my eyes away, however, I shifted my gaze and landed on a figure. As it came into focus, I saw it. Lying on the side of the road. A corpse.

It was the abandoned Steak & Ale that had closed nearly a decade ago, though I knew the last time I'd been there was long before that. There were no boards, no graffiti, and, overall, very little evidence of decay, save for the busted "e" on the plastic sign that rendered it STEAK & AL. It was as if all of the diners, waiters, and owners had collectively decided to go home one night and just never return. So, it sat there, unwanted, unnoticed, and unattended for years; a memorial to herb roasted prime rib and Hawaiian chicken.

Orange and white traffic drums hung from the chain that blocked the entrance, swaying in the breeze like a toddler swinging his legs in a vinyl booth, anxiously awaiting his roast beef and French fries. That was the fun part. The difficulty always lay in getting past the vegetables, but each time it happened in the same unavoidable way. The waitress, probably named Jackie or Karen (they were always named Jackie or Karen), would deliver Dad's root beer, Mom's water, and my Shirley Temple and leave us in a cloud of Davidoff Cool Water For Women. I'd grope my straw and get a good three or four stabs at the cherry sitting at the bottom of the glass before my parents whisked me towards the salad bar. While Dad went straight for the beets and hard-boiled eggs, I'd fall in line behind Mom and watch as a deluge of broccoli, carrots, and baby corn descended from the sky and onto my plate.

When the moment presented itself, however, I'd quickly abscond to my father's side at the dressing station. Without even looking down I could always tell he knew I was there from the way one corner of his lip would curl upwards. "Red or orange?" he would ask.

"Orange! Orange!" I'd shout to the ceiling.

"Tell me when," he'd reply as he scooped and ladled and scooped and ladled, eventually giving up when every single speck of green was hidden under a thick blanket of Russian dressing. Mom would watch in frozen horror as I'd return to the table with my platter of salad soup and wash it down with heaping gulps of sugary fizz. And, as the bubbles ticked my nose, I'd catch a smile creeping through her quizzical stare while Dad sent the ice in our glasses clinking with vigorous laughter.

I sailed past the restaurant that night as I'd done a thousand times before. But in my rearview mirror, I watched as a memory peeked over the building's hollow bones, a flicker in the void, a scrape of light through the darkness; the crescent moon.

> *I have seen death in the half moon,* a world awake and a world asleep. A war between two paramount forces set ablaze on a starless battlefield. Clashing and charging, shield to shield, churning up the dirt with their heels and never once looking around to notice that they haven't moved an inch.

"I thought there would be more lava people," said the mess of auburn hair and pale skin behind me as she fished a stick of gum out of her purse. When my best friend, Ellie, had decided to accompany me on my sojourn to a family wedding in southern Italy, I'd failed to tell her just how much walking would be involved. The ultimate city girl and lover of all things steel and automated was a fish-out-of-water amongst the ruins. A skyscraper in the desert. As one of her heels sunk into the uneven cobblestone streets of ancient Pompeii, I grabbed her elbow and broke her impending fall.

There was a positively eerie feel to the place as the September sun beat down on the first-century walls and sidewalks, baking the thousands of tourists brave enough to venture through this hot clay oven. Narrow alleyways and long courtyards revealed to us all manner of weird and wonderful relics. Empty plinths sat where statues one stood. Fossilized corpses littered the streets, arms extended, reaching for someone or something dear to them in their last moments. It was as if life had been freeze-framed and at any moment, Rod Serling would round the corner and begin to assemble a plot device.

But what would have been completely lost to me as a child now left me positively bewildered. We wandered through forests of columns with no roof, so tall you'd swear they held up the sky. We sought shelter from the buttery, thick swelter under a canopy of stone pine. I flagged down the drink vendor's pushcart and exchanged the last four euro in my pocket for two sopping wet bottles of Chinotto. As Ellie wandered off to dip her feet into a fountain walled-in by ancient graffiti, I sipped my bittersweet soft drink and rested my back against one in a long line of smoothed-out trunks.

Off in the distance loomed Vesuvius, the great destroyer, the sleeping giant. Its stoic silence betrayed a total lack of shame, surveying its damage and taunting anyone who had anything to say about it. This quiet moment of reflection, however, was to be short-lived. A young boy, too busy to notice rivers of melting gelato running down his arms, noisily crossed my path, kicking a rock and shrieking as it became airborne. His mother pulled up the rear and gave winded chase, yelling something in German that I couldn't understand. As he led her through a passage into one of the hundreds of mazes that snaked through the city, I glimpsed the world in a way I never had before. I saw a young couple sharing a slice of focaccia as they sat in the doorway to what was once someone's home. I saw a father teaching his young daughter how to spin a top on the altar of a centuries-old place of worship. I saw Ellie tearing pieces off of her panini and tossing them to the gaggle of birds that waded around her ankles. "Check me out! I'm feeding the Pom-pigeons!"

That day I marveled at how so much life could fill a place of death; how, despite being at odds, two potent and opposing agencies agreed to co-exist in a sacred place. I stood on the border of two worlds with a passport in my back pocket and watched as the half-moon mixed lilac into the blue, creeping softly over the simmering horizon.

> ***I have seen death in the full moon,*** *wholeness amidst the nothingness, the aught against the naught. A glow that sifts through the shutters, it jostles the sleeper awake, tricking the eyes and bathes the weary skeptic in belief.*

My mother still lives in that house by the sea, the house where Dad silently slipped out the back door the morning he took his last breath. People often wonder, to this day, how she can stand to reside in a home so mired in death. It began at the funeral, really. Once the requisite "Sorry for your loss(es)" and "He's in a better place(s)" had been uttered, the subject of real estate inexplicably became of paramount concern. It happened the same way each time: one of the faceless humanoids would grip my shoulder reassuringly and draw near, brow furrowed, and mutter some derivation of "Your mom's not gonna keep that house, is she?"

Absence of tact aside, I couldn't help but find it astonishing how no one seemed to realize that, at one point or another, we have all lived in a place where someone has died. It's as if we operate under the assumption that a fresh coat of paint, some treasured tchotchkes, and a couple of throw rugs can somehow absolve an objectionable past. What's more, I couldn't help but find it impossibly hilarious that anyone might have the unmitigated nerve to assume they know your story better than you do. Loss is subjective, and it's punishingly individual. In that individual loss, however, are a thousand threads that continue to tie you back to a person who's no longer there. And my mother's house is a veritable quilt.

Considering his brief residency, Dad's overflowing love for his seaside citadel waterlogged the place so profusely that the paint was on constant verge of chipping. His cigar cabinet still sits in the same corner where it's always sat, and on summer weekends, I'll stop by to pop open the door and check if there's enough water in the humidifier. But, more realistically, to catch a whiff of that familiar scent that always seemed to perfectly complement a triple spritz of Givenchy. The fig trees he so delicately transported have taken root in the backyard, blooming once a year with a flourish of fuzzy green buds. With their return, I pluck the first one I see from its branch, bite off the end, and suck out the honeysweet seeds just exactly how he taught me to. I feel him in that place more so than I've felt him anywhere else. He lives in the studs and the joists and speaks in knocks and creaks.

As for why my mother continues to live there, that's no one's business, really, and I don't ask her about it. But if I were to wager a guess, I'd say it's because she feels a comfort there, the same comfort that envelops me when I visit. More than that, though, I believe she lives there for all of the days that my father didn't get to.

I can sort of see why those on the outside might view that house as a tomb, but the fundamental misunderstanding there is that a tomb is a dark place, a place for death. That house was built for life and though, yes, death did visit, it was only for a moment. Life, however, stuck around. And each object, each remembrance, is the reflection of love and light that pushes through the darkness like a full moon in a hollow sky.

Nine. One. One.

There's a reason we say the clock has a face. There's a reason we gave it hands. It is the personage of time. Time, which is measured but not wielded. Time, which, despite our best efforts, flows only forward. Forward unbendingly. Sometimes pleasurably. Often punishingly. But always, always forward. So, humanity, in its vanity, did what it does best. We lassoed the unseen forces from the periphery—those to which we remain steadfastly subject—and assigned them a physiology. We constructed them in our own image, on our own terms. This, in part, was a flattery, there being no greater distinction than sharing that which makes us distinct. Just as unmistakable, though, are the limitations of our own architecture. Giving time limbs and appendages was to weigh it down, to drag it into the mud with the rest of us. There it could be wrestled. There it could be tied to our wrists. There we charmed it with words: appeals that it might hasten derision when it cheated. Giving the clock a face made it mortal; it gave us something to scream at. And it listened. And it ticked. And it learned. And it remembered. Because the clock has more time than we ever will. Because when we gave it form we gave it features. We provided the mechanism. We taught it how to talk back.

The first time was an aberration.

The three of us sat at the dinner table in our customary L-formation like it was any other night. Dad had his side so he could see the TV in the family room. I'd been shipped across the oak slab years earlier, when my vertical gains had begun to impede the view. (Either through peaceful acquiescence or some unseen rock-paper-scissors tournament, in the battle over my increasing longitude, Mom had drawn the short stick). Now twenty-one, I'd all but eclipsed the horizon, save for the moments when I was hunched over, inhaling my plate.

That night I seemed to be the only one eating. Though the television blazed as it always had, it was nothing more than a soundless swirl of pigments. Sentient spin art. To my left, Mom chided Dad's distracted eyes into tail-tucked obedience. "You can't keep ignoring this. I don't care what he says, it's getting worse."

My ears pricked. I chewed the same bite of food into a paste, raising and lowering my fork in pure theatre. The worry in her voice was out of place, and it sent a rash down my backside. This was the woman who'd once sliced her finger to the bone and finished cooking dinner before tending to her injury. The same woman who had to be goaded into taking me in for an x-ray after I'd fallen down the stairs and couldn't stand up. She'd thought it was a bad bruise. It was a broken foot. In fact, I'd only heard her voice thistle with such sharpened concern once before. When

Dad had the headaches. When he couldn't walk more than a block before needing to sit down. When we'd found out, soon after, that he'd been millimeters from a heart attack. "A widow-maker," the cardiologist had called it.

Here again, half a decade later, nothing had changed. Her disquieted timbre echoed like a bad dream in the open-mouthed flail towards consciousness. "I hear you wheezing. Last night it was so loud I couldn't fall asleep. I just lay there listening to it."

I heard something, too. Air escaping. Not from my father, but from myself. A collapsing balloon, I watched the world grow larger around me. From my seat, I peered over the edge of the table through adolescent eyes. Next to me, two mountains loomed, holding up the sky. Their words the distant roll of thunder.

Above the range, a flash of neon lightning. Electric blue premonition by KitchenAid.

9:11. 9:11. 9:11.

The second time strained coincidence.

It started with one doctor's visit. Then the follow-up. A few markings on the calendar, a few innocuous diagnoses. First, it was allergies. So, Dad pickled himself with saline spray and took enough antihistamine to turn the Beringer Vineyards into Sun-Maid Raisins, and we thought that would be it. Yet, that was not it. Then, they said asthma. So, he puffed up like Popeye on inhalers. But the antagonist antagonized.

Soon, it came to be that the calendar became contested grounds in a gang turf war. Slashed with the reds, blacks, blues, and greens of specialists, tests, and lab-work appointments, it closer resembled the underside of a railroad bridge. In the white spaces, I carved out little moments for schoolwork. I allowed myself to muse about post-college life and what that might look like. I mined the internet for periodicals, research to pad my senior portfolio. But the axe overhead was undeniable. Pulling it from its perch, I bring it down upon the keys, thinking a few light swings might dull the blade, might make it harder to slice through the air. I pound out a question to the oracle. It offers back "chronic bronchitis." Sounds like a bad cough. Sounds manageable. The axe feels lighter. So I place it down, close the tab. There's the clock. 9:11.

I picked up the axe.

The times after were a blitz.

Tear into the bedrock enough and a seam with eventually open. When it does, it spews. Methane, coal, sludge. A cornucopia of carcinogens to drown in, gag on, crumble under. Too far in, by then. Have to dig down to rise up.

The more I dig, the harder it becomes breathe. Digging pollutes the air, makes it unlivable. I kick sediment into the atmosphere until I choke on words like *progressive, degenerative, irreversible*. Night after night of spiraling down digital rabbit holes send me out into mornings a chattering husk. Any moments of composure swiftly sullied by a dreaded call. *Attention. The 9:00 train is running on an eleven-minute delay.* I turned away from clocks, but they still found me. *9:11.* An unsuspecting glance to the corner of my computer screen goes off like a siren. *9:11.* A text message notification begs a question. "Are you there?" *9:11.*

The departure board at Penn Station clacks like rocks against a window. The universe wanted my attention. *And the universe would not be ignored.*

Astrologers call them "master numbers." Mystics, "angel numbers." It's all the same. Energetic codes from the fates, life trying to break through. They tell us that they are not omens. They are not to be feared but, rather, interpreted against the framework of our own lives. From there, we can uncarth the deeper meaning.

> *Consider the numbers separately. Measure their individual significance.*

Nine. Compassion. Empathy. Long associated with endings.

Eleven. Instinct. Intuition. Gut feeling. Knowledge without rationality.

Consider what they mean together.

Nine-One-One. Injury. Agony. Long associated with endings.

Nine-Eleven. A violation from the inside. When we weren't looking up. The sky fell.

> *Consider what they mean to those around you.*

"Maybe it means help is on the way," said Mom.

"Maybe it means we're calling the wrong number," I whispered into my shoulder.

> *Consider...*

The time the envelope came in the mail, I wouldn't open it. Not that I couldn't have stealthily resealed it. But the paperwork wouldn't tell me anything the NEW JERSEY

I'M NEVER FINE

PULMONOLOGY ASSOCIATES lettering hadn't already. The packet was thick, like the mucus gumming up Dad's lungs. There was talk of breathing tests. Spirometry—a word I'd never asked to learn. There were long, dusty stretches of weeks until "the next available appointment." As if no one could smell the urgency. As if this wasn't someone's son, husband, father. As if he was just a warm label on a fresh manila folder.

I filled those weeks running tallies of calamitous possibilities, thinking somehow omniscience could deaden the impending jolt. I avoided faces, both human and horologic. I stopped wearing watches, blackened my radio with electrical tape, answered my phone with my eyes closed. I took later trains home from school and asked for closing shifts at the restaurant. I served food that turned my stomach while making a meal out of my cuticles. After work, I'd sit in my car long after the lot had emptied, leaving only when I was sure my parents had gone to bed.

The night before the doctor's visit, I made no sound entering the house. On socked feet, I crept across the family room, smelling of garlic and lemon butter sauce, and sat against their bedroom door. I listened. I wrapped myself in the signature vibration of my father's snoring, a sonic quilt threaded with memory. Only now the memory was tinged with wet gurgles. Every exhalation the sluggish moan of a mangled harmonica. I sat there for some time; I don't recall how long. All I recall is sending each wail off into the shadows like a passing train, my father with them. A cowering child, I gave the man to the darkness, not to save him but to save myself. From having to lose him.

Nine. Compassion. Empathy.

My father had a sinus infection.

Eleven. Knowledge without rationality.

The time it mattered came as thunder after the strike. Seconds marking the distance from a storm already gathered.

The April sun baked the road with a July heat. Too nice to be inside slinging rigatoni. A band of truants, we played sick to dip our feet in the freezing, brown ocean. The salt in the water dried the girls' hair into ringlets of crunchy seaweed, its spray crackling against my skin. It felt like home. Not the one I'd left four years ago, but the one that continued to change the sheets should I decide to come back. Same room, new fixtures. A stop along the way. But the world felt open. The spring glow said, "We'll leave the light on for you." With uncertainty feeling more hand than fist, I hung my dirty Chucks from my fingers and walked home with sand in my toes.

At the sound of the screen door, a voice from inside the house hushed itself. Around the corner, Dad angled away as I entered the kitchen, phone to his ear. He listened more than spoke, every so often breaking the silence with the reflex, two-syllable response of someone trying to process the last sentence while the speaker has already moved on to the next. "Ah-huh." "OK." "Mmhmm." "I see." The bray in his voice sanded down to the grain, so wooden I wasn't certain it was him until he turned around.

"Hey, buddy." He moved across the room with a press-on smile and picked up where he'd left off, rinsing dishes in the sink.

"Anything wrong?"

"No, no." He turns his head, not really looking at me, not really looking away.

"Who was that?"

"Oh, just the doctor. I've got to go in for some more tests."

"What for?"

"Well," he slides a clean plate onto the rack. "That spot on my pancreas got a little bigger."

And he pulls another dish from the suds. And I burst out the door to the slosh of cups and cutlery.

The world meets me closemouthed. No rustling branches, no birds, no breeze. Not that I would hear anything over the pound of *pancreas, pancreas, pancreas* that threatens to rupture my eardrums. The word is an epitaph that I carve into the blacktop, pacing up and down the driveway. I know that word. It's the word that follows "died from..." It's the word that topples titans. People with deep pockets and bottomless resources, each of them swallowed whole by a tiny splotch two inches right of the duodenum. Nothing good ever starts at the pancreas. But plenty of good things end there.

This understanding doesn't come like a slow creep. It's an ambush. There's no universe blinking out a signal through a timepiece. In fact, I don't even care to check the clock. Because I don't need to. Because if the fates cry wolf when there's nothing wrong, what does it mean when they're tight-lipped?

On my knees, on the lawn, I'm short of breath. With each stilted intake the earth amplifies. The grass radiates, phosphorescent chartreuse. The heat prickles the back of my neck. The colors blend, swirl, saturate, spin out as the picture settings of life are dialed to their highest marker.

Then the knobs break off. They don't go past ten. But I'm at eleven. *Eleven. Intuition. Gut feeling.* I'm at eleven, staring down a nine. *Nine. Long associated with endings.*

Here I am again. At the mercy of numbers. Consumed by time. Only, now I stop myself. I stop because I can't go back. I stop because I won't make the same mistake of wringing my hands about time while ignoring the time at hand. So I move, only forward now. Forward through the door. Forward through the kitchen. Forward to the easy chair where he sits and grabs the remote. And I grab the hand that grabs the remote, and I sit on the ledge of the brick hearth, and I look into the eyes that look upon me like a child who's skinned his knee.

"What's the matter, kid?"

I know I should be strong here. But I'm weak and I've fallen. I know I'll soon be the one to have to pick him up, but for now, I curl into his arms and empty my sobs down the back of his shirt. He tells me it'll be all right. And I want to trust that. But we've been here before. When we stopped looking up, but for a moment.

When silent hands snapped our necks backward. In time to watch the sky fall.

Part Two
Pathology

At the Castle Antonia

Whatisit?

In a tangle of wires and tubes, the father
springs back to life with a question.
A gurgle, as machines bubble and wheeze,
filtering blood spiked with twilight;
antiseptic cherry cola, shaken, swollen
and placed back on the shelf.
Against mercurial fluorescence, floating,
figures in robes of mineral wool;
bend forth, revealing disciples, hands
cupped to catch the mystery
of faith from half-woken lips.

Isitcansuh?

No answers. Only shushes
and a cradled face. He has fallen
for the first time. Behind a scrim,
discolored khaki on a ceiling track,
a thousand passion plays are performed

I'M NEVER FINE

at various stages. Reluctant audiences,
who overslept in Gethsemane,
sweat to catch up while, elsewhere,
on the other side of the curtain,
Pontius Pilate, lobbying for life, flips
off a microscope and washes his hands.

Wading Toward Willamette

Somewhere between Snake River Crossing and Fort Boise, my wagon wheel broke. This, in and of itself, was not a major concern, as I'd managed to wisely trade three hundred bullets for a spare from an Indian outside the general store at our most recent trail stop. We'd be moving again in a matter of seconds, that I knew, but the pace of the repairs were hampered by my notion that this setback was, perhaps, a sign. **NAN** still swelled with fever, curled up in the back, the damp rag on her forehead long dried from the heat that had beaten down on the canvas for days. That, coupled with an ox that had been visibly limping since morning, would normally have me setting up camp to rest for at least forty-eight hours. But, as the mess of black clouds that had clung to our tail began to peak over the horizon, I glanced over at our paltry supply, a mere shadow of the stockpile with which we'd left Independence at the beginning of our journey. **PA** continued to doze, unfazed by the jolt and drag of the wheel collapse. **MA** looked up from her sewing to offer a less-than-convincing smile before returning to her work, attempting to rejoin the mess of frayed threads that had once been **PA**'s socks. As the lot of them disappeared behind the close of the front flap, I was left alone.

There was no doubt that each one of us would welcome the rest, but even with bare-bones rations there was no way the food reserve could be stretched over two more days. With only sixty-five miles left to go, I knew I could get us into Boise by tomorrow morning if I kept us at a grueling pace. But with the trail ahead tricky and uneven, the slightest mistake could assure our arrival with a lame ox, a cracked axle, and a fresh corpse. So, here I was, a young man of twenty-seven, on the edge of a decision that would ensure either the survival of my family or their annihilation.

Save the drips of light spilling through the venetian blinds of the window on the far wall and the glow of my laptop screen, the room was otherwise blackened. The heat kicked off in the utility room with a rather violent shudder, sending its final wheeze rattling through the air vents before it, too, joined the silence. My eyes, however, remained unmoved, locked onto the monitor that screamed back at me in bright neon:

> `Broken wagon wheel. Would you like to try to repair it?`

The Oregon Trail (as crudely rendered in the Minnesota Educational Computing Consortium's version 1.2) splashed across my corneas in all its two-dimensional splendor, thanks to a Windows 95 emulator I'd pirated some years before. But just before my fingers could rush to the aid of my beleaguered, pixelated kin, a soft knock pulled me toward the door. On the other side stood my mother, wearing an expression of desperation not often seen outside of parole hearings.

"What are you doing in here?" she asked, speaking barely above a whisper.

"Just on the computer," I nodded toward the device breathing hot air into a pillow on the narrow bed.

"Well, could you come out here and help me?"

The look in her eyes required no explanation. Following her out, I left my 1884 family hungry, tired, and stranded on the plains of Idaho.

The midday air hung heavy with gray, punctuated by flashes of green from outside the windows as neatly groomed shrubs and ornamental trees twisted in Hurricane Sandy's gale-force *harrumphs*. The New Jersey coastline hadn't seen a storm like the one meteorologists were predicting in over a century. Not knowing what to expect, I'd driven down the day before to help my parents ride out the storm in their new home on the Barnegat Bay. They'd moved in just four months prior, after Dad's release from Columbia Presbyterian where doctors had removed a tumor, half of his pancreas, his gallbladder, sections of his stomach and small intestines and—as far as I knew—replaced it all with crushed newspaper and old wigs. The recovery thus far had been rather brutal, hampered by weekly infusions of atomic-grade chemotherapy that made it impossible for his system to heal from an already punishing operation.

With my father laid up, I'd spent the morning moving the cars to higher ground, tying down the porch furniture, and rolling the barbecue grill into the garage. Though we'd hoped the forecast was an exaggeration, doing nothing was too great a risk. So, when the power conked out for the third time and gave no inclination of an imminent return, our sullen brigade had piled into Dad's Chrysler. And, as the bay churned in the rearview mirror, we'd heaved inland toward the relative comfort and warmth of the Jubilee Junction Adult Living Community.

In the kitchen, my grandmother, waist-deep in her fridge, evaluated the inventory from which to concoct a menu for her newly arrived company. I didn't have to glance inside to know dinner would be an eclectic smorgasbord. By then, she'd all but given up driving and relied on bi-monthly visits from my aunts, who would take her grocery shopping and to one of the litany of doctors' offices she frequented. Still, even if the shelves had been recently replenished, she wasn't known for coming home with much more than some loose fruit and deli meat. We decided it'd be best to just lean into the mystery.

Mom called me over to the couch where Dad had taken up residence not long after our arrival. It being the only piece of furniture purchased after the Reagan administration, the cushion still had some bounce and thus was our best chance at maximizing his comfort. He'd already lost a good third of his original body weight (though we tended to round that figure down in front of him), so keeping warm had become a high-ranking priority, one that called for an increased effort with each passing day. My mother returned from the master bedroom with a stack of mothball-marinated blankets, and we set to work smothering his shivers, fluffing and tucking until he was nothing more than a head in the mouth of a paisley python. "Thank you, Alina," he offered, lifting his eyes to her with love, gratitude, and as of late, a growing measure of diffident apology. Her absolution came, as it always did, in cradling his face and pressing her lips to his forehead.

I sidled up next to him, hoping that he might siphon some of my heat and began my watch so that Mom might find a quiet corner and a few minutes to herself. Instead, she set to work emptying the cabinets and proceeded to wash every single piece of upturned glassware that sat on the shelves.

"There's nothing wrong with those!" Gran interjected with a slam of the refrigerator door. The woman, whose back had been turned almost completely toward the sink, had the twisting range and binocular vision of a desert owl.

"Ma, look at this!" My mother extended her hand, in possession of a juice glass with water stains that would've had Jackson Pollock consulting lawyers.

Gran snatched it from her grasp and scuttled off to hide it somewhere. She'd insist on drinking from that glass—and only that glass—for the duration of our stay just to prove her point.

Quietly seething at her inability to stop the unsolicited deep clean of her kitchen, she relocated to the mud-brown recliner in the family room, which she'd maneuvered earlier so that it was facing the couch. Settling in, she rested her chin on an upturned fist and proceeded to stare at her ailing son with wide, wet eyes that never blinked. This had become a habit of hers, ever since Dad's diagnosis, and one that she felt she had a right to. Dad had learned from earlier protestations that engaging her on the matter would only result in a prolonging of the activity. So, in an effort to skirt the impending argument, he'd simply close his eyes and will himself invisible.

In short order, he'd slip beneath consciousness with my grandmother hot on his heels, as if she could trail him even in his dreams. I did my best to stay close for a while should Dad wake up in need of anything. It didn't take long, however, for the five available channels of network television to be stretched to their absolute limits of entertainment. As the octaves of symphonic snoring deepened, I softly extracted myself and made my way to the living room. On the far side of the unlit reach, my mother stood silhouetted against the gauzy draperies, peering out at the sky, looking for any sign of the storm's waning. Meanwhile, Sandy was merely settling in, raking her fingers across the aluminum siding and thwacking the metal doorknocker like an uninvited and most unwelcome guest.

Back in the guest room, I lifted the lid of my computer to find my fictitious family of pioneers just as I'd left them: still hungry, still tired, still stranded, and desperate for instruction or intervention from a higher power. Somewhere there, between human and human representation, between design and configuration, it became increasingly difficult to separate the real from the simulation. Both scenarios were inordinately randomized. Both were seemingly subject to the rules and limitations of a game of someone else's creation. Both were preset at levels equally severe. If the musk from the bed sheets were any indication of the last time they'd been changed, both shared a certain aromatic unpleasantness. The most apparent difference for my trail-going faction was that, with the stroke of a few keys, I could bring about salvation. For one family I could right the course. I could make things better.

And with a flick of the space bar, that's exactly what I did. Into the evening, again and again, I ferried my simulated kin through the hills and pitfalls of 2D terrain toward a new life. With each reboot, my skills grew sharper and my sight grew blurrier until eventually the true task became discerning what was real and what was the game.

```
Weather: rainy
Health: fair
Food: <5 pounds
Next landmark: 57 miles
```

By night the power had returned, and thanks to the foresight of city developers who'd buried the lines, it would stay that way. Sandy continued to air out her grievances in the streets. I pounded the dirt, pulling my wagon down the ridge toward Soda Springs for what must've been the twenty-fifth time. I was quickly becoming an expert at nineteenth-century pioneer life—at least the interpretation as presented by the MECC. Not since mid-afternoon had I unintentionally stewarded a family member to their death, and thanks to my sharpshooter's eye, I'd hunted more than enough game to ensure no one's portions would be meager. The strategy was pretty simple: maintain a grueling pace; rest two whole days for every passenger who falls ill; ford every river unless it's deeper than your oxen are tall, in which case caulk the wagon and float. That was it. Grueling pace, rest times two, ford or float.

Outside my fortress of solitude, grueling took an altogether different form, one more emotional than motional. In the den, Mom straddled the arm of the couch watching to make sure my father guzzled down every sip of his protein shake. Her eyes glossed over as she deflected my grandmother's repeated objections to the fact that Dad had elected to sleep on the couch that night. Convinced that he would surely turn over in his sleep, tumble to the tile, and shatter into a million pieces, her offerings of the master bed nonetheless were met with polite but unyielding rejection.

So gathering up her powder blue nightgown, Gran marched off in a cloud of indignation, returning minutes later to line the floor with bathmats and throw pillows.

Dinner that night was about as rough-hewn as predicted and edible in only the most abstract of terms. At the center of the table sat a paper plate upon which towered a stack of bread slices, each one a different hue, shape, and level of freshness; each one clearly the individual butt-end of loaves that had once been but were no longer. Pulling a selection from the top, Mom packed its concave center with a few tomato slices and a whole bunch of hope. To my right—and to my amazement—Gran worked her way through a dish of over-nuked baked beans and lettuce leaves as if it were the most normal thing in the world. The three of us ate quietly, filling the void with percussive ice clinking and the rake of our forks.

From the communal plate, I snatched what appeared to be a semi-soft shard of Swiss cheese and clamped it between my molars. Applying an unanticipated amount of pressure, I broke through the skin with only the briefest of seconds to celebrate my victory before the force of the rebound snapped my head back against the wall. In the living room, my father turned his face downward in an attempt to bury his chortles into the blanket cocoon. Even Mom had to shove another slice of bread in her mouth to muffle the laughter. Whatever the genesis, the comedy was a welcome relief, an unlabored breath. It felt good to help, even in the most insignificant of ways. So, as I rubbed the back of my head, I proceeded to gnaw on my cheese with the subtly of a Labrador, hoping for an early checkout come breakfast.

```
Weather: cloudy
Health: fair
Food: 0 pounds
Next landmark: 4 miles
```

As a touch of blue began to seep into the gray of the morning sky, Sandy departed, leaving only a stiff breeze in her wake. Out in the street there wasn't so much as a single branch askew or a roof shingle displaced from the stretch of prefabricated, mass-produced, single-story homes that could've doubled for game pieces on a Monopoly board. It was a typical October day, a new game. The world had hit restart.

Inside, **PA** waited on the couch, watching **MA** empty concerned whispers into her phone as she slingshot back and forth across the room. Next to him sat a neat pile of sheets and duvets that he'd clearly folded out of great optimism the moment he'd awakened. That optimism would be tempered by word from their neighbors that the houses on their block remained without power. And with no power, there was no heat. And with no heat, there was no going home.

The three of us stood in a vacuum for an indeterminate amount of time, perhaps hoping that our concentrated effort might will a solution out of the air. Revelation by osmosis is impractical. The cold hard facts pointed toward an indefinite extension of our stay, tossing my mother and me right into survival mode. And as the familiar smack of house slippers echoed down the hall and sent our ears to throbbing, we hugged **PA**, vaulted into our coats, and leapt for the car.

I'M NEVER FINE

When on the Oregon Trail, it's sometimes necessary to leave your kin to fend for themselves in order to serve the greater good. When provisions wane, the able-bodied break off from the path and use their wits to track and hunt game: whatever it takes to keep their clan in the bacon. In that moment, driving down Highway 9, my mother and I were similarly tasked. There being no discernible greater good than laying our hands on sustenance that would see us through for at least the next few days, we sailed past empty strip malls and through desolate intersections in search of perishables that had yet to pass their sell-by dates. Radio reports squawked about power restoration in patches of town that included stores, some of which had already re-opened their doors for business. Without much knowledge of the landscape, our North Star became the traffic signals, lifeless and colorless and about as useful as charms on the arms from which they swung. That is, until a clap of bright green announced that we'd stumbled our way onto a section of the grid with some juice.

Under the emerald beacon, our wagon deposited us into a Shop Rite parking lot whose already limited capacity suggested we were far from the only settlers in dire straits. Managing to squeeze into a narrow corner spot, we made our way toward the entrance, zigzagging through carts that flung themselves erratically like loosened cattle. Their drivers, too far out of earshot, craned their necks as they wrenched open their trunks, sharing clandestine reports with passersby who would then break into a sprint. Sure enough, inside, a melee was in full swing. Bleary-eyed staff fielded queries and grew extra sets of arms, doling out guidance to the hungry, the crazed, and the sweat panted. Down each aisle, shoppers plucked from half-empty shelves, not even looking at what it was they'd just thrown in their baskets. Apparently, word was the storm had stalled all incoming supply trucks and the stores had already taken a major hit from doomsday preppers in the days leading up to its landfall. With the next shipment not scheduled to arrive until midnight at best, Mom and I shared a look that said, "To hell with the carts," and peeled off in opposite directions.

When on a hunting sojourn away from your encampment, rules still apply. Though you may be flush with ammunition, it's important not to be overzealous, as no matter how many kills one may amass, none may carry more than one hundred pounds of meat back to their wagon. As such, pragmatism must always remain a guiding principle. Sidestepping screaming toddlers and narrowly avoiding a concussion from a wayward swinging door in the freezer section, I traversed the aisles, stacking up my kills. Over one shoulder I flung an economy-sized bag of Colossal Crunch, over the other a pack of frozen, boneless honey-barbecue wings, steaming like a fresh carcass. Under each armpit sloshed a gallon jug of Diet Peach Snapple. The more I picked up, the more my run slowed to a waddle, leaving myself more and more vulnerable to hazards that sprung like weeds.

```
A motorized shopping cart has
       blocked the aisle.
         Lose 5 minutes.
```

However, now and again detours can drop you exactly where you didn't know you needed to be.

```
    MOM has located an
       abandoned cart.
```

I'M NEVER FINE

After dumping my haul and taking another frantic pass, snatching up some chips and salsa in the process, we piled our spoils into the wagon and sped home to rescue **PA** from the elements to which we'd left him exposed.

Triple-bagging each hand, I elbowed open the front door to learn we'd arrived not a moment too soon. "Ma, stop staring at me!" my father's frustration rattled the tchotchkes and sent the clocks in the hall chiming out the hour. We filed into the kitchen, the *shish* of the shopping bags on the counter proving to be the exact diversion necessary to defuse a shouting match he'd never win. Immediately, my grandmother's ears pricked up and sent her shuffling from her perch in the living room. She proceeded to fuss at the two of us, bemoaning our need to go shopping and taking the tacit rejection of her cuisine as a personal affront. Mom stocked the fridge as I emptied the contents of the bags, locking eyes with my father's glare. The crease of his brow accused me all the way from the other room. *How could you leave me here alone?* But as we stepped into the line of fire, absorbing the shock of my grandmother's deflected dissatisfaction, I caught relief creeping out of the corners of his eyes.

```
Weather: cool
Health: poor
Food: 25 pounds
Next landmark: 162 miles
```

Day three played out much in the same way as the previous two, with dreamy pupils twisted tight in the sober light of morning.

Your house remains without power. Lose a day.

MA and I worked to keep **PA** comfortable, fed, and ungawked. We drew from our supplies and filled ourselves at the table while **NAN** staged a silent protest. Refusing to acknowledge our invitation to share in the bounty, she pulled a spoon from the utensil drawer and spent the next half hour excising the remnants of white flesh from an otherwise rotten pear.

Empty seconds turned to hours that, by and by, we managed to fill. Dad sat with his arm around Mom, her head resting on his shoulder until the absurdity of court show after court show inevitably resolved unconsciousness. At select intervals, we woke him up and pumped calories into him—sugary drinks or soft-boiled eggs. Anything that easily slid down the gullet. I changed his pillows. Mom played solitaire in the kitchen. I filled myself on iced tea and shuffled my two-box sets of *The Office* through my disc drive until they were lightly toasted. My grandmother found hidden vantage points from which to stare at her son. We took turns acting as his human shield.

That's what we learned cancer to be: a lot of waiting. Players in a game, we fell into a preordained set of circumstances and bought into the illusion of control. Biding our time until the next prompt flashed on the screen and called for a response, we filled the moments between scans and infusions and specialists and therapists. A thousand little choices between the big ones to convince us the game could be outsmarted.

It should be noted that the little choices are not arbitrary and, at the very minimum, serve to distract from the situational severity. Upon reaching the Big Blue River Crossing the game will ask "Do you want to look around?" While it offers nothing more than a poorly animated landscape against a tonal melody, the vista obscures the fact that the last river washed away eight sets of clothes and two passengers show symptoms of typhoid. So it was not hard to give into the pure entertainment offered by my grandmother as she spent the afternoon straw polling the three of us on what we wanted for dinner. The choices were simple enough: spaghetti or bowtie pasta, yet the absence of an opinion allowed what should have been a snap decision to derail the entire evening. One by one, she'd ask us the same question, and one by one, we'd offer back some deferential iteration of "Doesn't matter, Gran. Whichever you like." But the computer is not programmed to understand indifference. Until the question is answered, game play cannot proceed. Which is why, when upon the seventeenth cycle I chose to make the executive decision, we learned a lesson in what can happen when time and energy are squandered on the senseless.

```
    GRAN doesn't have enough
  bowtie pasta. Lose your mind.

            Weather: warm
            Health: fair
          Food: 10 pounds
      Next landmark: 17 miles
```

Like a canary sunrise over Chimney Rock, day four smothered us with light. Whether it was my laptop overheating at the foot of the bed or the news that power had been restored to my parents' block, an unseasonable warmth railed against the November chill. With one hand I shoveled gobs of cereal into my mouth, stuffing the still-open bag into my backpack along with the rest of my belongings. In the hallway the front door stood open, veiled by the exhaust from the car idling at the foot of the driveway. I left the surplus of the foodstuffs to our host, and with kernels of Malt-O-Meal spinning into my dust, joined in the goodbyes and supplemental waves as **MA** tried not to leave tire marks on the street.

Another hill conquered in the series of hills that sit between Independence, Missouri, and Oregon's Willamette Valley. Another bend in the trail that we angle into because the game was never about how quick to the finish line but, rather, how many cross it. So we fixed the wagon wheels and adjusted the rations and bartered for clothes and rested when needed and did whatever it took to get us to the next depot, all the while believing that we were catching up, catching on. Because we failed to realize that the program already knew everything it was going to throw in our way long before we hit START.

Pulling off the parkway, the town looked more or less untouched, save for some off-kilter mailboxes and the occasional displaced pool tarp. It wasn't until the tear of rubber through standing water that things began to seem amiss. With each block passed, splash became splatter became snarl until squelched into silence against the underside of the car. As we slowed to a stop, tiny waves lurched forward from the grill, continuing on without us until the surface was still as glass once again. From where we sat it was impossible to tell the depth, and not wanting to choke the engine, my mother turned to park down a dry street just a couple of blocks away. Walking through the yards of nearby homes, the three of us assessed, not speaking, not even looking at one another. We mashed our dread into the mud and grass under our shoes.

Across the pebbles of our neighbor's driveway, the footsteps ceased. Before I lifted my head, I knew what I was going to see, but I wasn't prepared for the order in which I would see it. First the roof, then the second-floor windows, then two-thirds of the front door. . .then two-thirds of the front door, then the second-floor windows, and then the roof. The house was sinking, ankle-deep in a reflecting pool with nothing to do but to watch itself slip beneath the tide. From the corner of my eye, my father wavered, steadying himself against a wooden piling before nearly collapsing down upon it. Here it was, the moment I was supposed to help. That was the prompt awaiting my response. But I couldn't ford this river. I couldn't float us across it. There, with no task left to distract me, I looked at the crouched figure of my **PA** and saw not the man who started the game, but the two-thirds that remained. For the first time, I wondered if he'd even see Oregon at all.

Food Fight

Recalling the order is the easy part. "Two hot dogs. One with chili, one with mustard and sautéed onions. Cream soda. Barq's if you got it." I present it to the Dewey Dogs counter clerk with no less assurance than if I were providing my home address. It's written into my code, a learned sequence programmed years ago. From countless stops at unmarked white trucks sporting a blue-and-yellow umbrella. At the sight of one, my father would cut across three lanes of traffic and shave some serious tread off his tires as he pulled onto a shoulder stop, one likely abutting a set of railroad tracks. The location may have changed, but the order never did. I'd toddle up next to him and listen as he barked his request with zeal through a window that reeked of pork water. When it came to food, Dad was never ambiguous. From a high-end steakhouse to a service-station mini-mart, he knew what he wanted, how he wanted it, and what he wanted it with. The real genius of this exactitude—at bit persnickety, at first listen—only revealed itself after sampling. With a chomp and a swig, my uninformed palate would come to learn how the spices of the chili enhanced the umami of the meat while the subsequent sweetness of the cream soda cut the saltiness of both, finishing off the experience with a most satisfying bite. From that point, there was no going back. An aesthete in training, I took every opportunity to develop inarguable taste, ordering from the cafeteria at my father's office like an even tinier Napoleon. "One poppy-seed bagel, toasted on both sides. Half butter, half margarine. And a Yoo-hoo. Chilled, if you got it."

Exchanging my cash for a warm paper carton, I'm halfway home before I realize the misstep I've made: the soda. The cream soda. The cream soda Dad can't have. The cream soda Dad specifically asked for despite carbonated beverages filling the topmost bracket of his post-Whipple "no-no" list.

The Whipple, or Kausch-Whipple, (also known as a pancreaticoduodenectomy) is an invasive surgical procedure most often performed to remove cancerous tumors from the head of the pancreas. The procedure dramatically reorganizes the digestive system, cutting away parts of the pancreas, bile duct, small intestine, as well as part of the stomach. Remaining organs are then reconnected, after which the system must learn to adapt to its new setup, frequently resulting in varying degrees of digestive discomfort.[1]

Caught between the compulsion to fulfill his ever-rarifying hankerings and not wanting to send his swollen, healing guts into turmoil, every traffic stop becomes an opportunity. I snatch the bottle from its bed of crinkled paper, and to the horror of any drivers in view, shake it violently beneath the steering wheel. The bubbles pull to the surface, pressing their way up the bottleneck towards the cap. I crack the seal, twisting just enough to release the gas but not enough to wind up with a lapful of soft drink. I repeat this process as many times as can be across the two minutes it takes to reach the house, each time producing a shorter and shorter crown of fizz until, on the last shake, only one or two straggling bubbles meet their end at the surface.

With each second the hot dogs become increasingly cool and decreasingly viable. Accepting that the beverage has been thoroughly flattened, I carry it in to my waiting patron. The smile that greets my armload of fixin's immediately douses any worries that his desire may have abated in the time it took to meet it. I lay out the spread as pleasingly as I can muster, allowing him to extract the frank he finds most appealing before following in kind. His movements are delicate, almost timid, as if one wrong move could scare away his appetite. I mirror him without knowing it, believing I might exert some telekinetic power over the proceedings. Whatever the foolish method responsible, he takes a bite. It's not quite the rabid munch he's known for, but its existence at all nourishes me more than the meat mashed between my molars. I know that as long as there are hot dogs in the world, we're going to be okay.

Some studies indicate nearly 68% of Whipple patients develop new gastroenterological symptoms, including acid reflux, indigestion, and diabetes-specific conditions due to decreased pancreatic enzyme and biliary excretions. These symptoms range in severity and persist over time, affecting a significant impact on overall quality of life.² Long-lasting changes in taste perception are also believed to be attributed to the procedure, granting further credence to theories of endocrine involvement in the gustatory system (taste stimuli).³

Somewhere during those first months of recovery, the doctors decide to reevaluate the treatment strategy. Dad's handled the surgery well, and with his system largely bouncing back, the prevailing endorsement is to shift toward guerilla warfare. "This is a nasty fight," says the oncologist, with practiced restraint, "against a foe with an eight-out-of-ten rate of recurrence." Initially scheduled for a targeted form of therapy meant to focus on disabling cancer-specific mutations, Dad's overall heft and vigor position him as a candidate for a more aggressive regimen of chemotherapy. "Folfirinox," he proceeds, meeting each one of our gazes to ensure there is no mincing of words. "It's a particularly potent cocktail. We often refer to it as the 'atomic bomb' of chemo." His words are stark but not altogether unfeeling, the gristle shorn over years of sending countless mothers' sons into hot conflict.

FOLFIRINOX is a combination of five chemotherapy agents: Fluorouacil (5-FU), Leucovorin, Camptothecin-11 (CPT-11), Oxaliplatin, & Gemcitabine. Used primarily for the treatment of metastatic or locally advanced pancreatic cancer, the drugs are administered intravenously every two weeks. Side effects include, but are not limited to:

increased risk of infection (due to drop in white blood cells), tired/breathlessness (due to drop in red blood cells), bruising (due to drop in platelets), sick feeling, diarrhea (severe in over 11%), hair loss, sore mouth, liver changes, watery eyes, sore/peeling hands and feet, brown skin around injection site, numbness in fingers/toes, brittle/chipped nails, sensitivity to sunlight, loss of appetite, heart problems, blood clots & difficulty swallowing.[4]

Whether it's the former soldier in him or the incendiary nature of the language being fired his way, Dad agrees without question. "Let's do it." Dr. Caplan clicks his pen and stoops forward, offering his hand in a manner almost Pattonesque. "I wanna hit you with everything I've got. You're a big guy. You can take it." I can't be sure, but I swear the wall behind him dissolves into an American flag, rippling in the wind.

Dad handles the first few rounds with spirit. He's a little tired, Mom shares, but it hasn't made him sick. He fills his time touching up paint around the house, on conference calls with the stockbroker, paying bills on the computer; anything to feel useful. Aside from waning portion sizes at mealtime, he's shouldering. She drives him to and from his infusions on strict instructions not to let him behind the wheel for at least twenty-four hours afterwards. It's not illegal, but with the potential impairment of vision and motor skills, the prospect is enough to have Geico sending claims adjusters into witness protection.

On one of those early days, I dip into personal leave and tag Mom out of the relay so that she might return to work with some semblance of heartsease. It's a gratifying opportunity, not only to play chauffeur but also in the incidental nostalgia of playing hooky with Dad, even if it is just for a doctor appointment. Midmorning, we sail up an empty parkway, bereft of the suckers currently goopifying at their desks. The CD changer shuffles among a half dozen mixes I've burned for him over the years. Over a hushed "Dirty Diana," he asks me about work, about friends, about my coming twenty-sixth birthday. There's no written rule, but from the way he avoids the subject, cancer chat is banned from the cavity of his Chrysler 300, the 2.2-ton tank in vanilla clearcoat. Not a handful of years ago, after wrenching his dream ride from the belly of Bucks County, PA, he'd hung his double disco balls from the rearview in a flagrant nose-thumbing to practicality. Now, as the ornaments spin to deflect a new, intrusive world, he asks that I not accompany him inside the treatment center. "It'll be hours," he says. "Go to the mall." Like I'm still a teenager.

It doesn't take much coercion on his part, largely because I'm just as anxious as he is to separate that world from ours. Instead, I drive for a bit. I walk the length of the Monmouth Mall twice and twice again, picking up everything, buying nothing. I kill time at The Bath and Body Shoppe, sniffing candle after candle until I reach the point where the world will never not smell of dark walnut and tonka bean. Eventually he buzzes, and I pull up to find him waiting right where I'd left him. He clambers in and looks at me like he'd just snuck out of detention. "Wanna go get White Castle?" I do not. But the fact that he wants it—wants anything—makes it the most delicious idea I've ever heard.

The Castle Combos passed through the driver's window are an ambitious order, soon filling the car with a cloud of beef that's enough to bring the leather upholstery to tears. I tear into some crinkle-cut fries while Dad cheats a few sips of my Diet Coke as if it's contraband. He extracts the first slider from its sleeve and wastes no time in devouring half of it in one bite. His chewing is more methodical, more choreographed, but he gets it down and goes after the remaining half with a smidge less gusto. Any flavor from the tissue paper patty and its bed of onions and pickle seems lost on a sandwich that is ninety percent bun. On the second bite, he's taking smaller bites, swigging caramel cola between each in order to douse the bread and defibrillate his taste buds. Through his silence it becomes clear that old tricks fail to produce the desired effect. Something is not sitting right on his tongue and his slowing breaths betray a swift bankruptcy of excitement. He sighs, regarding the burger as if it has let him down. By the time he ventures a third, flecks of onions flesh fly out the passenger window in a last-ditch attempt to make the thing more edible. But after a dubious nibble, he resigns the burger back to its brethren. The rest of his lunch cools on the dash.

In addition to an increase in taste sensitivity across all domains, 54% of patients reported an unspecified change in smell, most notably that of fatty, sweet and meaty food.[5] Often foods once previously enjoyed become difficult to eat or digest.[6]

One of the quicker discomforts to bear in a chemo-soaked world is the growing need to infantilize the patient. At first, it's cute, treating them to their favorite meals. But cuteness pimples and pocks into a much more unflattering yet vital part of the process. Soon the game becomes less about "what does he like?" and more about "what won't make him dry heave?" Eventually, when the list of things he can stomach can fit on my palm with room left for an epilogue, everything becomes much more elastic. The rules stay the same, but their letters can be rearranged.

"Is this really *one* egg?" He crouches down to inspect the mound of scrambled farm-fresh innards that nearly tumbles off the edge of the plate.

"Yes, one egg," Mom stares, lips pursed. "A big egg." She breaks for the sink and begins to rinse dishes that she's already rinsed while Dad forks a yellow glob into his mouth, still half-convinced he's been hoodwinked. He's not entirely wrong. Neither is she. Technically, it is one egg. It just happens to be a jumbo-sized egg with two yolks, locally sourced from one of the scads of organic ranchers within arm's reach. It's not a cheat, we convince ourselves; the workaround being that the three of us stand on the same side of the cause. Like folding spinach into brownie batter or hiding broccoli in a grilled cheese, parents engage in subtle subterfuge for the sake of their child's wellbeing. Our case is not dissimilar. Only this child is wise to our tricks, mainly because he invented most of them.

With no other option, the two of us are left toiling to maintain a constant lead. Each time he begins to sniff out a hidden ingredient, we've already moved it five other places. It's a forced resourcefulness, developing this skill set I never knew I would need. On the one hand, most of the standard nutritional guidelines are out the window—and with the doctor's blessing, no less. A nutrient-rich diet is critical, but we're dealing with a body at once healing from trauma, fighting active disease, and regenerating from its bimonthly poisonings. "Get calories in him any way you can," we're told. So, no one says boo when he uses half a bottle of ketchup to make his eggs go down easier. No one stops him from snacking on the black licorice and jellies in the cupboard. Even if it means keeping an insulin pen perpetually cocked, should he only find satiation at the bottom of a Chuckles wrapper, we'll happily make him target practice.

I learn to smuggle organic unflavored protein powder like it's cocaine. It hides well, especially in meals with a distinct flavor profile, things like cream of mushroom soup or chocolate pudding. It does not mix well with eggs. However, the mixture does develop a paste-like consistency that would prove handy to bricklayers. On occasion, when Dad's not looking, I'll even goose his Ensure with a spoonful. Of course, a little ingratiation comes in handy there. No one thrills at a freshly popped bottle of liquid chalk, no matter how large "Café Mocha" is printed on the label. But offer it in a chilled mug from the freezer, and it goes down a little easier. Not to mention, the mug holds a bottle and a half.

Dinnertime gives the phrase "negotiating table" new meaning. Night after night, Dad sidles up to a plate that Mom pretends she didn't overfill. He takes a few initial bites and plays foosball with the rest, hoping that movement might be confused for actual eating. We employ tactics from both corners, all in anticipation of the inevitable appeal. "Can we make a deal?" Dad mewls, peeping upwards over a scrunched nose. Mom saw this coming, hence the heaping portions. The two of them go back and forth. They haggle over bite sizes and protein vs. veggie ratios, engaging in all manner of civil manipulation. Dad lowballs, Mom flirts. In the end, he's excused to the couch after washing down something just shy of a normal-sized meal. And it's fine if it's a little bit less than desired. Because he's trying and because we made up for it a dozen different ways throughout the day. Tomorrow there will be a dozen more.

> *It is thought that taste change is a result of damage to the cells in the oral cavity, especially those sensitive to chemotherapy drugs. One such drug commonly associated with these taste changes is fluorouracil (5-FU).*[7]

In all of history, no movement hasn't seen at least one disciple fall victim to a lapse in resolve, however fleeting. The noblest of those that lived to make the textbooks held fast to a single ruling principle: leave no man behind. The faltering don't fall without the strongest to provide a boost. Sometimes quite literally. "Time for your Boost," I hand Dad the frosty goblet—his third or fourth for the day—which he greets as one might greet a sloppy kiss from their mustached aunt. "It's butter pecan!" My excitement fails to sell him on the idea, partly due to everything tasting like metal and partly due to his diet growing ever more liquid-based. When the drugs turned his tongue to sandpaper, even the most undercooked proteins may as well have been shoe leather. With breakfast now comprising nearly the entirety of his solid intake, we make up for the lost nutrition with new, higher-calorie shakes on a new, higher-frequency schedule.

"I'll drink it later." He places the mug on the coffee table and angles himself entirely away from it. The shakes have been a subject of contention for weeks, but with some light haranguing, we get him to empty the glass. The dicey part is learning just how far he can be nudged, mainly because we understand that this has evolved past childish obstinacy. A major defect that comes with subsisting largely on fluids is that they don't magically solidify between input and output. What enters flowing exits quite the same way. At lightning speed. As a result, Dad's trips to the bathroom grow not only in rate of occurrence but also in duration of stay. When he emerges, what little color he had before going into the bathroom has gone the way of his last Mixed Berry nightmare. He's shorter of breath every time, huffing and bracing himself against counters and barstools on his trudge back to the couch. And, when he finally arrives, what is there to greet him? Another frozen, foamy surprise. That which is spent must be replenished, even when the problem is the cure.

> *<u>Fluorouracil (5-FU)</u> is classified as an "antimetabolite," attacking cells at very specific phases in the cycle in order to interfere with DNA/RNA synthesis. When cells incorporate these substances, they are unable to divide. Side effects (in greater than 30%) include: diarrhea, nausea, poor appetite, taste changes, watery eyes, vein discoloration, low blood counts.[8]*

Leucovorin is a reduced folic acid used in conjunction with chemotherapy drugs to augment their effectiveness. The drug can enhance the binding of 5-FU to an enzyme within the cancer cells, extending its life, and subsequently, its anti-cancer effect. When given in conjunction with Fluorouracil, the side effects of 5-FU may be more severe.[9]

"He just goes and goes. Nothing's helping." Mom clasps her hands, praying for an answer from across the room. Receiving her prayers is no idol, but a lithe, bespectacled man in blue scrubs who taps back in response, summoning all the emotion of a court stenographer. He turns her pleas into bullet points, shooting back a reply without ever looking up from his keyboard. "I have him on every antidiuretic known to man." With a little more interest he might almost sound disinterested.

To be fair, Dad doesn't contribute to the conversation. He sits between us, aloft, alternating between staring at the wall and down at his shoes. Were it not for the crumple of exam table paper under his scantiness, one might not even know he's there. But that's not his job, to draw the notice of some blasé gastroenterologist. There's only one person in this room on the clock and he's more preoccupied with his workstation on wheels than his actual work. *Look up!* I want to scream. *Look at him! Half the man is gone. You might realize that if you'd once bother to meet his goddamn eye.*

If he offers something constructive after that, I don't hear it. I break him down into a string of clicks and tones. That's my silent retribution, I suppose, to render the man no less a nuisance than we are to him.

> <u>Camptothecin-11 (CPT-11)</u> *is classified as an "plant alkyloid" and "topoisomerase 1 inhibitor." Attacking during various stages of division, topoisomerase inhibitors interfere with the action of topoisomerase enzymes, which control the manipulation of the structure of DNA necessary for replication. Side effects (in greater than 30%) include: diarrhea (both early and late forms), nausea, vomiting, weakness, low blood counts, hair loss, fever, weight loss, poor appetite. Less commonly: shortness of breath, cough, headache, dehydration, insomnia, chills, skin rash, flatulence, mouth sores, flushing, heartburn, swollen feet/ankles.*[10]

To some extent, it's irrational to expect an outsider to care or to appreciate the magnitude of the situation. That irrationality comes in handy when excusing how we distribute our antipathies. If nothing else, it is just another activity to bind us. As long as there remains a consensus. All of that changes when I come down the stairs and catch my father slumped over the sink. At the sound of my footsteps he jolts, but not quick enough, retracting his arm at the end of which hangs an upturned mug emptying its last few driblets of froth down the drain.

"Don't tell Mom." He's sheepish, half-smirking, like he's gotten away with something. He leaves the glass in the sink and heads back to his easy chair, leaving me to inspect the sink where a ring of creamy residue confirms what I already know. And I'm not sure what's worse—the fact that he's been deliberately trashing vital nutrition or that he thinks my discovery can be twisted into some fun little father-son secret. A game. I actually think about it, for much longer than I should. What amounts to no more than a matter of minutes can feel like forever when the choices are either treason or assisted suicide. But I damn the instinct to heed the father. I climb the stairs and disclose my findings. Mom leaps, descends, and pretends to notice the glass on her own. He doesn't buy it. "He told you, didn't he?" They go at it for a while.

For the next few days, I get nothing from him but dirty looks. He expects an apology. Somehow, he's confused any action against his starvation as one of a traitor. Somewhere along the way, he started to see us as enemies. Nonetheless, I'd sooner inject protein shake into his eyeballs than participate in his self-destruction. He expects an apology. He's got a long wait ahead of him.

> <u>Oxaliplatin</u> *is classified as an "alkylating agent." Given in combination with 5-FU and Leucovorin, it is cell-cycle non-specific, working to stop cell division during the resting phase. Side effects include: difficulty swallowing, short of breath, jaw spasm, abnormal tongue sensation, chest pressure (when exposed to cold), peripheral neuropathy, nausea, diarrhea, low blood counts, fatigue, loss of appetite, fever, headache, cough, generalized pain.* [11]

Longing as we all do for some interlude wherein we might return to our corners, the lack of a bell's pardon means the gloves never come off. Unable to stop the treatment, to stop the side effects, to stop feeding him leaves the three of us with one arm protecting our faces and the other swinging wildly at the air. The higher the toxicity of his blood, the more tainted my father's attitude toward us becomes. Before long, every meal is a brawl. It begins with a groan, followed by a refusal that swiftly devolves into shouting. At the height of the melee, I slip out of the house to the end of the block where I wade knee-deep into the bay and throw my fists against the tide, again and again and again. The desire to be virtuous would have me ascribing my frustrations to his disease or to some somatic sharing of his pain, and that may be partly the case. But, right now, more than anything else, the anger is pointed directly at him, at his willful inability to see reason. To see how simple it all is, how his options are either eat and live or starve and die. In the face of that realization, however unpleasant, even the most obtuse among us would shut up and swallow our damn food.

"You're not gonna win!" At the bottom of the entryway, I return to sounds of the scuffle, still in process. A dining room chair slides against the floor above my head as my father shushes his way back towards the TV room, the floor barely registering his footfalls anymore.

"Me, win?" My mother's tone reveals our shared incredulity. "Don't you understand? Every bite you take is a win for you, not for me. You think I want to do this?" On some level, I know he knows this, that we're not his adversaries. The immediate and omnipresent threat of voiding himself to death does well to keep this reasoning buried. On the very bad days, when he's too exhausted to argue, he'll return to the bargaining table, promising to eat extra cookies with his nightly glass of milk if he can skip dinner. That worked for a while until a battalion of ants led us right to the broken bits of wafer he'd shoved under the couch. After that, the dukes went back up.

At the first impasse, I make my way upstairs to find the table cleared. Mom lays out five Oreos on a plate and sets to pouring a heaping glass of milk. From the other room, Dad angles his head to catch my reemergence. "Where'd you go?" he asks with a tinge of offense.

"For a walk," I respond. Peeling off a strip of seaweed from one of my still-wet legs, I toss it in the trash and regard the dish of chocolate discs, wondering what kind of night lies ahead of us.

"Don't be so dramatic," he answers and turns back to flipping the channels.

<u>Gemcitabine</u> *is an anti-cancer ("antineoplastic" or "cytotoxic") chemotherapy drug. It is also classified as an antimetabolite and functions similarly to 5-FU, damaging the RNA or DNA that instructs cancer cells on how to copy themselves through the division process. Side effects (in greater than 30%) include: Flu-like symptoms, fever, fatigue, vomiting, nausea (mild), poor appetite, skin rash, low blood counts, temporary increases in liver enzymes, blood or protein in urine. Less commonly: diarrhea, weakness, hair loss, mouth sores, difficulty sleeping, shortness of breath.* [12]

Not long after he emerges from his latest infusion stumbling like a drunk, Dad returns for a reckoning with the medical team. "Your body's just too weak," says Dr. Caplan, steadying a clipboard over his chest so as to obscure the giant hole in his defense. "We'll pick things up again once your levels are back where they should be." A mild protest ensues, largely superficial. Dad laments the idea of suspending his treatment but concedes without much arm-twisting. Though no one will admit it, beneath the confusion is a pinch of baked-in relief. As a patient, my father would sooner burn his castle to the ground than abdicate to his disease. As a caregiver, counseling him to ease up would be misinterpreted as an absence of belief. The simplest blessing, it turns out, arrives not as a choice but as a directive.

The "chemo vacation" doesn't abet some abrupt dissipation of Dad's symptoms nor does it inspire any easing of procedure around the house. There are still pills to take, mixtures to gag upon, and the occasional dustup, albeit ones more restrained in tone and nature. His body has been pummeled too vigorously for too long to snap back the way we all hope it will. But the possibility is enough to cling to. Because if we're to believe anything that can happen will happen, then it's not unthinkable for a little magic to be juiced from the ozone.

As with most atmospheric anomalies, on a late-April day, several intractable elements eventually arrange themselves in a manner that subverts the forecast. Dad wakes, rosy; he's rousted at the prospect of escaping the confines of the living room, even if it only means tagging along for an afternoon's worth of supply runs at the town commons. At

Costco, he ditches his cane for a shopping cart and weaves through mile-high aisles, indistinguishable from every other warehouse pillager aside from the whoops that emit upon completing each objective. Not since *Hatchet* has a man been so excited to lay hands on canned belly tuna. In the Christmas Tree Shoppes, as he tests the "lounge factor" of a six-piece rattan patio set, what's remarkable is not his choice in style but his choice to still be around come summer. So indefatigably jazzed is he, so lusty for life, our suggestion of having dinner out that evening is met with a slaphappy "Sounds good!"

Outside the Bonefish, we await our seating on another patio set, one whose mildewy aroma suggests it was only recently plucked from winter storage. Early spring has settled on the Northeast with cotton winds that sheath the skin. The unseasonable warm front frees Dad to throw an arm around my mother, to share a pink sky without an onset of oppressive shivers. From my vantage, in the ebbing daylight, his scant limbs might not be that of a sick man at all but of one lanky with youth. Inside, he peruses the menu with an interest that could be confused for sincere were it not for a familiar snarl of the lip laid bare in electric candle glow. Yet, upon prodding, what is presumed to be disgust reveals itself as hesitancy. "I could really go for lobster, but it's pretty expensive," he frets. "GET IT," Mom and I clap back with a fervor that could reanimate the sashimi at the neighboring table. And so he does. And with the help of a little melted butter, he manages to down two whole lobster tails without even a hint of dissent. Maybe he takes a couple forkfuls of succotash or whatever lines his plate, but even if he doesn't it's still the most he's eaten in one sitting—at least, in recent recollection. Even at the arrival of dessert, he volunteers a few scoops of strawberry shortcake into his mouth. None of us are hungry at that point, but even if it means a cheese plate, coffee, after-dinner drinks, filling the salt shakers, and helping the kitchen staff mop up, this has become a concerted effort to stretch the moment as far as a waistband can endure.

Whether this is or isn't the start of a sweeter season matters little. It's the anomalies, the promises of summer, that carry us through the spring. Trouble is: our preoccupation in seizing the unseasonable is preconditioned on overlooking the glorious concurrence that allows for its being. Only after the summer turns up a washout, only then, in warm recollection, does it come to mind that the earth had to lean closer to the sun, the wind had to break, the solar rays had to hit the ground at a steep angle and just so happen to concentrate their energy on the very patch of dirt that held us. All for an impermanent pleasance. Then, after the fight is called and assessment reveals how every bite for my father was a horror show where morsels once favored now tasted of iron ore, burned with each swallow, churned in a swollen and scarred stomach only to spill through a tainted system where five drugs waited to twist every expenditure into a paroxysm. Only then, when I realize how it was so much more than shutting up and chewing, can I take the totality into account and instead choose to appreciate everything that had to happen to make a singularity possible. How, at once, his tongue had to remember flavor, how the bile had to recede, how his stomach had to settle and recall its function, and how a legion of side effects had to suddenly become ineffectual. And how miraculous it all was.

The Bottle is Irrelevant

"Joe, for the love of God, stop! I know what's in the box."

My father stops in his tracks, halfway across the dining room. Admirable as his efforts are to proceed double-time once the crunch of wooden steps echoes up the half-pace stairwell, the cane in his left hand and the cancer everywhere else has significantly dialed back the number at which the needle on his odometer tops out. By the time Mom hits the landing, he is just a few feet shy of the pantry, just a few feet shy of stashing the eBay parcel tucked under his arm behind the decade-old liquor bottles or, perhaps, neatly hidden beneath a fort he'd construct out of three family-size bags of Lay's Wavy Originals. Hiding anything from my mother is an exercise in futility, even for an Olympian-level bootlegger. Her trained eye can pick up even the slightest displacement of effects to the point where, years prior, upon fishing a nearly translucent seed from the weeds of a paisley-print carpet, she'd exposed my father as the refrigerator bandit who'd absconded with one of her Italian cucumbers. As such, every newly established alcove within their walls retains an interminably short shelf life.

"Please tell me it's not another one." Mom stands in the frame at the top step, arms hugged to her chest. Her tone cuts into the air, sharp at first but softening as it carries, almost as if there remains a pinch of belief that she might be wrong about the box's contents.

Dad flinches, hunched, stands facing away. A gray tree frog hoping to blend with the crags and ridges of oak bark, he tenses up to confuse the senses. One last-gasp attempt to trick the eyes of his pursuer. As is the way of the mischievous, though, an abrupt shift in posture occurs as a reaction to being discovered. Back straightened, he about-faces and makes his way toward the kitchen island, eyes-forward with a swagger to suggest that this has been his ultimate destination all along.

I've only known my father to ever have one setting when it came to dispensing his affection: overkill. This was never to compensate for some verbal impotence or as a response to any feelings of inadequacy. That was just how he worked. His love was voluminous, both in sound and serving size.

At eight years old, I decided to go into the Italian-ice business. By that, I mean I was going to position myself at the foot of our driveway with a hand-crank ice crusher and hock my syrupy wares to the scant supply of drivers who made their way down our dead-end street. And, by that, I mean I was banking my fortune solely on the ability to browbeat potential customers with my moon-faced charm. And, by that, I mean "Buy my goop, so I can buy my Jeep. Specifically, a Jeep Wrangler. More specifically, a Jeep Wrangler 4x4 Power Wheels by Fisher Price. *Adult supervision required.*"

When I breathed this million-dollar notion to my father, the next thing I knew he was towing the box for our

Magnavox 71-inch TV from the recesses of the detached garage and into his workshop. A week and several failed attempts to peek at the proprietary goings-on later, I was invited inside to witness an unveiling. Before me stood the gargantuan container, only it had been entirely transformed. The beige exterior, with all its printed branding and technical specs, had been painted over in a solid shamrock green. From the front protruded a retractable awning, striped with yellow and complete with semicircle valance fashioned from the cardboard that had been carved to make way for a serving window. Along the bottom of the window, just high enough to rest my scrawny elbows upon, ran a narrow counter space on which to churn the ice and douse the crystals in rainbow-colored sludge with a swirl and a flourish. Presentation was everything. Round the back had been cut a special swinging door for employees only, easily functional thanks to the spherical wooden knobs affixed on either side. Suddenly, all the Price Club boxes I'd lugged home over the years began to make sense. Turning a value pack of Top Ramen into a speedster by scribbling racing stripes into the sides or punching portholes into a case of Welch's Fruit Snacks so as to explore the ocean's uncharted depths was not a youthful eccentricity, but something that had been pre-written into my genetic code. A line drawn directly from my father to me using every shade in the Crayola 64 Big Box.

The next day, my first brick-and-mortar location opened at the curb of 30 Oak Street. After all his work, it seemed only appropriate that Dad serve as my first customer. Cranking out cold shards into a Dixie cup, I smothered them with orange slime from one of my upturned squirt bottles and slid the finished product into his waiting hand. He smiled and offered me a dollar, a gesture that, even to an eight-year-old, felt inappropriate. Turning down a buck, though, was bad business. Sucking on the tangerine iceberg, he suggested I market the product as *granita* instead. "It'll sound more exotic," he slurped. I dismissed the thought outright, flattening George Washington's face onto the bottom of my change box and grumbling. "People will think I'm selling rocks."

Dad smiled and returned to the house, leaving me to build my roadside empire. By early afternoon, I'd swapped my shavings for the sticky pocket change of the local kids and sweat-logged singles fished from the back pockets of bike shorts. Neighbors took a break from yard work to fetch a cold treat and support my entrepreneurial spirit. But, on a street for which the phrase "the road less traveled" is generously applied, I'd tapped the full potential of my consumer base by mid-morning.

Closing up for lunch, I aired my inclination to shutter the business over a peanut butter and jelly sandwich. After some fatherly encouragement, though, I returned to begin the afternoon shift. It was then that familiar faces began to return to my cardboard kiosk. My morning customers returned in intermittent but rapid succession, first once and then, as the cycle ran through, once again. "Gotta try all the flavors," they'd smile and extend their hand with payment at the ready. The progression of the afternoon was marked by the dwindling levels of syrup in my caddy. Mom replenished my stores with blocks of ice as quickly as she could, but the turnover was so great that water just couldn't freeze fast enough. As the gaggle dispersed to their homes in the summertime dusk, I wheeled my stand back to the garage amidst visions of a growing franchise.

    Emptying my squirt bottles into the sink for rinsing, I ran to tell my father of my commercial triumph. But finding him dozing on the recliner, I decided it might make for better dinnertime conversation. No sooner had I turned to head back toward the kitchen than my eyes caught sight of an anomaly, whipping my body back around. Sure enough, in taking a second look, Dad remained snoreful and unconscious. Only, at the end of his left arm, his leather billfold also rested. Half-clutched. Half-open. Far thinner than it had been earlier that morning.

Dad places his cane in a nearby corner and lays the package on top of the kitchen island. He offers no words, moving about as if nothing is out of the ordinary. As he rummages through the utensil drawer, Mom slinks from her spot on the landing and steps into place a few feet to his side, catty-cornered. From her new vantage, her spouse cannot obstruct her view by any sleight of hand that he might employ.

    A shock of clinking tin gives way to the extraction of scissors. Dad separates the blades with one withering hand and steadies the parcel in the other. Pressing the tip into the groove between the flaps, he drags the shears with surgical caution. It's a slow pull, deliberate. He is no fool. Playing the advantage of his condition means not having to explain why he handles the instrument with the dexterity of an arthritic old man. It also means delaying the inevitable reveal and subsequent reaction, a scene most assuredly already running through his head. Would that the packing tape could run on forever.

Flaps freed, they open to the ceiling. From beneath an amorphous crash of bubble wrap is lifted which, when unraveled, lays bare the visage of an antique perfume bottle. The body of the bauble runs the length of my father's hand from tip to wrist. From where I stand, in the next room, it appears to be blown glass, dark purple with honey marbling and clear diamond-shaped embellishments running the perimeter of the base. At the top sits a gold metal atomizer from which a fringed pump of a similar hue swishes downward like a cat's tail.

The mere sight of the thing is enough to confirm my mother's assumptions, upon which she begins to audibly deflate. It's not quite the reaction I would have expected, especially considering her growing collection of them. Truly, over the last few months of weekend visits, I had noticed bottles of a kindred aesthetic begin to amass on the bathroom shelves. Each one differed in shape and palette, but all were of a similar style and period. Soon, enough had manifested that I'd started to wonder if my parents were slowly robbing a vintage parfumerie. Or, worse, they'd become garage-sale vultures. My mother never having been one for clutter, it was admittedly out of character for her. But since they were clearly on display, I hadn't thought to question it.

Now, however, face buried in her hands, it seems the withheld inquiry is about to be addressed.

In 2000, the American League's New York Yankees and the National League's New York Mets would find themselves pitted against one another in the World Series for the first time in forty-four years. To a fourteen-year-old who'd spent his adolescence trying and failing at nearly every sport, this was not an item of particular note. My two-summer tenure in Little League was more than enough to drive home the fact that, of all the places the future might find me, a stadium-center victor's podium was a bad bet. If I wasn't in the dugout silently rooting for my own team to strike out thereby sparing myself the terrifying trudge toward home plate, I was relegated to the outfield, feverishly grinding to achieve a Zen state through my unfailing mantra: *Plea sedon'thitittomepleasedon'thitittomepleasedon'thitittome.* But even the most athletically inept have our moments in which the crucial intersection of fear and excitement drive a connection to the deep-seated competitor in us all. In those situations wherein a ball might find itself hurtling in my direction, I exhumed my inner sportsman, thrust my glove into the air, twisted my neck to the ground, and prayed for death.

Still, having grown up in a baseball family, pure exposure alone was enough to make avoiding the event a statistical unworkability. My bubble of ambivalence broke wide open on the night of Game One, ruptured during a foot-stomping rampage at Aunt Bee's. Relatives and friends, both human and canine, piled into the den; a fondue pot of Brooklyn and Queens transplants melting with the native Garden Staters, forever without a home team. The eyes of the nation, having zoomed in on the intrastate rivalry, pushed juice through the power lines, supercharging the air. In Manhattan, the transit authority—a billion-dollar delay factory—moved almost overnight to skin-dueling subway trains with Yankee pinstripes and the signature Mets blue, orange, and white. Radio waves jammed as the Baha Men altered the lyrics of their biggest hit. *Who let the Mets out?*

Who, who, who who? This was only to be out-kitsched, days later, with the release of an original recording, a dialectal ode to the Bronx Bombers, "Haya Doin' Yankees." The atmosphere was suffused. It was as inevitable as oxygen. Even the most extreme outliers had no choice but to open up and breathe it in.

The commotion was easy for me to buy into. Dozens of bodies packed in, swarming around the screen, eyes glowing with ultraviolet blue fluorescence. We filled five scoreless innings with seven-layer dip until the Yanks snatched two runs in the bottom of the sixth, releasing a cloud of Frito-laced screams. When the Mets took an immediate lead in the seventh, half the crowd launched into the air while others pummeled their soles to the ground, shaking the earth with a rage not seen since Godzilla leveled Downtown Tokyo. By the ninth inning the game was tied and I was fully converted. Running on taco pinwheels and Coke Zero, I mirrored the moves of my cousins and uncles as extra innings gave way to superstition. Thinking it would bring about success, we spun our caps three times around our skulls each time the Yankees came to bat. I fisted barbecue chips into my mouth in short intervals, returning immediately to the same exact position I'd held when the Mets had earned three strikes in rapid succession. It was a spectacular madness, and as our team squeaked out a victory just shy of the game's fifth hour, I watched my body hurl skyward in the twin jumbotrons of my father's bewilderment. Of all the evening's abrupt swings and pitches, his son's unfeigned celebration was a heat straight out of left field.

The Yankees would clinch the series in five games. Not two days later I would be pulled out of bed in the early morning October darkness. "Dress warm," Dad whispered before hurrying down the stairs. Jeans over long johns, I staggered into the kitchen where my presence triggered an unfurling that wiped away any remnants of sleep. There, in the dim yellow light, the top half of my father's face poked over a stretch of poster board that obscured just about the rest of him. A trifecta of opposing championship teams was scrawled along the top border: *Padres. Braves. Mets.* Each one in black lettering. Each one with a thick, red line skewering them, and underneath, in big, block print, one word: *THREE-PEAT.* There was devilment in the air, underscored by the rumble of coffee percolating on the stove and confirmed by the skin that crinkled in the corner of my father's narrowing eyes.

  We skimmed along the New Jersey Turnpike, northbound, a single ripple on the glassy surface that would soon be churned up by commuter traffic. Truants, the both of us, steeped in the Manhattan air and a breakfast of Red Hots as we scouted out a spot along the barricades that lined Broadway between Battery Park and City Hall. In the time it took me to understand the full significance of Derek Jeter's hitting streak, onlookers joined, adding to the collective cloud of mustard breath. By eleven am, the sidewalks were a parted sea of white-and-blue-clad fanatics discussing dynasties, arguing about who should be cut during the off-season and laughing into their Anthoras about all the work they were missing in order to be there. When the news crews lit up their satellites, Dad made sure I was front and center, sign in hand, that I might receive all the glory any wandering camera lenses had to offer. When the champions rolled past, a squash of navy-jacketed varsity men endorsed my clever wordplay with a wink and a thumbs-up. I threw my fist to the air, collected shoulder slugs from chummy revelers, and emptied my voice into the blanket of sound and glitter that dappled the streets.

Never once, in all that time, did I feel out of place. Never once was there a beat to consider how there were those far more deserving of the patch of concrete where I stood. Never once did the light in my father's face shine any more or less bright than it had when I started that Italian-ice stand or enrolled in summer drama camp. After years of conscientious abjection of interest, I had arrived, late to the game. Yet everything that could be done had been done so that I might be welcomed into this world and feel licensed to participate as an equal. So that, when the "Thank You, Fans" flag waved at the end of the procession, I could count myself among those addressed. The pomp of the circumstance was not rooted in having done something right, but simply having done something together.

The 2000 World Series would clock in as the lowest-rated in history at the time. Critics would attribute it to a lack of interest outside the Greater New York City area. The following morning, my mother and father would send me to school with a note explaining the prior day's lack of attendance. Unfolding it in front of me, Sister Regina, a teaching nun, read it out loud. "Please excuse Joseph's absence yesterday as he was called to witness a historic event." Under the brim of her habit, she rolled her eyes, choking on the penultimate term. "Historic."

Wasn't it?

Mom rakes her fingers down the perimeter of her jaw, leaving streaks of white where the blood used to be.

Nighttime pours in through the windows and creeps along the floor, pushed down by the ceiling's halogen glow. So sharply is she focused in the foreground that the picture behind her melts into strokes of blues and reds and yellows. Stretched, her lips open as if to make room for a scream that will find itself—as it always does—strangled by guilt. So, she stands, an Edvard Munch in pastel, filling the room with silent bellows until her soul is hoarse.

"I just don't understand how many times I can say it." Her words return with the color in her complexion. "I thanked you for the first one but said it wasn't necessary. I obliged the second one because it arrived so soon afterward. By the third one, I politely requested that that be the last."

Dad can't look at her. Can't look at me. Can't look anywhere but through the cut glass phial he spins in his hand, refracting the light. He has nothing to say for himself.

"But you just kept going. Even after I asked you to stop in every way I could think to ask you. You keep buying ..."

He spins the bottle.

"... and buying ..."

A glint of light skids across the floor.

"... and buying."

Then cuts across the top of my wrist.

"I'm at my wit's end. So I'm just going to say what I'm not supposed to say." She steadies herself against the back of a barstool as if the next words are going to hurt. "I don't want that." The bottle hovers at the end of her pointer finger. "I didn't want the first one. I didn't want any of them. I know your heart is in the right place. But God help you if I see another one of those damn things show up."

Mom turns to the stove, proceeding to stir some peace into a boiling pot from which bursts of liquid have been meeting their sizzling end on the hot steel. It's about the only peace she'll find tonight, but it's a reminder of what a steady hand can still achieve. In an airless room, however, there's nothing for the frustration to do but hover until it finds a new host. Breathing it in, Dad rests the bottle back in the box that gets tucked back under his arm. He palms his cane, a mere decoration in its inability to protect against sentimental slips. One made further extraneous by the umbrage that steels his spine. Still, as he beats the rubber pad against the wood a little firmer than usual, it ekes out meager value as a conduit in passing his anger to the boards. So he passes across the room and thumps up the staircase, off to withdraw from a host of active auctions where he is, undoubtedly, the highest bidder.

About a month before Dad died, I signed the lease for my first apartment. At twenty-seven, it was hardly my first time living away from home. Ever since college, I'd hung my hat in all kinds of shared spaces: company intern housing, a smattering of condos and townhomes split between anywhere from two to upwards of ten people. I even spent a year living with my aunt after my folks had moved closer to the water. But this was to be the very first serving of square footage that I could lay sole claim to.

The place wasn't much. A second floor converted garden apartment in a complex on top of one of the Highlands' steepest hills. The rental office claimed it was originally constructed in the '80s but were a geologist to count the layers of lacquer and dust that sat between the oxygen and the hardwood floor, I'm certain it would've dated back to the Cretaceous Period. Four rooms featured black iron fixtures affixed to walls a shade of white not often seen outside of an asylum. Along the breadth of the galley kitchen hung "certified cabinets," a distinction announced by official stamps on the inner doors and one that made me wonder how many people were living their lives ignorant of the counterfeit cabinetry currently housing their cups and dishes. The terrace looked out onto a parking lot. The air-conditioner unit cooled the living room and not much else. To me, though, it was everything. It was everything because it represented an end to months of searching for an affordable space from which I could access work but also from which I was no more than an hour's drive from my parents' home where Dad remained in steady decline.

"You know we need to help him." My father muttered to Mom not quite out of earshot shortly after I'd shared the news. Sure enough, that same day we rolled up to the discount furniture store with the intention of finding a couch and a small dinette set. For my father, the walk from the car to the entrance in the June heat may as well have been a trek across the Sahara. He hadn't been off the house grounds in the weeks since the doctors had deemed him no longer fit for chemo. Yet, he remained unflinching in his determination to join in the selection process. So, in fetching a courtesy wheelchair from the service desk, we lowered him into the seat and dabbed at the beads of sweat that formed atop his eyebrows. From the way his chin drooped it was evident the exertion was already more than his body could handle. But being off of the couch had seemed to freshen his resolve.

The summer crowds off sinking in the sand left the store virtually empty and us relatively unbothered. In the circulated air, I pushed us across the showroom, cornering ottomans and weaving through neatly assembled layouts. Now and again, Dad would point to something he liked, and I'd hit the brakes so that we could both give it due consideration. Each time involved lifting him from the chair and helping him onto the upholstery so that he could weigh in on both look and feel. This happened over and over as we worked our way across the expanse of classic rounds, retro squares, sectionals, hard wedges, sloped arms, straight backs, high backs, wingbacks, and barrelbacks. Back and forth I carried him, and at no time was it ever anything less than a joy. Because in a store where it couldn't be easier to feel like nothing more than a piece of furniture, it meant the universe to do what I could to ensure he was an active part of the process. It was no secret how hard it was for him just to be there, yet in those few short hours, he came alive in a way I hadn't seen in maybe a year. We sat and talked, and I rested under his arm in a thousand different living rooms, both knowing that he'd never get to see mine. I think that's why he forced us into the car that day, to make sure some piece of him would.

I no longer live in that apartment at the top of the hill. When Dad passed, all the problems I was too tired to notice became noticeable. In a world where everything was temporary, I bought a place a few towns over out of some intense need for the illusion of permanence. But the couch was there, and the couch is here, and it will probably live in my next place, too. It loses its shape a little easier than it used to, and I often have to beat it back into something resembling the likeness of a sofa. Now and then I think about getting rid of it, making a change, wiping the slate clean. The mere inkling feels somehow treasonous and I often banish it after a few seconds. Maybe because aside from myself and the small allowance of snapshots on the walls, it's the only item to have known him, felt him, learned the curve of him. That's the funny thing about a couch. In them, we become embedded. They settle around us and soak us into the fabric. Try as we might to smooth out the notches and grooves, they settle back in. The fibers remember.

A descending swarm of thumps announces his approach, and Dad emerges from the stairwell, the bottle still clenched in his right hand. He moves a bit slower now, the trip up and down having burnt off some of his intensity. But he remains as mum as he's been all night. Touching down onto his easy chair, he rests his cane on the armrest and frees his other hand to join in cradling the violet liability in his lap. And that's where it stays.

  I watch him for longer than I should, longer than I care to remember. There's something about the way he runs his thumbs along its uneven elements, the purposeful imperfections. It's almost as if he believes he can spread it even, soften the roughness. If he just keeps at it, he can restore the balance. But despite his delicate repetitions, the bottle remains unchanged. An observation he meets with a pout as he sinks further into the leather, growing smaller than a man has ever been. It's another in an extended series of little images that break me more than any of the big things. In the macrocosm of terminal illness, the big things, the world-enders, are expected. What's unexpected, though, are the host of tiny atrocities that occur as part of the fallout. It is those tiny atrocities that manage to cut deeper by presenting themselves as fixable when, in reality, we are just as powerless to remedy them as we are to remedy the illness.

    I'd learn later on that, some weeks prior, due to his ever-weakening grip, my father had accidentally dropped and shattered an antique bottle of French perfume he'd brought home for my mother during their early years of marriage. The way Mom told it, she was unruffled by the circumstance, stopping only for a single tick to mourn the loss of a memory before cleaning up the mess and moving on. Problem was, as my father crouched to scoop up the fragments, he mistook any twinge that her face may have betrayed for something of far greater significance. Cancer has a funny way of magnifying everything tenfold, another charming byproduct of the upside down. As such, Dad responded the only way he ever had, the way that led him to Frankenstein a TV box into a Dairy Queen and pull his kid out of school for some mad parade. He responded the way he would when putting his already depleted body at mortal risk all for the chance to act like a parent one last time. Understanding he'd never be able to track down an exact replacement, he chose instead to replace one bottle with dozens of them.

    So, he did a few searches and stroked a few keys because he could do so all his own. The disease hadn't yet taken that part of him. It was a way to feel useful, a way back to himself. My mother knew it, even if she hadn't in the moment. That's why she'd humored it. Eventually, though, the bottles piled up until she lost sight of the man behind them. So she screamed under the weight of his love before it buried her alive.

But love it was. Just mistaken by people looking in opposite directions. Whereas my father looked to us and saw that he'd become a labor, saw the things we were forced to take on to compensate for his perceived deficiencies, we saw only an endeavor of distinction, the privilege of being for the man everything he had been for us. Where my mother saw meaningless bric-a-brac, my father saw a way to fill the void, summoning the degree of his power to make sure his disease couldn't pick her pocket as it had his. So yes, she screamed. She screamed that he might look up. She screamed that he might meet her gaze and see what it reflected back. That cancer could never diminish him, that she'd sooner smash every trinket she owned if it meant keeping him alive, that the bottle was irrelevant.

A Comedy of Errors

*"He that commends me to mine own content
Commends me to the thing I cannot get.
I to the world am like a drop of water,
That in the ocean seeks another drop;
Who, falling there is to find his fellow forth,
Unseen, inquisitive, confounds himself:
So I, to find a mother and a brother,
In quest of them, unhappy, lose myself."*
                              Antipholus of Syracuse

ACT I
SCENE: Neighborhood Medical Center. A nurse's station in the post-critical care unit. Mid-morning.

"You can see where he fell right here."

The NEUROSURGEON points to an image on a monitor, his finger landing on a dark gray splotch that sits at the bow of the brain. Not forty-eight hours prior, my FATHER had been found at home bleeding from the side of his face, unable to comprehend or answer any of the questions put forth by the paramedics. Now, in the hum of the intensive care unit, after days spent at the end of the MRI waitlist and more frequent sightings of custodians than physicians, one well-placed demand to speak with Dad's caseworker had nurses and doctors crawling out of the ventilation, offering us everything short of a mai tai. "And what about these?" MOM asks. She motions to a handful of faded spots in the same vicinity as the first. "Similar bruising, but older." He shifts to allow us both in closer, continuing.

"You can see they've begun to heal. By the looks of this, I'd say he's been falling for weeks." From my vantage, the entire front half of Dad's brain bares the markings of a dairy cow. "The frontal lobe," he draws a circle around the bovined area, "is the seat of personality expression, decision-making, and social behavior moderation." The sound of my mother's scribbles fills the gap between my ears as I stand, agog, retinas painted with gray matter. "Luckily, the damage is not permanent," the SURGEON maintains, doubling down on his efforts to appease. "But this would certainly explain his demeanor."

Dad's infamy clearly preceded him, and it was well-earned. Upon my arrival at the emergency room, no more than an hour after the ambulance, I had been greeted at the door by a disorderly bellow. "Goodbye, Alina!" The voice was recognizable. The same could not be said for the rancorous tone that gave it shape. Sure enough, following the echoes down the hall, I came to find its source, squirming against a NURSE actively trying to apply gauze to his wound.

"Joe, please let her do her job," my mother shushed from the bedside, trying to corral my father who, at that moment, appeared to be spring-loaded.

"Goodbye, Alina!" His message, unchanged, rang louder from this distance, drawing ire from the patients and impatience from the staff.

"He's going to need to quiet down," prodded the nurse before drawing the bay curtain closed. From the look on Mom's face, she'd been deflecting Dad's dismissals since the moment they'd gotten him on wheels. Whether my presence might soothe or sour him I'd never learn as, no sooner had I stepped into his sight line, she wrenched me to the other side of the divider. Nevertheless, the ensuing quietude confirmed our invisibility as an effective pacifier.

In the time it takes for Mom to whisper the details of how she found him, how they got to the hospital, and her concerns that Dad may have suffered some attack, an ER DOCTOR shuffles up with the results of his preliminary blood work. His platelet levels are at 45,000—a precarious deficit from the normal range of 150,000-450,000—likely due to adverse effects of his chemo. This, they believe, is the cause of his blackouts. He'll need an infusion of fresh frozen plasma and platelets to get his counts back where they should be.

"What about his head?" The effort required to download information whilst interrogating distracts Mom from tempering her volume and the uptick in pitch sends Grendel into frenzy.

"GODDAMIT! ARE YOU STILL HERE?" Beet red, Mom bends from the conclave to shove her face between the curtains and confront the creature.

"Be quiet!" she mumble-shouts. "I have to talk to your doctor. Now, shut up!"

Feeling an all-too-common rumble begin to work its way up from my stomach, I leave the doctor to shuffle his one piece of paper in a feeble attempt to pretend he's not listening. Behind the scrim of an empty bay, backed in a corner, I gird myself for an eruption of everything I've suppressed over the last five months since his surgery, three since he started chemo. Every swallowed lump, every ghastly image drunk, every poison statistic gagged upon had been slow cooking like some septic goulash, rising with each day, building pressure, waiting for just such an event to break the seal. Throat clenched and eyes welled, I prayed that the row next door might drown me out. The shakes do come and the tears do flow, but as my jaw lowers, what I'm most unprepared for comes emptying from between my chattering teeth. Not sobs, not screams, but guffaws. Sheltered by the bluster of my father's calls for Mom to take an unequivocal hike, I expend the air from my lungs so rapidly that there's no time between cackles to refill them. Under oxygenated, my legs noodle, give out, and leave me to silently seize my way down the wall into nothing more than a human pile of wheezes, bobbling somewhere between crying and cracked.

What delivered me behind the curtain initially was a prevailing concern for preserving decorum and treating the situation with the seriousness it demanded. What holds me there until I can wrest composure is the notion of being taken for a sociopath, some unfeeling maniac laughing at his father's plight and his mother's distress. The thing about cancer is how its enormity behooves an intense sense of focus from those it engages. That very preoccupation is all too easy to conflate with the belief that there is only one way to feel about something. It's what forces my mother to cry, if she does at all, behind closed doors—this need to exude resilience. It's what has me suffocating unwarranted laughter against the hands pressed to my face—this duty to reverence. It's what drives my father to face each day with the vigor of a victor—that is, until something comes along to damage the mechanism filtering his anger. As close to mortality as this affliction delivers us, it has a distinct knack for blinding us to what makes us mortal.

 His filter removed, Dad no longer reflexively modulates his words nor the amplification with which they're delivered. Whereas before mealtime was a negotiation, however cordial, he now takes to the table like a feral cat to water. His hisses and sprays are nonexclusive, grazing a DEPARTMENT STORE ASSOCIATE who refuses to honor the original price to replace a flood-damaged washer unit. "THAT'S NOT FAIR!" The sonic boom from Dad's dissent is enough to knock off a couple of points from the Sears stock. Though, admittedly, it does beget a quick discount and profuse capitulation. Still, it's at home where Mom and I catch the brunt of his earnestness. Coarse as it may be, the incessant grinding succeeds in a gradual stripping away of our veneers, unexpectedly freeing us from any betrothal to etiquette. Yes, every hard-nosed barb and display of insolence is appraised with consideration to his condition, and as such, is granted a measure of slack. But head injury or no, there comes a point after racking up one too many hits where compassion falters and innate imperfections create an environment where my cancer-riddled father is roasted for being an unendurable turd. Maybe it's necessary. Maybe it's necessary to chew him out when he marches into the living room and changes the channel without bothering to ask if we were watching the TV. Maybe it's necessary to flee upstairs and hunker in the den, even if he's clanging his way to the landing thirty minutes later to decry: "You just *left* me down there!"

It's a nasty jaunt; this trip through Carcinoma, and at times, the nastiness must be abided. If only because it saves us from being crushed under the weight of propriety. Nastiness requires truth, requires love, can engender love through its expression by no longer weighing it down. I can feel two ways about something, about someone. I can yell at a man and honor him. When the world turns cold, I can bring him warmth for all the times he did the same for me. When darkness comes early, I can string lights around the windows to kindle color and brightness. I can make a holiday for him because he's weak and so am I. But I'm strong enough to know that the same man who bristles at me will shoulder into five layers of clothes, wrangle the steps, and tread into the freezing December night. Beholding the twinkling façade I've festooned, he will reciprocate with similar brilliance. "The wreaths aren't centered."

"Every why hath a wherefore."
       Dromio of Ephesus, Act II, Scene II

ACT II
SCENE: Monmouth Medical Center. An emergency bay. Some months later.

With a keen ability to materialize in one place and flare up in a completely different hemisphere, this particular plague calls for a level of reconnaissance not seen since

Where in the World Is Carmen Sandiego? Routine imaging scours the entire body for any sign of metastasis, and as is often the case, casting a wide net can ensnare all manner of oddities. Complications are to be expected, everything on the medication package inserts detail. There are warnings of nausea, fevers, traveling pain. Even the syncope can be explained away, thanks to the low blood counts from the chemo cocktail. But, when another call from the emergency room pulls me out of an exhaustion coma at 11:30 pm on a Thursday, I have my mother repeat herself to confirm my stupor hasn't clouded her speech.

"Pneumatosis," the doctor spells it out so Mom can jot down the word in her notebook. Leaning over the bed, he rolls up the hem of Dad's undershirt and gently presses his hands to the abdomen. "Do you feel any pain?" My father simply shakes his head and exhales through his nose. Everything about this visit to the ER is unlike the one just a month prior. When the results of Dad's latest scan prompted a call from the medical team urging my mother to have him admitted, memories of the local hospital's second-rate performance history had her driving nearly forty-five minutes out of the way. At Monmouth Medical, a quiet urgency seems to command a higher standard of efficiency. From Mom's calm, almost deadpan delivery of "we're in the emergency room" to the militaristic scuffle of medical slippers under nurses and specialists who attend Dad in clean formation, a lack of a qualifier stymies a marked severity, keeping the collective terror alert stuck on "moderate."

In the middle of the swarm lies my father, this time sitting above the sheets in his sweats and ball cap. Back reclined and hands behind his head, they scope and poke him, but if there's annoyance, it doesn't register on his face. "I don't understand it," one of the MDs approaches my mother, actually scratching his head. "His scans show pockets of air in the lining of his colon, but no perforation. Anyone else would be in extreme agony right now. But this guy," he points at Dad as he lounges behind sleepy eyelids, "he looks as if he could be on a pleasure cruise." And it's true. Though the tranquility he displays modulates my quantifiable reaction , that does not make the situation any less problematic. Dad will be admitted to the ICU, the team explains, for a few days of observation. The situation is serious. Should it progress, invasive measures will be taken. There's talk of emergency surgery, intestinal removal, and the mention of a colostomy bag does well to raise the hair on my arms. Yet, amidst all the huffing and puffing, not a strand is askew on Dad's chinny chin chin. He remains, still and obedient, fielding questions and answering mostly through nods. The doctors ask if he understands what they're saying, chalking his naiveté up to the head injury. But each time they return to nudge his midsection like Play-Doh and talk about air in the bowels, the curl of my father's lip reads less of innocence and more of a man tickled at the thought of being hospitalized for a fart joke.

Over the next few days, he's monitored, checked, and checked again. Every expert brings their theory. "It's because of his low white-cell count." "It's the chemo." "It might just be diverticulitis." The ideas change but the situation stays the same. Eventually, after a lack of consensus, a surgeon will declare him stable and "nothing extraordinary." "Sometimes the intestine just heals itself," he says, signing the discharge papers. They shoot Dad up with a leucocyte booster and wheel him out the door just as full of hot air as he was on the way in. Maybe the whole ordeal could be dismissed as just more time wasted for a bloodline already bleeding time. But, if nothing else, for once he gets to be the abnormality without having to pay for the distinction with body parts.

"If everyone knows us and we know none,
'Tis time, I think, to trudge, pack and be gone."
Antipholus of Syracuse, Act III, Scene II

ACT III
SCENE: Monmouth Medical Center. Another emergency bay. Some months later, but fewer than before.

One of the byproducts of becoming an ER regular is an ability to navigate disconnection. Between arrival, admittance, and consultation my father's case history is downloaded more times than a Beyoncé album. The trouble therein is that the nature of emergency medicine is to concentrate on the presenting issue and to only dally on the most pertinent facts. That crucial detail, coupled with the ever-lengthening archive of names, dates, dosages, and dilemmas in my mother's purse, often means sending off doctors to find a solution before they fully understand the problem. For a cancer patient, I come to learn, every tiptoe through triage is one of Shakespearean complexity. Nurses are the arbiters of clandestine meetings, deference, and puffery which gains counsel with kings, vital messages either get misinterpreted or misconstrued to the detriment of their speaker, and more often than not, someone ends up having to drink poison. Even worse, however, is how the plot is never contained, frequently involving separate narratives occurring simultaneously across kingdoms. Each informs the next, baffling when considered alone, yet illuminating when appreciated in chorus. For the players, unfortunately, such great distance can hamper the transmission of information. That is, when the messenger isn't shot along the way. As a result, impulsivity leads the powerful to act without comprehending the gross state of affairs—and violently, at that. Should anyone make it to the end, to be sure, it is not because someone did not try to kill them.

The nurse feeds a needle into the vein she coaxes out of the crook of my father's arm, just south of the warm front spreading across an area once home to a bicep. "I'm placing him on and IV of Vancomycin," says the doctor, running her thumb across the perimeter of a yellowy-purple nebula. "It's the standard antibiotic we use for Staph or MRSA, which I think this is." To my right, Mom notes the internist's last name from her badge and presses like a hungry reporter.

"Can you spell that?"

"Of course," she nods, giving Dad his arm back. "V-a-n-c-o-m-y-c-i-n. We'll want to keep him on the liquid for one or two days. After that, he should be okay to go home and finish the course orally." The idea of another pill or puncture doesn't put a song into any of our hearts, but we've been here enough to know the direct route home always involves a toll road. And, in any other play, that would be the end of it. But, in this comedy of errors, an exit stage right is just the cue for an entrance stage left.

"It seems superficial," the INFECTIOUS DISEASE SPECIALIST traces the stigma in a manner similar to the white-coated figure who came before him. "I'll order a CT scan just to make sure there's no internal involvement. He'll be here for the weekend." Our regard for their hypervigilance makes it easier to let them toss Dad through the microwave again, especially with the repeated assurance that the benign culprit has already been identified. Like the word itself, though, he who puts stock in assurances is an ass from the start. Not a day passes before a PULMONOLOGIST breaks forth, bringing news of blood clots, two to be precise. Enemy factions, likely dispatched by the cancer, are holed up in encampments at the base of my father's lungs. Should they travel, the consequences would be swift and fatal. With no time to lose, the pulmonologist orders a Heparin drip and tasks it to liquefy the coup.

It is a well-meaning exercise; one that likely would have worked had a HEMATOLOGIST not decided to interject. As it turns out, thinning the blood of a man with already scant resources is a risky gambit. Sure enough, when they find blood in Dad's stool, they replace the Heparin with a blood transfusion. There's worry of internal bleeding. He needs an ultrasound. At 1:30, they cut into his groin and feed filters to his lungs in order to anchor the clots. That evening, he gets more blood, red and white. On day four of the two-day stay, a GASTROENTEROLOGIST wants an endoscopy, wants to look for the source of the blood. "Are you aware of the air in his bowels?" On day five, gastritis, inflammation of stomach. Not the cause of the bleeding. His left leg is swollen. It's attributed to the clots. Blood thinners again, this time with careful monitoring. A colonoscopy on day six removes a small polyp, also not the cause of anything. On day seven, he's retaining fluid. They draw a sample. Day eight. "Negative for cancer cells. He's just prone to infection." His kidneys shut down on day ten. Enter NEPHROLOGIST. It was the antibiotics from day one. Off he comes. More ultrasounds, EKGs. Check the kidneys, check the heart. They're coming back. Slowly. On their heels, the skin rash everywhere: groin, sides, lower back. More antibiotics. Different antibiotics. Day fourteen. "Are you aware that his bladder is not emptying?" Enter UROLOGIST.

In all, it takes twenty-six days for every "-gist" to get the gist and to get my father stabilized. Over that time, he gains and loses about fifty pounds, most of which is fluid. They determine that the infection that began the saga is not infection at all but an irritation from the liquid retention caused by the cancer caused by the pen of some psychotic celestial playwright. It may be the fact that we're resigned to their mercy or it may be that false prophecy allowed for the neutralization of a very real threat. Either way, it turns out easier than anticipated to forgive the missteps. Because even after all the swords thrown at him, even with recovery just beginning, even battered and more than a little worse for wear, Dad still steps into the sun, an unlikely survivor. And there, amidst the bodies, is fresh air and purpose. "Don't pay for the TV service," he prays. "I never used it."

"He is deformed, crooked, old and sere,
Ill-faced, worse bodied, shapeless everywhere,
Vicious, ungentle, foolish, blunt, unkind,
Stigmatical in making, worse in mind."
       Antipholus of Syracuse

ACT IV
SCENE: Monmouth Medical Center. The intensive care unit. Barely one month later.

The last call that rolls in from the hospital doesn't shock any less than those that came before. It just tends to pass quicker. As they rack up, I learn to read the warning signs: how things sounded on the phone the night before, what Dad looked like the last weekend I visited. Then, of course, any time "Mom Cell" lights up on the screen outside of five-to-nine pm it's a hard indicator that something's up. I expect their news before they deliver it, often answering the phone with one hand and slipping a shoe over my foot with the other. To some extent, the body adapts and learns to regulate instinctively. But while repetition sets the movements into the bones, memory recalls air bubbles that threaten everything and mean nothing and a skin blot that means nothing and threatens everything. Without a clear definition, "emergency" becomes a pliable word, leaving the mind to waver until a more solid reactant presents itself.

"I think he may have had a stroke." Mom passes the words through the three fingers she holds to her lips; as if the squeeze might slow them down, soften the collision. Behind her, Dad sits upright, his legs draped by the top sheet of another bed on wheels. The image has become so commonplace it's begun to resemble a scene out of *Willy Wonka and the Chocolate Factory*. Grandpa Joe spends the days tucked away, watching the light pass across the wall. The placid expression he wears never fully obscuring a hunger for more life that gurgles somewhere inside. His stare breaks when I step into view, giving way to a smile that can only be described as one of pure, unadulterated warmth. "Joe, do you know who this is?" My father's head turns to meet Mom's question as she scoots down next to him on the mattress but returns quickly to me. There's an excitement in him, almost as if he's been waiting for this, waiting for me to return from the candy store so that he can witness as I fish a golden ticket from the mouth of a freshly shorn chocolate bar.

"Hello, Joseph," his eyes widen to reveal whites that have taken on a lemony hue. Try though I do, initially, to dismiss it as a trick of low-grade, institutional halogens, the shade does not diminish when I move to block the light. And there, bent at the waist, an inch from his nose, I find it. Gold. After all.

"Do you know where you are?" Mom asks.

"The hospital," he looks to her for confirmation.

"That's right," she nods. "Which hospital?" Dad peers into the air between her and me; the narrowing of his eyes and protrusion of his chin suggests the answer hangs just out in front of him. So close he could catch it with his teeth.

"Saint Joseph's!" he exclaims, so very proud and so very wrong, but I don't have the heart to correct him. Instead, I take his hand and hold it, saying nothing but tightening my grip when the silence seems to run on too long. At some point, he's going to realize he doesn't know where he is. When that happens, at least he'll know he's not alone.

A CAT scan rules out a stroke, much to the attending's expectation. From the moment they saw the mustard glow of his skin, the prevailing suspicion was a liver malfunction. And, when blood tests come back practically reeking of ammonia—re: intellectual impairment—he's admitted.

Until they can convene a medical team, the concern for the time being becomes reducing the toxins in his body, finding workarounds to compensate for his liver's decision to phone it in. To flush his system, they pump him with sugars—a giant laxative designed to accelerate bowel movements. It's not the most pleasant news for a man who's spent the last year of his life pummeled by gastric distress. The bright side is that he probably can't remember any of it.

To our chagrin, Dad has to spend Father's Day convalescent. Mom and I rush out and buy him a tablet, something he can use to run out the clock. I load it up with games, word searches, uncomplicated things that won't confuse him and that we can do together. To teach him 3D Bowling, I must first help him ball up all his fingers, except for the pointer, then guide it across the glass toward the center pin. After trailing his hand off the edge of the device a few times, he gets the knack of it and the two of us go back and forth, taking time between tournaments to test his recall.
"Dad, do you know when I was born?"
"July."
"Yes, July. What year?" A pause.
"1926." It should be crippling to witness this decline. Surely, the pang registers somewhere. But the idea that my sixty-seven-year-old Dad, who sits directly to my left, believes I'm twenty years his senior proves just too hilarious and insulting to ignore. So, I laugh, another wheezing, rib shaking, not-enough-oxygen-to-produce-a-sound laugh. Only, this time it's out in the open, with no curtain to crouch behind. Before shame can press a boot into my chest, the bewilderment plastered between my father's ears melts into a fit that mirrors my own. He knows he got the question

wrong. But if he's taking his cues from me now, how wrong could it have been?

In fairness, it will never feel totally right, not as an inside joke and especially not when outside parties get involved. When the nurses deliver a roommate to the neighboring bed, the scene merely doubles down on farce. From the moment the gurney wheels in, its inhabitant reveals himself as captive to a similar delirium, bleating like a yak while infected blood from two botched knee replacements marinates mind and body in ruination. The groans fill the hours, receding—*MAURA!*—only during patches of clarity in which the man will scream—*MAURA!*—for an invisible woman until the tide washes him under again. Startling as each jump scare may be, it bows our trio into laughter time after time; not at the plight of the beleaguered, but at the innate comedy that comes in discovering that the mangled bovid is a malpractice attorney. Following that revelation, it's impossible not to see every howl as the addition of another "0" to the lawsuit being drawn up in some bunker of his addled brain.

If there is a vulgarity to the proceedings, it's because humor always requires some manner of capitalization. That's why a joke is said to come at an expense, either of ourselves, of another, or, more than likely, both. Laughter is the result of a conscious effort to reject the alternative. Of course, it would be just as easy to come apart in my seat, powerless to do anything but watch from the audience as my father goes a little bit mad. Instead, I choose to acknowledge that he's held on to the important things. He knows who he is, he knows who we are. Perhaps, fortuitously, the malady allows him to forget the sickness that begets it, even if it is just for a few days. So, wherein each return visit we collect victories ("What did you have for lunch, Dad?" "Hot dog."), there are an equal number of setbacks ("Did the doctor come to see you?" "Hot dog.") But, in that light, the only choice is either to surrender to the levity because— *MAURAAAAAA!*— consider the alternative.

"We came into the world
Like brother and brother.
And now let's go hand in hand,
Not one before another."
Dromio of Ephesus

ACT V
SCENE: A room of one's own. But not an emergency room. At least there's that.

Part of the mastery of a life within the nation of illness comes in adapting to a new system of measurement. Things are much easier to compartmentalize when they actually come in compartments. Diseases, especially chronic ones, are measured in stages (1, 1b, 2a, 3XL, etc.). These being stages of progression, they're largely relative to units of distance. The medications used to go after such diseases are distributed in milligrams or milliliters. These are less abstract, most solidly seated in the category of units of volume. Pain, the oft-intractable side effect of illness or trauma, also can be gauged. Within the confines of hospital walls, nurses and doctors will frequently ask patients to rate their pain on a scale from zero (no pain) to ten (unimaginable, unspeakable anguish). Such a tool, while helpful in aiding medical staff in assessing the level of urgency each particular case requires, doesn't meet the criteria of distance or volume. Rather, much like temperature, it is measured in degrees, essentially hinging on one key differential: how hot it can get before we burn up and die.

For the most part, the system works when applied exclusively to pain of the physical variety. Though, the idea of the scale itself implies that pain can be finite, even when its apex is vague and purposely all-encompassing. Categorizing a feeling as unimaginable only works as long as life agrees to never ever hit any harder than it does right at that particular reading. But there is another side to pain; it is no offspring of some damaged nerve, no footprint on a negative, yet somehow no less injurious than its brother. It is the pain of the inert, of the helpless watcher subject to a repertory of repugnance. For those relegated to the stalls, pain is too easily described as sympathetic when, in actuality, it comes as a result of our mad desire to siphon the agony of a loved one. Because of this communality, shared pain has a wider range of impact, and as such, can be measured in distance. However, given the limitations of our own proportions, each individual also has a defined threshold of containment. We can ladle all we like from the punch bowl of suffering, but there will come a point where the cup overflows.

The trouble then becomes how to quantify something not so straightforward, something that comes in degrees and grams and inches. While I won't soon be presenting my findings in front of the Nobel Committee, I have, in my experience, discovered a broad, but applicable, unit of measurement. Each of us, for every traumatic event we encounter, is equipped to withstand only *so much*. We can hold only *so much*, weather only *so much*, carry away only *so much*. Once we receive too much *so much*, when our level of *so much* has been exceeded, there comes the inevitable spillover. And in our blind haste to keep moving, we will slip on the drippage and fall flat on our asses. Right there, in the heat of the mania, bums ablaze, is where it becomes not just appropriate but necessary to give in to the comedy, to laugh at the string of unfortunate events that has dropped us to the floor, leaving us to steep in the puddle of our own mess.

It is no mistake that the word "hysterical" can be used to describe fits of sadness, confusion, rage, and hilarity. Rare is the occasion for a patient or caregiver not to feel some combination of all four. Nonetheless, inside that very ambiguity is the license to let go of one and cleave to another for as long as the body needs to filter out the surplus. Cancer can be funny and needs to be funny in order to cut the despair. Along the way, it tries to kill us a thousand times, in every conceivable fashion. It turns men into monsters, makes balloon animals of their bowels, impersonates infection so as to choke the insides, and manages to steal from the vault for good measure. It is Elizabethan drama, bedroom farce, and murder mystery all at once. It's bad theatre. But the worst productions can be spectacular in their failings. If only *so much*.

Nice, Clean Margins

There's a phrase you can pick up if you spend enough time kicking around cancer wards: *clean margins*. It's what surgeons look for when they decide to go Gordon Ramsay on the pesky nibs and knobs of us that start to go bad. *Nice, clean margins*. It's what they ask the lab to look for under the scope as the patient lies spatchcocked on the operating table. Clean tissue free of visible disease. The hi-res go-ahead to lace you back up. Maybe they get a little greedy while they're in there, slice off a little extra, a little more than they really need. Just to be safe. Just to avoid having to open someone back up. There's another phrase you may be just as unfamiliar with, less medical in nature. *Green leaf volatiles*. It's that sweet, dense funk of fresh- cut grass, a scent so visceral, it practically smells electric green. So entranced have we grown with this smack of summer, so transfixed, we got so busy bottling and selling it, we failed to learn that burning on our mantles and dangling with our delicates is chemical warfare. Methanol, ethanol, acetone. Our lawn's violent emission in response to damage. A dirty bomb we suck down like a slushie. So blind drunk, we cut a little closer, drop the blade a notch or two below where we should. Maybe we nick some roots along the way, leave a few knuckles bloody. Long as the lawn is even. Long as it buys more time. Surgeons do it to avoid going back in. Groundskeepers do it to avoid going back out. It's all just an exercise in buying time. So, you missed a spot. No matter. Step back and the margins look clean. So, the knuckles bleed. No matter. Step back and the grass will hide it. So what if, from this very moment, it all begins to grow back with a vengeance. Step back, step back, step back. Far enough where the view is clear and the smell is splendid.

And the grass stops screaming.

On Respecting the Layers

When surgeons cut into men, they drag the scalpel slow and precise. On some level, each one of them has done this before. They start on pigs and then try their hand at dissecting the cadaver of some soul either altruistic or, even in death, scheming for a free cremation. Time, tide, and thousands of supervised hours eventually lead to the operating room, pulsing with a light that burns a shadow clean off the feet. There, amidst the clicks and hisses, and breathing through a paper mask, they begin at the close, learning first to suture and cobble together the living tissue recently sliced open by doctors far more practiced. It is through this exercise in reverse that they become intimately acquainted with how much damage the knife actually inflicts. That it is not just the skin that must be cut to get to the guts of a person, but also blankets of subcutaneous fat, fascia, muscles, tendons, ligaments, and in some cases, even ostium (the lining around the bone). It is, as some physicians refer to it, "a seven-layer cake." Only after mastering the art of reconstruction does one then graduate to tying off vessels, then to excisions, then upward through the myriad levels until the steel-stomached and persistent hold a blade to the unbroken flesh of someone's mother or brother. And they will drag, slow and precise, a hand steadied by respect not just for the numbed-out human beneath them, but for the layers of them. Even as proficiency begets a routine that, in other worlds, might encourage a tendency to play cowboy, the grip never loosens. The drag never accelerates. *The layers must be respected.*

My father had a bypass scar—an eight-inch gash down the center of his breastbone that the years had faded into a pinkish splotch obscured by tufts of curly, black chest hair. In a way it was cool, especially if you're the sort that's prone to romanticize. Like death itself had come for him and stabbed him through the heart, only to watch the intended victim draw the sword from his chest and brandish it in pure sport. But the reaper doesn't stand for mockery. Not for long. As the nurse peeled away the medical tape beneath the scar, a new line from the gauze emerged, a continuation of the very same path, marked by staples that ran down the length of his abdomen, through the navel, stopping right above the groin. It was a clean cut, proficient, almost compulsive in its need to match the original. Like scribbling pupils onto a late Modigliani, it was as if someone perceived incompletion and took up the cause to finish the job.

His wound bathed and redressed, Dad was left with little else to do but scab, drawing the gown across the bandages out from which wisps of rust-colored iodine poke. To his left, Mom sat, head bowed and spilling every observation, every vital reading, every fluff of pillows into a thickening spiral notebook:

> Feels better. He is on fluids & IV. Stomach tube is unclamped. They suspect his stomach is not ready for solids yet. Tomorrow they will clamp stomach tube and see how he reacts. Although his eyes are hazy, he still looks better than yesterday. He looked fatigued yesterday.

As long as he kept down his own juices, it meant that they could remove a tube. It meant his organs were remembering how to do what they do. As long as she jotted down doctors' names, demeanors, vague assertions, and siphoned answers in a manner that would put a stomach pump to shame, it meant we knew more today than we did yesterday. Each of them had their jobs, tasks to mark progress and cross off the hours as days extended outward. In that stretch, I felt the length of every minute. And in need of an official capacity, I named myself watchdog, fixing on the doorway to the hall, ready to pounce the minute the spectacled surgeon should arrive with a folder tucked into his armpit.

This was day nine. Nine days since they'd cut my father open like a Thanksgiving turkey and removed his giblets. Four days past when we'd been told the pathology report was due. The report that would either rebuff or confirm the surgeon's opinion that the mass removed from the head of Dad's pancreas "felt like cancer." Five days, he said, it would take for the results to return. But, when a leading expert— the only man qualified to deliver the findings—is called out of town for a speaking engagement, so must the possibly terminal wait. And wait. And pack the empty space with crossword puzzles and word searches until you shove the book aside when, while sniffing for "fetal" among a random assortment of letters, "f-a-t-a-l" pop up like deadly kernels gone as quickly as they're found. And when four channels of court television prove ineffective at distracting the eye from the rustle of a room-dividing curtain, laps up and down the steps between floors prove mildly successful as filler. Until, of course, I lose track of how long I've been gone and return to the room, questioning through huffs if I have missed the arrival of the oracle.

Do that enough times and the exasperated parents will send you out scouring for food that doesn't arrive on wheels. Not that Dad is allowed solids or, between Mom and me, there's a single appetite to be found. No, it's a foolish errand. One that each of us acknowledges in the silence knowing full well that there's nothing edible to procure in all of Washington Heights. Or maybe it just seems that way. In either event, I wander, staying within relatively close proximity, stepping through the glass rotunda, watching recent releases wheel out into the sunshine as hopeful arrivals step through the opposite side of the revolving door. One out, one in. The population never changes. Across the street, a banner hangs from the parking structure. AMAZING THINGS ARE HAPPENING HERE. I want to believe it more than I've ever believed anything.

When enough time has passed, I corral a couple deflated sandwiches from a pub a few blocks down, heading back before the grease can eat through the paper container. In the room, they wait for me. Mom's notebook sits folded closed on her lap, Dad sits folded upright in the bed. Both faces painted with a hopeful severity, a color I haven't seen since the day I was fitted for a back brace. It's not what we wanted, but it's better than it could have been. Early stage two. Out of twenty-one lymph nodes tested, only six affected. He'll need chemotherapy, once a week for six months. Then, a re-evaluation. They hold hands. And I think: *that's it, right? Six out of twenty-one ain't bad. Surely, they got it all out.*

Somewhere in the back of my mind a child wonders aloud. *How long have they known?* He asks, "if that's the whole story, why the rehearsal?" But, for now, his queries are lost. A banner thwacks between two poles as forgotten sandwiches cool on the windowsill. AMAZING THINGS ARE HAPPENING HERE.

I want to believe it.

The skin folds, right where the underside of the arm joins the chest. Right where your knees pucker, standing up. Where the inside of your elbow creases as the arm bends. Langer lines, they're called. Human topography. The direction in which collagen fibers align. These fibers grow, weblike, designed to withstand tension from all directions. Cut along the Langer, or just parallel to it, and the skin tends to heal quicker, better. It finds its way back. But not every surgery affords such consideration. Some operations, for instance, those of the chest cavity, require perpendicular bisection. In these cases, doctors have little choice. They must violate the line. And even when all is closed up properly, fibrogenesis conducts itself randomly. New tissue grows in mismatched order, beyond the boundaries of the wound. It puckers, inflames, and heals, leaving behind a new layer of skin that differs in pigment and in sensitivity. A mark that remembers the trauma.

The immediate world of a post-op cancer patient has very little to do with recovery. Removing a tumor and the outlying tainted tissue remains the medically agreed upon initial course of action. In the operating room, doctors carve out generously, taking more than they need to decrease the margin of error. The patient, hovering several inches above death, waits with their innards exposed to the world while carpaccioed slivers of themselves are rushed under the light of the microscope. Little by little, bits are shaved and clamped between glass in the hopes of preserving whatever usable fraction of an organ remains. Slide after slide, the pathologist examines the gross characteristics (weight, color, size, consistency), then the microscopic attributes (size, shape, features of cells). This process occurs on a loop until the tissue comes back clean and the team in the OR, believing they've removed all discernible evidence of cancer, begins to put Humpty Dumpty back together again.

"Discernible," is, itself, a tricky word. Still, it more or less fits. In surgical oncology, the name of the game is removing what can be seen. Doctors will couch their observations and noncommittal statements with phrases like "to the naked eye." This is not a trick meant to skirt litigation. It is a reality. It is why the next words out of their mouths are "metastasis starts at a cellular level." It is why cancer is fought in a militaristic manner. It is observed with drones and satellites. Yet, even the most powerful camera can't pick a single radical out of a gathered crowd. So, they move in and chop off the cabal at the head, hoping the extremities will wither and die. But they never do. They just go into hiding and stew for a bit. So, the espionage begins, the wiretaps. Physicians eavesdrop through the blood, sift amongst the body's internal chitchat for markers and antigens that tumors release to the stream. All of this reconnaissance takes place not so much in anticipation of a subsequent attack, but rather, in step with active offense. When battling cancer, the prevailing strategy is, and always has been, to go scorched earth. Blitz now, ask questions later. Cities are leveled with fire from above. The rivers are poisoned because everyone drinks from it, innocents and enemies alike. The imaging and the blood work search for targets, yes, but also for bodies.

As a son, I come to learn most of this indirectly. Being at work makes it impossible to attend every infusion, checkup, weigh-in, and progress report. On weekends, I'm downloaded with what I'm sure is the sanitized, edited-for-TV network cut of the topline updates. Not because my parents feel I can't handle it but because they're parents and no matter how old we get they forever outrank us. So, I fill in the blanks, sneaking peeks into my mother's journal:

October 10th, 2012: Five months post-surgery. Tumor markers at 665. Down from 926 in July.

The numbers are reassuring. It's the scans that terrify me. Each time they toss him on the belt and send him through the machine like a carry-on bag, I wait for the moment when we're ushered aside and told they have to open him up. But as the months roll by, the results remain inconclusive, stymied by sheets of scar tissue that frost the area: a Betty Crocker occlusion. That is how it's translated to me, by extension. And as much as I throw myself down digital wormholes to explore every prescription and stage and statistic out of a skepticism that doctors could feel or care for my father as deeply as I do, I take the word of my folks as scripture. Despite my doubts that a sophisticated piece of imaging machinery designed to peer through muscle and bone is somehow incapable of seeing past some jumble of fibers, that topic remains the one exclusion from my Google search bar. Because in that I recognize the devices employed to shield me, I also know the difficult pills cannot be held behind a child-protective lid.

Perhaps I indulge it. To an extent, regardless of age, our originators never shed the urge to plop us in high chairs and spoon mushed beans into our waiting mouths. To an extent we never lose the urge to lap it up, clapping our pudgy fingers together to encourage the exercise. But even if the Pull-Ups hug my waist a little too tight, accepting the limitation also allows for a firewall. It establishes leads that are off-limits from my investigation, so that it actually becomes possible to exhaust myself. I could pour through pages on targeted chemotherapy and scroll through message boards about survivor stories and research the success rates of the most recent clinical trials. Obeying the parameters keeps me leashed, closes the circuit, and in the absence of a new subject, guides me toward articles that are variations on what I've already read. Then variations of variations; same words, different order. "Persistence Pays Off For Edward Zellinga." "Carmen Reyes-Hiroya: Still Here, Fighting Every Day." "Ronald DiCicco Never Gives Up Hope." Spooning from the same bowl over the course of months. Until the stomach begins to turn. Until what once satiated a hunger now gives rise only to a sourness of the tongue.

The beauty in that distaste is a freedom. The drug loses its effect when the dosage cannot be increased. Through sober eyes I begin to realize that knowing the chemical makeup and compound compatibility of medications isn't going to make them work any better. To read about "Ronald once again enjoying the activities he loves" or how "Carmen considers herself a walking miracle" doesn't change the fact that my father is neither Ronald nor Carmen. Without the desire for a hit, closing the laptop screen becomes the easiest thing in the world. And from behind, the planet comes back into focus; the story that has been unfolding the entire time I've been looking down. I help my father assemble shelves in the garage and watch him organize his tools, file taxes, polish his Bburago diecast model cars, sit on the deck watching the Phragmites sway to Simply Red's "Sunrise." There are little differences. He moves a bit slower across the room and medical restrictions have extracted an evening glass of liqueur from between his fingers. But they're all temporary sacrifices, steps in our dance beneath a veil of tissue. Up to and until its dissolution, I put my faith in the design of my architects; I align with the direction of the fibers. All to accelerate the healing.

The process of new tissue production is referred to as "fibrogenesis." This gets set into motion as the body reacts to injury, replacing the damage on every level with new proteins and fibers that explode in outward arrangement—like a firework—resulting in the formation of a scar. On the surface, a surgeon might extend the length of an incision, thereby reducing strain on tissue and often resulting in a scar that disappears almost completely. For superficial cuts, this is favorable. But, if such care doesn't extend to deeper wounds, suitable healing can be impeded, causing fibers to grow irregularly, stiffen, and calcify. For some, flexibility becomes hampered. For others, joints freeze entirely. Shoulders lock, necks jam, and unblemished patients are left to wonder why they cannot look any way but forward.

Emerge the perpendicularities. The stumbles, the shakes, the phone calls at 12:45 am "We're in the emergency room." Late-night drives southbound on the parkway, a jacket covering whatever I was able to throw on before falling out the front door. It's dark cutting through the Pine Barrens, almost peaceful. The way the trees brush against a midnight blue sky has a hypnotic effect, drawing the eye away from the odometer until red lights appear in the rear-view.
 "Why we in such a rush tonight?"
 "I'm sorry. I'm trying to get home. My father's sick."
 "What's wrong with him?"
 "He has cancer." A pause. The light in my eyes clicks out.
 "Just…slow down." I remind myself to feel guilty later about using his illness to get out of a ticket.
 It becomes almost routine. Explaining his history to doctors who've never met him as they attempt to describe some biological oddity. Hours pass, sometimes days. He's released. He goes back to the oncologist. It's all to be expected, we're told. The toxicity has built up. It has its effects. It's working. Nine months, he's beating the odds. His numbers are stable. We'll soup him up, give him blood, give him fluids, give him physical therapy. A young woman comes on weekends, walks him to the kitchen stool. He lifts his legs off the floor, does arm curls with two-pound dumbbells. Each time he bounces back, a little more diminished but never less resolute. His face withers, but not his

expression. Not once does he allow anyone in his orbit to believe these are anything other than expected annoyances, laughably surmountable. "Sometimes it's necessary to go a long distance out of the way to come back a short distance correctly." Edward Albee doing wrist bends.

We're comfortable with the long way. Centuries of idioms profess it produces the best result. Not only that, but time is time, whether fought or bought. So we flank him—Mom on one side, me on the other—yet he maintains a lead, just a few steps ahead. After all, it's his route to chart. So focused are we, though; so poised are our hands to catch him should he falter that we cannot look any way but due north. And it's a useful distraction. It keeps our eyes glued in one direction so that whatever misgivings the wind kicks up might be heard but never lingered upon. Not as long as he keeps moving.

The problems come when we stop. When I wake to find the fire smoldering and the camp deserted. On a cloud-covered Martin Luther King Jr. Day, I drive down to watch the house. This is what I say, but no house needs watching when the owners have only stepped out for a common consult, a briefing on the latest results of the latest scan. But something tells me to be nearby, and then I'm nearby, convincing myself I can pack the time with work. For the first hour, I open and close documents. For the second, I clean my inbox. For the second-and-a-half hour, I walk between the kitchen and the dining room window that looks out over the driveway. Nothing moves; not the clouds, not the branches. Only the seconds, as they stretch into the third and fourth hours, make it more and more difficult to explain the delay. The mind ambles, calculates the distance to and from, factoring in traffic that wouldn't exist on a Monday in January. Even then, they should've been home. Emerge the cross-sections, the asymmetries, what they may have found out. Matters that warrant painstaking explanation. Or worse, matters that force the concerned to drive in circles and search for detours while they figure out how to soften the blow in translation. That's the issue with stopping—at some point there's nothing left to do but look around and wonder.

Intruding upon the wondering is a garage door that sets the entire house vibrating. Calm as a catastrophist, I'm down the stairs, ready to surrender my irrationalities to the pillars of reason. This time, though, my father passes through the frame, not so much a pillar but a stump. Slower than I've ever seen him he clinks at the ground with his cane, looking up without quite ever meeting my gaze. "Hello, Joseph," he greets my chin and moves past to scale the stairs. Behind him, Mom sloshes in, her stride slackened by a knee-high water no one else can see. In her left hand, the clutched notebook; in her right, the small of my father's back. No words are exchanged. Not between them. Not between us. Not until they reach the top of the stairs. As if, by then, the story hasn't already gone softcover.

Two people had walked through the door wearing faces I'd only seen before in the mirror, that of those given no choice but to confront the alternative. Up to that point, procedure had been our center of gravity. Chaotic as it was, even chaos can become procedural if it has a point. With the point removed, chaos gives way to silence as the planet rolls off its axis, dizzying the mind until heartburn swallows the speech. Even as the equilibrium settles, the throat aches in a reluctance to follow down a path diverged. And as my parents disappear atop the landing, I remain below, five toes touching where silence violated the line.

In a PET scan—short for *positron emission tomography*—patients get injected with a special dye that contains radioactive tracers. These tracers, once absorbed by organs and tissues, are designed to gather in areas of high chemical activity. Passed head-to-toe through an imaging system, the PET scan captures the body in a detailed way that reveals concentrations of radioactivity as bright spots, indicating a burrow of active disease. As conditions like cancer have a higher metabolic rate than those non-cancerous, the PET scan can track progression at a cellular level, succeeding where all other scans fail. This is also highly effective in denoting a clear differentiation between fibrosis and recurrence.

On the eighth floor of the Herbert Irving Pavilion is the Pancreas Center at New York Presbyterian Hospital. Within the center are the offices of some of the world's leading pancreatic surgeons. Inside one of those offices, a team—including the very man who removed my father's own cancerous mass—pore over the most recent renderings of his insides. Further in, just a few doors down, we wait, the three of us, for their consensus. There's a little less of us than there was the last time we sat here. And a little more: a new spot on the head of Dad's pancreas, two more on the liver. I didn't personally see the imaging, but with his tumor markers up to 4,000, I imagine it looks something like a nighttime descent into Las Vegas.

In the days since the quiet violence, we begin to move with new intent. There's an urgency in our steps, wind in our sails from the gusts of doors closing all around us. We take appointments, seek opinions, shuffling his wiry frame across the Tri-State Area in the hope for a pill or an epiphany. Arm in arm, we lead him, one step behind us now—and there's the difference. He comes willingly, without argument, possibly because he knows the answer already exists as a few megabytes on a hard drive. But we won't speak it out loud, not until someone walks through that door and confirms it. That this is no longer a rescue mission, but one of recovery; that this is not about saving his life but about saving as much of it as we can.

A tumble of sounds, stern hoots, and shushes of rubber soles roll down the hall, quieting into whispers that gather in the light from under the door. Over the *flap* of my mother's search for a clean page, Dad turns his head and looks me square in the eye. For a moment, there is nothing. Too many words hang in the air for me to pick from. He knows. He knows I know. He knows I want to fix it. He knows none of us can. It won't stop him from trying. "Don't worry," he says, the corners of his mouth lifting. "They're gonna make it sound a lot worse than it is."

I nod. I find the energy to smile back, to show that I believe him, whether or not I do. That's why we cut parallel, so as to limit the damage. I won't violate the line, even if mine has already been. Because beneath his grin is anger, is fear, is confusion, is grief—all stacked, all holding it up. So, I smile back because I can see them now. The layers must be respected.

Loud, Quiet

Her tears were wilting my French fries. Not that it mattered. In yet another booth of yet another nameless highway diner, appetite had once again become a memory. Only, this time, the reason had shifted. Patrons within earshot did piss-poor jobs of hiding their curiosities, crouching behind foggy partitions and menus slashed with syrupy dribble. They took their turns glancing between turns of laminated pages that ripped through the silence like the pull of Velcro. But, neither that nor the soft tones of Lite FM snowing from ceiling speakers nor the stovetop gristle that popped between swings of the kitchen door was enough to dull the whimpers coming from across the table. Each one of them sending pangs of pure anguish through the woman's face, contorting it ever more into the face of some stranger; some loud, quiet thing. I watched my hand as it moved to offer itself across the divide, giving up halfway, and pushed my plate out of sight instead. My mother was crying. And I wanted to leave.

My reflexive indifference was not lost on me. However, it was impossible not to feel like some agreement had been violated. Over the last thirteen months, the two of us had racked up a lifetime's worth of rewards points at cruddy eateries like this one. We'd find some dimly lit corner and stab at chef's specials, feeding on each other's lies while cancer fed on my father in some hospital down the road. Over the scrape of stainless steel against ceramic, reassurances lobbed back and forth, cutting through clouds of carbon dioxide and fryer oil. *"Once his kidneys bounce back, he should be able to start chemo again." "Elevated markers on the blood test, but no new lesions on the scan." "Gastro thinks he found a drug that should help with the diarrhea." "He looked good today. Maybe, if we bring him some ice cream, he won't put up a fight."* That was the deal. That was the tacit contract: to exchange stone-faced placations while trying to bury our terror under heaping gulps of all-beef patties and grease.

This was no crying game. Crying was for under blankets and into pillows. Crying was for the elevator in the parking garage after pretending to leave something in your car. Crying was for the shower, where not even God could tell the tears from the running water. But in the light of day, there was absolutely no crying in cancer.

To be fair, there isn't a child ever prepared to watch their parent come undone, not even at the age of twenty-seven. I had no barometer, no learned mechanism. No instruction booklet for "How to Console the Consoler." It was like watching some lost, deleted scene from *Raiders of the Lost Ark* where, faced with momentous peril, Indiana Jones drops to his knees and weeps softly into the collar of his worn leather jacket. Up until this point, we'd been navigating the same temple, getting tripped up by the same booby traps. All the while, I'd maintained indelible faith in my brazen, hard-nosed navigator. Now, though, it seemed we'd hit one snare too many. The walls had crumbled, the boulder was rolling right for us, and Indy was in the fetal position. *Get up!* I wanted to scream. *Get up, you fool! Don't you see what's coming? We have to run!* But I didn't. I stood, watching the shadow loom larger and hoping against all hope for some secret door to reveal itself.

My mother dabbed at wet, swollen eyes, emptying her grief into a paper napkin that grew increasingly translucent. Behind her very own Shroud of Turin, she dissolved into a collection of flesh-toned streaks. I prayed for it to soak up all of her pain, for some loaves-and-fishes miracle that would return and fortify her iron will. Until that could happen, my emotional stopper would remain firmly in place, forcing a backlog of familiar cynicism. As the pressure built, I palmed at a sugar caddy in disarray searching for even the tiniest way to restore balance to the universe. Facedown, I spilled the contents onto the table and shuffled the sweeteners into tiny mounds. The whites slid back into place nicely enough, but with each subsequent sob, I found myself jamming the pinks, blues, and yellows in with a force that ruptured their pregnant bellies and until the air swam with white particles. By the time the final sleeve of Splenda shouted up at me to "Share the Love." Mom had sensed my displeasure. "I'm sorry. I'm sorry," glottal, she fought through heaving breaths to regain herself.

Stewing in my own embarrassment, I flicked the caddy back to its slot amongst the condiments, avoiding her eye line. "It's okay."

I wish I could say, at that point, I let up. I wish I could say I took her hand and held it, closing out the rest of the world and offering a heartfelt validation. I wish.

This weeping figure was unknown to me. Rifling through my memory, I fought to call up a single image of my mother ever in such a state, coming up dry. By all accounts, including our own shared history, this woman held a relationship with hardship most intimate. Having lost her own loving mother at age nine, she and her sister were forced to leave Italy to come to America where they would suffer under the hands of their father. A crippled man unable to earn a living, he turned his frustrations on his own flesh, defenseless against a second wife who emasculated him every chance she got. *"She'd egg him on and he'd hit us even harder,"* an ocean separating them from a family that would forever mark their absence with two empty settings at their dinner table. *"Please cry,"* he'd plead between throws, *"just cry and I'll stop."* But she wouldn't. *"I just stood there and stared right back, never letting him forget the man he used to be."*

In that house she marked the days of her sentence under the regime of a warden who never missed a chance to remind her *"There's only two ways you leave here: with a ring on your finger or in a pine box."* Despite not asking for a protector, the neighborhood saw fit to send reinforcements. At a local picnic she caught the eye of a slightly older boy who lived a few blocks over. From that time forward, she'd find him waiting, day after day, for the chance to walk her home from choir practice; a home she'd finally free herself of when she married that boy a few years down the line. Soon after the honeymoon, though, misfortune found her new address. Manifesting as a tiny mountain range of tumors that laid waste to her ear canal, it silently siphoned the sounds from her world. Still, as she began to sink into the hushed quicksand of her own scar tissue, that very same neighborhood boy—now a man—would swoop in to pull her up by the arms to prevent her from losing sight. *"You can either feel sorry for yourself, or you can keep moving."* So, she kept moving.

And she persisted. After the miscarriages, the experimental treatments, and the pregnancy that nearly left her in a wheelchair, she had her baby. After the years of exhaustive physical therapy, she walked. After the numerous reconstructive surgeries to her middle ear, she heard. After the father's deathbed atonement, she forgave. After the layoffs, she worked. After the husband's heart scare and the triple bypass, she dressed his wounds. Then when adenocarcinoma came for his pancreas, his appetite, his humor, and his identity, she drove him to treatment, she coaxed him to eat, she made him laugh, and she reminded him of who he was.

My mother was the stone from which life could not get blood. Yet, here she was, in front of me, bleeding. And without the tools to tie off the vein, I sat there and let it spill and pool and rise until the riptide swallowed me down.

Stomach half-empty, I'd certainly had my fill. Dropping a wad of cash onto the table, it was all I could do to bring a swift end to this meal and an even swifter exit out to the car. We spent most of the ride back to the hospital in silence as Mom tilted toward the passenger window and let the breeze wick the remaining liquid agony that shimmered in the corners of her eyes. I palmed the wheel and drove on autopilot, trying to untangle any words from my knotted tongue that might bridge the widening gap between us. But under every loosened snarl were two more just like it. We pulled into the parking lot so I could drop her off at the entrance. Sliding into the sun, I watched as her spine straightened with each step along the sidewalk until, as she slipped through the sliding doors, she'd returned to the pillar I'd always known her to be.

Finding the closest available spot, I slid the car into place but left the engine running having recently discovered an idling motor's effectiveness at masking the shrieks of my customary pre-visitation breakdowns. But, over the grumble of the exhaust, though disturbed, I found myself unable to bring any tangible element of reaction to the surface. Distracted by my mother's miraculous transformation, I replayed what I'd just witnessed over and over again. Stone by stone, she'd reassembled herself, readied once again to deflect the bleak tableaus of the intensive care unit. That was the transaction, I suppose. When a loved one stumbles and gets scraped, we speak an unspoken oath not to reflect their pain but to remain steadfast so that they might regain their footing. That was the contract to which my mother was beholden, not to mine but to the one she'd struck with the only man in a lifetime ever to hold her up.

Unbeknownst to me, I'd signed my name to a similar covenant not minutes ago on a sticky vinyl bench. Mom was down, not out of weakness as I might've believed, but because she knew there was no fix. Dr. Jones had no more tricks up her sleeve. This was the finale. But, in lieu of allowing her the freedom to mourn, I'd chosen to chip away at it. Staring out the windshield, I finally felt the dynamic complete its shift. For as long as my mother would need to cry, I knew I would no longer be able to. I would shore up my pillar with numbness and indignation, whatever it took to maintain a rigid but obliging façade. If there were any foundational deficiencies, they were my own. As I cut the engine, I resolved to stop punishing her for them.

How to Shave Your Dying Father

I - Prepping the Skin

I fill the metal bowl in the sink three times before the tap finally produces water warm enough to soothe. Little curls of steam dance along the surface. Still, it's nothing you'd brew your tea with. At the bottom, the crumpled facecloth springs to life, knocked conscious by the heat. It twists and pulses, like a white jellyfish, chasing the tip of my index finger before I leave it to soak in bewilderment.

Across the room, Dad lies in the hospice bed that we'd pushed against the window; the top half of the frame inclined so that he might catch some of the morning light. His lips move without sound, engaged in deep conversation with the ghosts at his feet. "They see people," the visiting nurse whispered to me earlier that day. "When the end is close, it's not uncommon for them to receive visitations from loved ones who've long passed on." I believed her instantly. Not because she'd said so emphatically, but instead with the cadence of someone to whom that notion was no more remarkable than the weather.

Apparitions or not, this was a man for whom entertaining guests always meant a neatly combed head of hair and a clean-shaven face. The son of a barber, he'd spent his childhood sweeping up clippings and watching every breed of gent—from mechanics to bankers—invest their hard-earned dough in a daily skim of the razor's edge. Barbicide pumped through his veins, blue and clean. Appearance for him became a reflection of a man's civility, of his humanity.

Trouble is, humanity is the first thing cancer comes for, and the victory in that fight is a game of controlled surrender. Like Washington's retreat from Brooklyn, you give up a city so you can fight for the country. Patients give up tissue. They surrender lymph nodes and organs and limbs because anatomy is not identity. Identity is smiling at your son as he holds you against the toilet tank so that you can relieve yourself with dignity. It's murmured gratitude to those who clean and dress your unsteady frame. It's a fresh shave that you might converse with heavenly callers while looking like your best self.

Wringing most of the water into the basin, I stand over my father and apply the damp cloth from ear to ear, tucking slightly under his nostrils so the man can breathe. There is no real preparation for a moment like this. No guidelines. The path to preservation is littered with crippling opportunity. We accept the fact that I am to perform the very last shave on the man who performed my very first. Still, while it may not be a cure-all, in the face of a tough decision a hot towel can indeed soften things up.

II - Choosing the Right Tools

The art of shaving, with its catalogued varietals of creams and gels and buzzers and blades, is a matter of individual preference. For most, the correct combination of apparatus is discerned only after years of burns, nicks, and bloodshed. Once arrived upon, though, a man's tonsorial cocktail becomes as sacrosanct as a Macallan 25 to the discriminating scotch drinker.

My father's particular mixture consisted of equal parts Gillette Mach 3, boar brush, and Bay Rum soap. Classic and contemporary, it was an impossibly cool composite that brought shame upon the spray can of Barbasol and Fusion5 razor that normally darkened the corner of my vanity. *Any man that needs more than three blades might as well shave with a butcher's knife,* he'd say, scraping the foam from his cheek and dropping a few more clouds into a sink full of gray sky. Meanwhile, I could take a cheese grater and barely put a dent into the five o'clock shadow that seemed to cling to my face for dear life.

From the bathroom, I fetch the supplies, tossing out a worn, scummy cartridge and fitting a new blade onto the wand. Running my thumb over the dry bristles of the brush, I search the canister of shaving soap for directions but find only the promise of "maintaining rugged good looks." Simple as it might seem, when there's only one shot at doing something right, the obvious has a knack for unlearning itself. Through repetition, men come to know the contours of their own face so well that we could shave in our sleep. But point the razor in the other direction and it becomes open-heart surgery.

Emptying the contents of my hands onto the TV tray, I arrange them neatly and make my acquaintance. Water, wine, and host, in this moment, these are the gifts I can bring to the altar. Faithful, present, and an offering to the Father. *May the Lord accept the sacrifice at your hands…*

III - Applying the Cream

He closes his eyes as I press my hands to his cheeks. Softly. Since he stopped talking, it's more difficult to tell if something's hurting him. Using the backs of my fingers, I massage the last of the water into his pores while checking to make sure he doesn't wince. Underneath the cloth, his skin glows, alive and pink. If I angle my hand just right, I can block everything from the neck down and pretend like he's asleep, like he could flutter open at any moment and spring to the kitchen for a cup of coffee.

The towel goes back in the basin and the lid pops from the soap canister. I am overtaken by a waltz of rum and bay leaves, and as they spin, the world gets smaller. Without knowing how, I am four feet tall, just barely able to see over the edge of the vanity. Dad runs the brush under the faucet and squeezes the surplus dampness from the bristles in the crook of his thumb. Then, like a mad conductor, he swirls the tips against the top layer of soap, faster and faster until it crescendos with a substantial gooey lather. A stop, the music halts for an instant as he holds the baton aloft, only to begin again. Legato, this time. Broad strokes connecting.

I follow the beat. One, two, three. One, two, three. Rinse, squeeze, lather. I'm short of natural rhythm but teach me the steps and I catch on quickly. The brush drips with freshly frothed cream, and I lean over my dewy patron. "It's just me, Dad. I'm going to give you a shave." His lips part, but nothing emits save for a whiff of sourdough from the plaques of candidiasis. That's not his scent. Yet, every time he breathes out, he has to smell his own decay.

I paint over the corrosion. From the earlobes, across his cheeks, I move in tiny circles. No one tells me why; it just seems like the thing to do. With each run of the brush, another element of the bouquet flourishes. A little bergamot across the chin, clove and cinnamon under his nose. Down the left, right, and center of his neck: ginger, black pepper, vanilla. The beauty of the process reveals itself as I go. Melodic, aromatic, and bracing, the dimensions tease my receptors in a way gel from a can never could.

He smells like himself again. Lather-bearded, he rests as little black spurs begin to poke through tufts of cream. The brush suddenly makes sense. I see how it makes the hairs stand at attention. I see the madness in smashing canned goop on your face if all it accomplishes is a flattening of the beard. But mostly I see how, whether or not he knows it, my father continues to teach me.

IV - Handling the Razor

It's important to give the foam a minute to set that it might soften the root of the hair, making it easier to shear. This time can be used to become acquainted with the razor. Each make and model, while designed for similar application, is inordinately different in its architecture. Dad's Mach 3 was an uncomplicated tool; a triple-blade cartridge that sat atop a symmetrical silver handle. Simple, unpretentious, and a stark opposite to the gizmo I was used to working with. A peacock of a thing with its anti-friction blades, precision trimmer, bright-orange comfort guard, and ribbed rubber grip, my Fusion5 looked like something they'd roll out at the North American International Auto Show.

Without the bells and whistles and optional rear bike rack, Dad's razor sits light in my palm. Afraid I might run the risk of applying too much pressure, I splash a flurry of soap on the underside of my arm to get a feel for how the blades drag against the skin. Gripping the base, I place the cartridge lightly at the start with the tip of my index. In a single, fluid motion, I plow a neat path through the snow. No tugs, no snags; just a clean pull I'm ashamed to be so proud of.

To be sure, it was a foolish and excessive amount of rehearsal for a procedure so basic, but there are no do-overs here. This isn't something I volunteered for. I never wanted to be in charge of my father's final anything. However, wants and preferences get chucked upon learning that the medical definition for palliative care is "every breath could be your last." So now that it came down to me, a nick or cut was no longer something a shred of tissue could clot. It was a scar that would likely never heal, a mark that he'd be buried with. It was a way to fail my father one last time.

I suppose the good part is you only have a minute to consider these thoughts. It's imperative to set to work before the foam dries.

V - The First Strokes

There's no way to straddle the bed. And attempting to do this while leaning over the head would require a straight razor and the skills of a seasoned barber—neither of which I possess. Still, I need to find a way to hold him steady because, in this transaction, at least one of us shouldn't be suppressing the shakes. So, I lower my knee onto the side of the mattress, taking careful steps not to mistake one of his legs for a ruffle in the blanket, accidentally crushing him. Turning his face toward the window, I rest my palm along the crest of his forehead and whisper into a near-translucent earlobe. "Dad...Dad, it's still me. I'm going to start, okay? You let me know if I'm hurting you."

Ah. That's all I get from him. Not permission or protest, more like acknowledgment. As if he's telling me: "Ah, yes. The boy who shaved his cheeks in an upward motion for an entire year, and now he's going to take a cleaver to my face. Have at it."

I pause to laugh. At my uncanny ability to add context where there is none. At the fact that the guttural noise I heard was likely involuntary and probably just the venting of acid reflux. But I like the fact that Dad's still digging at me. I like the fact that my hand's not trembling anymore. So I begin.

I place the blade just above the three sparse gray hairs that suggest what was once a sideburn. Starting in the more planar areas should allow me a few practice runs while limiting the odds of hitting a snag. In an undisturbed motion, I pull it halfway down the slope of his cheek, leaving behind a freshly pruned ribbon of turf. Into the basin go the soapy fragments of him. A swirl, a swish, and I finish the stroke. The work is good. Clean edges and well-maneuvered corners evoke more pride than the simple stroke of a razor should be afforded. Maybe it's the herbal cocktail smeared across his face, but he smells like fresh-cut grass. And now I'm lining up for another run.

Only, this time, I'm eleven. Pushing through the expanse of yard that sits in front of our old English Colonial, I round the trees and mulched flowerbeds with the exactitude of a Formula 1 racer. The Walkman at my waist beats out a mixtape pilfered from weeks of the noontime Hot 100. My lungs fill with exhaust and lawn clippings, and I am king of the earth, the king of the summer. Until I'm caught by the glint of sun off of silver aviator frames that peek around the corner of the garage.

He's watching me again. First it was through the sidelight, then the drapes of the living room window. Each time I catch him he scurries, only to be found minutes later posted at a nearby turret. I seethe, throttling the control lever. *If he doesn't trust me to do this on my own, he might as well do it himself.* So, I raise my pointer in accusation long enough for the mower to veer in the liberty of my one-handed grasp. Out of my mouth comes the scrape of metal as the motor housing rebounds, leaping into the air and cutting out dead upon landing. He steps from around the corner and I wheel the contraption to the side to survey the damage. There, poking through the dirt, freed from the brush that once hid it: the root of our cherry tree.

It is his cheekbone. My arm snaps back as soon as I feel the razor lift against it, and sure enough. The dusting of scruff had obscured it—the nodule poking through the sunken terrain of his face. But it doesn't bleed or even flush. The realization stops me from swallowing my own fist but not from picking up the stare of a single brown fisheye. All these years later. He watches me, still.

VI - Go With the Grain

One of the first lessons novice shavers come to learn is to "go with the grain," or shave in the direction of the hair's growth. Others may argue that going against the grain provides a closer shave as it bends the hair back, allowing a cut closer to the root. While this is technically true, pulling the hair away from the skin can be a harsh process often leading to snagged blades that yank out the hairs from below the surface. It many cases it also results in irritation, redness, and inflammation. However, to go with the grain does not necessarily mean the sacrifice of closeness for comfort. In fact, it often means having the fortitude to make the uncomfortable decision.

When Dad could barely stand after his last treatment, the oncologist said: "He won't survive another drop of chemo." The second opinion agreed, as did the third. So we stopped searching for a cure. When the surgeon said she could perform a procedure to open his bile duct, we asked what that would help. "Well, his eyes won't be yellow anymore," she replied. So we saw no reason to cut him open. When the caseworker brought up end-of-life care, she was clear about the options: "In-patient hospice can help to lighten the burden on the family during this difficult time." So we brought him home. Because it wasn't a burden. Because it was a privilege. And because the story might have started in a hospital, but it sure as hell wasn't going to finish there.

Going with the grain is not about giving up the fight, but rather, recognizing when the pain is self-inflicted. It's about understanding that we might not have been able to save his life, but we could save what was left of it. To pump Dad full of poison would not delay the inevitable. To subject him to a useless surgery would only siphon his collateral peace—an action for which we'd forever carry regret. Only when faced with them do the easy decisions reveal how deceptively painful they are.

There's a reason the wheat fields bend with the wind. It's not because they've surrendered. It's because they choose to bend rather than break.

VII – The Lip Area

Because of its sensitivity, the lip area is prone to excessive bleeding, even from the smallest cut. With its curls and divots, philtrum, and sulcus, the terrain is as welcoming as the dunes of Death Valley. One trick to simplifying is to have the patron puff out their cheeks, thus filling in the dimpled spaces and creating a more even surface on which to pass the blade. This tends to work best on those not already laboring to breathe. It also helps to be sure they're coherent enough to even understand the request.

"I'm going to do under your nose now. Okay, Dad?" Using my fingers as a guard, I push back his nose to pull the skin taut. In that moment, it's unclear which one of us really needs the reassurance. Yet, as his mouth closes in on itself, it's a reminder, once again, that he is more with me than I realize. And we are in this together.

Bit by bit, I prune patches of his upper lip, leaning in to inspect for accuracy and to assure that maneuvering to access a few rogue nostril hairs doesn't lead to an overzealous slice of his septum. Each strip of scruff to fall brings years with it until the face of a younger man begins to emerge. My chisel chips away at the weathered bits, loosening the granules of disease so that I might blow them into the air. So narrow is the space between us that it becomes difficult to tell which end of the world is up until I'm down on my back, a ball of flesh squirming against the marble of the kitchen counter. The legs of a hatchling kick toward the sky because he's cold and wet and unable to help himself. Frustration, a bile, howls upward from his stomach only to be choked down again when recognition steps through the gauzy range of infantile eyes. It is a vision, a comfortable outline developing from the negative. It is the one who grabs my crinkled feet and presses my toes to his lips, running them back and forth, trilling like paper against a comb. Vibrations run down my legs. I squawk and he does it again, even more vigorous the second time. He brings music to the world and I am the instrument he plays. And I am safe and I am loved. And we are in this together.

I scrape the last bit of cream from his face. We've switched places again, but not much else has changed. One of us is helpless. The other, desperate to help. Yet, where language fails, a familiar tune echoes. And he is safe and he is loved. And we are in this together.

VIII – The Neck Area

For most, it is advised to address the neck area last as the skin is a bit thinner and far more sensitive. This is also an area in which the shaver should not skimp on the lubrication. Generosity in application only further saturates the surface, creating the ideal condition for a steady glide of the blade. Since the skin in this area tends to be loose, craning the head back slightly will help to tighten things up, especially for a patron like mine whose once meaty neck now hangs. Puckered velvet curtains ready themselves for the close of the act.

Without the three hands necessary to cradle his head, to hold his neck taut, and to shave him at the same time, I have to wrap an arm behind Dad's back and lift him just enough to slide out one cushion from under him. He's trying to help. From the shudder in his chest, I can feel he's doing all he can to hold himself rigid so as not to flop backwards. But by the way his head slopes over the remaining pillow when I return him, it's clear he's spent his last ounce of strength.

Unlike the face, hair on the neck does not grow in uniformity. In fact, if the area was, it would resemble something scribbled by a spasmodic toddler. As if that isn't enough to inject caution into the proceedings, there is also the issue of his protruding Adam's apple—an article easier to broadside than a Buick. Palm to cheek, I inch across his lower jawline, sputtering along the narrows like a Sunday driver.

Give no argument to the detours and the end of the road still eventually rises out in front. Blacktop gives way to sand, a thick yellow ribbon that wraps around my father's neck. It's jaundice: a biological warning light, the symptom of a liver choked by malignancy. If I squint, I could almost confuse it for the reflection of noontime light bouncing off the bay and in through the window. But no trick of vision can silence the reverberation that shakes the walls. Disease might have taken his voice, but my father's throat screams.

IX – Rinse With Cold Water

Cold water is sort of miraculous. There are reasons why we feel an intrinsic need to splash our faces after voiding our guts, why it can wash away anything from the softest cries to body-wrenching sobs, why it douses the flames of searing panic. It is a physical, emotional, and psychological salve so powerful in its raw form that churches use it to immerse newborns and converts, believing it to have transcendental purification properties. When bodies ache, it fills the pores, soothes, and draws them shut, hushing the million voices that call out in pain. After aggravating the skin—a natural result of the shaving process—a cold rinse is an essential step in the finishing procedure.

Rinsing the bowl in the sink, I return with a freshly doused towel and begin to wipe away the cloud formations of Bay Rum that hover over the landscape of my father's face. I clean the crook of his brow and the corners of his mouth and then wriggle inside his ears. (Shaving soap always gets in the ears. Even if I don't shave, it just manifests. It's a phenomenon). With each pass of the cloth he glistens and grows flush, the body pushing blood to counteract the cold. A cross of the lips and they plump, as if ready to whistle "Reveille" from the bottom of the stairs, robbing me of the last five minutes of sleep before the alarm goes off for school. A span of the forehead and he's luminous, home from work, lifting me off the ground to press his cranium against my own. I marvel at his ability to go full Cyclops as he declares "One eye!" in his signature singsong.

The water pulls him to the surface and he bobs there for a while. But I can't pull him out. Not all the way. Should I try to grab him, the liquid escaping my closing fist will carry him away. Should I try to lift him, he'll drip over the edges of my hand. All I can think of is to re-wet the towel. Perhaps if I never let him dry up, he can float here forever.

X – Applying Aftershave

For those under the impression that an aftershave serves purely an aesthetic purpose—like kale and an orange slice on the side of a club sandwich—I should note that aftershave is no garnish. Not only does it help to soothe the skin and replenish moisture, but proper brands will also include an antiseptic agent that acts as an astringent to reduce irritation. While some might choose to forego this step due to the mild (but brief) burning sensation that follows application, they, in turn, miss an opportunity to kill rash-inducing bacteria. More than that, by sidestepping the heat they entirely neglect an invaluable privilege. After all, it is in those moments that burn that remind us that we're still alive.

Lit up like a firefly, Dad takes deep, restful breaths. I turn to the counter, dropping the towel into the half-rinsed bowl and grab the bottle of Pinaud Lime Sec I filched from his medicine cabinet. Against the sunlight, the liquid in the bottle glows neon green, looking more like sour apple drink mix than a heady topical. But the label says *Qualite Supérieure*, and I've always been a sucker for accents. At the twist of the top, the room is a citrus field, delivering on the bottle's promise of "a zesty lime scent." So powerful is the cloud that my eyes flutter to adjust, darting all over the room before returning to neutral. And that's when I see that I'm not the only one who's been knocked conscious by the fumes.

Dad lies on his bed, eyes gaping, waxed with stupor and cold sobriety. At first I blame his startled expression on the vapor until I notice that he's not looking at me. Once again, his gaze is drawn to the foot of the bed, and I know they're back. The visitors; whoever they are. It's impossible to know their names or the number of them, but I don't doubt their presence for a second. The wonder and disbelief on my father's face razes any argument that this is a simple, drug-addled delusion. He's got company, and I can't let him greet them as any less than the man he's always been.

With a couple splashes of the aftershave in my hand, I work the solution between my hands. Palms warmed, I lay a delicate coat to his cheeks, letting my fingers trail off his jaw and down the slope of his neck. Between my thumb and forefinger I rub a little into his earlobes and even run a streak down the length of his nose to make sure the smell lingers, to make sure every intake of breath is a validation.

As I lean back, he remains transfixed. Lips tremor, the conversation with his cosmic company bindingly proprietary. Whether this is a social visit or the arrival of the convoy with which he'll depart, it's impossible to know. Either way, I'm not ready. I don't think I ever will be. But he is. And that's the most I can give him.

The aftershave continues to set. Its alcohols and biologics will seep into the layers and cleanse the microscopic cuts invisible to the eye. As I place my nose to my wrist and fill my lungs with notes of floral and exotic woods, I beg that my own cuts find a similar healing.

The Space Between the Tenses

The last words my father ever heard from me were a complaint that he wasn't dying fast enough.

"I don't know," I offered my mother as she tucked Dad into the hospice bed he'd called home for the last ten days. Once the sojourn up half the staircase had left him hunched over, panting and sweating from the brow, visiting nurses had provided the wheeled trundle within hours of our call. Since then, the living room had become triage: the nucleus from which Mom and I could eat, work, and sleep never further than five feet from our patient by the window. From my post, peering over the back of the couch, Mom brushed a cool hand across his forehead then slogged across the carpet with a gait that suggested gravity held twice the hold on her than it did the rest of us.

Aside from the faint rise and fall of his chest, no other motion from beneath the blankets betrayed the fact that Dad was aware I was talking about him. Or that anyone was talking at all.

"I just don't think I can take another week off from work."

It was a Saturday night, and though well-intentioned, my fatigue-addled brain had once again failed to assemble a sentence representative of my true concern. After seven days of blood-pressure checks, handy-wipe baths, outfit changes, the fastening and unfastening of adult underwear, tongue swabs, leg massages, pain injections, and piggybacked quests to and from the bathroom our bodies ached with the tired satisfaction brought on by the understanding that we'd done all we could to preserve Dad's comfort and whatever measure of nobility remained. It was what I wanted to do, where I wanted to be—at his side until the end. Though the idea of hospice conveyed the imminence of the very end in question, Monday loomed and Dad remained in relatively stable condition. "He's still taking fluids," the nurse had said earlier that day. "Once he stops drinking, he'll last about two weeks."

The thought of leaving him seemed about as impossible as extending my hiatus from the television job I'd started just two months prior. I needed to be with my father. I also needed a paycheck. In the chasm between, my worry echoed with a petulance often reserved for the arrival of a tardy room service cart. And even in that context, its usage strains legitimacy.

To my left, Mom sank into the folds of the easy chair, flat as a skyline. Her narrow eyes sunk into her face, anchored by a thousand concerns far more pertinent than my own. Still, in her own inconceivable way, she managed to clear just enough room to take on her son's surplus anxieties without capsizing. "Let's take it one day at a time," she breathed as sleep draped black across the green of her irises. "We'll talk about it in the morning."

But in the morning Dad was gone. Despite educated forecasts of being pruned to death through slow dehydration, my father had instead chosen to have his last drink and decide for himself when the party was over. It was quick and quiet. More surprising, however, was how voluntary it appeared.

"His eyes were open," Mom said, cradling his face in her hands. "I woke up and saw him looking out the window. So, I said 'good morning' like I always do. Only, today, he didn't turn to me."

It was true. When I stumbled out of a stupor to the shout of my name, I'd found myself by her side, by the bed, gazing down at the vacant gawk that had occupied my father's face for nearly a week. He was still pink, still warm. Blood still moved through his veins; that last gush of hose water bursting from the nozzle, blithely unaware that the supply has been cut off. It was only when his chest didn't beat back against my palm that I realized what had happened. We'd missed him by minutes, seconds even. What lay before us was not so much him anymore as it was a reminder of him. Like it was nothing more than an early morning business trip, he'd crept across the floor so as not to wake us, poured himself a cup of the day, and took a sip. Deciding that was enough, he lay down and left himself cooling on the counter.

"Oh, Joe. Did you leave us?"

There was a crack in my mother's voice that she quickly choked down as if she half-expected him to answer the question. It wasn't an unfair thought. Even as she rained kisses onto his cheek, I found myself bracing for him to rouse. Up until that point, I'd never known my father as anything but alive. The lack of a pulse didn't suddenly shift his tense. Present doesn't simply become past when a passing is so present. Not when his face still leaned to take in sunlight, not when his smell still hung in the air, not when I could snake my fingers between his and find the soft, meaty mitt that used to throw my preschool chassis into the air and catch me on the way down. So we talked to him as if he were still there, held him as if he could still feel us there in the space between the tenses.

After a while, I left Mom at Dad's side and phoned the hospice agency as they'd instructed we do. It was well before normal business hours, yet their call service answered in two rings.

"Hello. I think my father has died." It was the first time I'd spoken the words aloud and they'd flown out so matter-of-factly. *I think my father has died.* It was an odd, albeit involuntary assemblage of words. What else was there to think exactly? Not being a medical professional, I suppose I couldn't be sure, but the lack of a heartbeat was a pretty telling indicator. Playing dumb, however, seemed to unearth an accidental mechanism for life extension. Embracing a lack of accreditation would allow me, in some preposterous way, to delay the codification of his death. Across the odyssey toward this mile marker there had been no task I was unwilling to perform in service of my father. But declaring him to oblivion? That was someone else's job. As such, I accepted the condolences from the sympathetic voice on the other end of the line, provided my father's name, and was told someone would arrive shortly.

Immediately, I called Dad's two sisters. In both cases, groggy slurs on the other end confirmed that I'd broken them from rapt slumber. In both cases, a swift overcoming of emotion found the receiver in the hands of their husbands who offered me kind words and an assurance that they'd be on the road within minutes.

From where I stood behind the kitchen island, the light shone through the blinds and bathed the other side of the room in a silvery glow. In it, Mom held Dad's hand to her lips and ran her fingers through the salt and pepper ringlets around his ears—the only vestige of hair the chemo had seen fit to let him keep. Placing down the phone, I lay my hands flat onto the marble slab and leaned forward to admire the silhouette. The distance, though slight, was enough to allow for a trick of the eyes. If I could manage to push the last several minutes from my mind then what I was seeing could be nothing more than one of Mom's frequent bedside visits. A simple, private moment between a husband and wife that was not to be disturbed.

Were I to reach out I could almost catch the glimmer in my hand. Like a lightning bug, I could clasp my paws around it so that I might preserve the fragile thing as long as I didn't squeeze too tightly. There it could live, fluttering and scurrying across my skin with its little stick legs. There I could feel it, watch rays of yellow-green drip from between my knuckles, reminding me that it was still there. Another way to preserve the present. Another gambit, but one that could mollify both child and adult: the child afraid to let go and the adult petrified that he may have wished his father away.

I must have stood there for a substantial blip as my next movements were to answer the call of the doorbell. From behind the tempered glass stepped an impish woman whose kind, long face sat under a tease of black hair. Though a stranger to me, she instantly took my hand between both of hers and looked up through rimless spectacles. "I'm so sorry, young man." Considering how many times she must have answered calls of this nature, it was jarring, the sincerity in her voice. Hospice had, surprisingly enough, been one of the bright spots over a fifteen-month trudge through the darkness, littered with snags and snares. Its "end of the line" connotations notwithstanding, every nurse, tech, and care worker had tended to Dad as if he was their own blood. After a litany of doctors hidden behind laptop screens and hospital nurses who'd cared more about turning over beds than who was in them, these people had seen our plane coming in with a busted landing gear. In discharging the most elementary of functions, they had looked my father square in the eye, had called him by his name, and spread foam on our runway through the restoration of his humanity.

I showed Peggy, the nurse, upstairs where she performed a similar hand cradling on my mother. Then, with the delicacy of a potter, she lifted my father's wrist, pressing her thumb to the underside. Checking her watch, a formality though it was, she gave the task every second that it was owed. Laying his hand back on his chest, she nodded once and knelt down to take Mom into her arms.

They held each other fast, the cotton on Peggy's shoulder swelling upon its reception of my mother's wet breaths. However long it took, Mom eventually gathered herself, palmed the tears from her cheeks, and sought guidance. "Should we call the funeral home?"

"All in good time," Peggy purled. "Don't rush yourself. Right now, you just sit with him and have your peace. Your son, too. And when you're ready, you let me know and I'll take care of everything."

With the sanction of her authority came a validation for my want to firmly preserve Dad in the present tense. Once again, we moved to hold him as we always would, tugging him back to the here and now. But, as Peggy faltered in her attempts to close Dad's already stiffening eyelids, it became clear that the past was already pulling from the other side.

As in any tug of war, it's crucial to have a solid footing. However, when your cleats sink into the soft ground, you begin to consider alternative measures. Fairness dictates that both sides should be evenly matched. But, with an invisible opponent, it's impossible to know whether the rules are being respected. And as the arm begins to strain, thoughts occur. Thoughts about the myriad of ways the unseen adversary has played dirty. Thoughts about how the deck has felt stacked in their favor from the very start. How, with your feet slipping beneath you and the victor preordained, there comes the sudden license to pull out a couple of tricks of your own. So when no one's looking, you add some more hands to the rope.

Dorothea was the first to arrive. The youngest of Dad's sisters walked through the doorway, head bowed, with her right hand splayed across her ribcage. When I met her at the foot of the stairs, we drew each other in. I hid my face in her tumble of brown locks while beads of melancholy fell from her lashes and turned my collar blue. It had been barely twelve hours since she'd last stood in that foyer, yet she felt like a long-lost friend. That someone with whom you share a history, but from whom time has extracted something. From that sudden extraction had emerged two new iterations of the same individuals. Same bones, but they didn't quite lock together like they used to.

Upstairs, Mom and Thea wrapped around each other, a briefly conjoined creature of sharp gasps. The lot of us hovered quietly on the fringe, attempting to offer personal space while remaining near enough to comfort or to offer an appendage on which to brace. Finding herself in the same mattress divot that all of us had occupied at some turn, Thea looked down at her brother and I saw, perhaps for the first time, just how many similarities the two of them shared. Though fourteen years stood between them, Dad and Thea had always seemed synched by the same timekeeper. Where life sprung from the ground they ran through with bare feet, laughing a little too loud, drinking a little too much, and never taking anything too seriously. They ticked. Physically, though, it had never dawned on me just how much Thea resembled him. The way her brow dipped, her nose arched, her cheeks filled, and her lips spread. It was all there. At once, it was all too possible to flip the image, to roll back the decades and bear witness to my teenage father marveling at his baby sister swaddled in her crib.

"Hey, bro." With a firm yank, Thea joined the fray and pulled Dad back to the present. She greeted him, not with a crack in her voice, but instead with the casual lilt with which she'd regarded her brother long before his convalescent days. She didn't pander. She never pitied him. Not even when he began to pass out from the high doses of chemo and it became necessary to compile a roster of volunteers to watch him in shifts. On her days, Thea would show up before Mom left for work and light up his face with that same "Hey, bro." No matter his mood, no matter his wavering willingness to comply, their shared brain gave her everything she needed to turn him around. While I never bore witness to the play-by-play, whatever magic she worked would get him to take his medication, eat his lunch, and gag down his chalky protein shakes. On Thea days, we knew Dad was taken care of.

Catrina arrived shortly after, just before the air in the room grew very thin. Arriving at the top of the stairs, Thea's older sister dashed toward my father's bed and knelt to the ground. There was a beat, rehearsed and executed as if called for by stage direction, and then the levee broke. With a great wail, she flung herself across his body, balling up the sheets in her fists, and calling out his name between throaty heaves.

To call it theatre would be to diminish the love she had for her brother. The love was unquestionable. However, even in the midst of my own languishing, I found it difficult not to wonder where all of her concern had been back when it could have been put to use. Since the moment Dad shared his diagnosis, Cat seemed to operate with the understanding that she could just ignore the cancer into remission. During his nearly two-week, in-patient, post-op recovery, she'd managed to shoehorn only a single visit into her schedule. Over the subsequent year and a half of treatment, with all of its relapses and unforeseen complications, she'd joined the roster of part-time caregivers in name only. On the days she would show up, it wouldn't be until long after my mother had left in the morning. Later, upon returning, Mom would find Dad sitting right where she'd left him, an empty bottle of Boost on the counter the only piece of evidence that Cat had gusted through. Only at the end, in those final weeks when the conclusion was foregone, did Cat's visits become more frequent. Only then had she cajoled her own daughters to visit their uncle on his deathbed, one of whom bringing her boyfriend along as if it were all some block party.

Mind you, I was not at all qualified to hold any of these actions to judgment. A thousand self-help books would make the argument that grief manifests in incalculable ways. Whereas Thea sought to retain a sense of normalcy through maintaining a casual and deferential cadence with her brother, Cat perhaps felt that refusing to acknowledge the existence or severity of a problem might be the very thing to snuff it out. In a scenario where a medically approved course of treatment involves pumping the patient to the gills with poison, no tactic can be deemed illogical. I had surely not been without my own selfish motives and inclinations, the most recent one occurring just hours before. Still, as Cat clutched and wailed, a sour taste ran across my tongue. After all the time spent avoiding the issue, here she was tossed across the man, prostrate, like some aggrieved mafia widow. While the rest of our conclave joined in the exercise of protracting Dad's life, Cat was all too quick to mourn its ending. While we pulled, silent but firm, to keep Dad moored on our side of the coil, Cat had begun digging his grave.

The morning pushed on and each member of the small gathering had their individual aside with my father, returning again, thereafter, in combinations of twos and threes. At no moment did we ever leave Dad alone. Mom remained by his side, almost steadfast. Peggy sat at the dining room table hand-in-hand with Dad's cousin Iris, the two of them joined in quiet prayer. Eventually, before we allowed the initial visitation period to meander into questionable duration, I gave Peggy the go-ahead to contact the funeral home. She excused herself downstairs and slipped out the front door without so much as a follow-up question, leaving us to bubble and collide in our purgatorial tank.

Knowing our window with Dad had been stamped with an expiration brought about a shift in the current. Though no one spoke it out loud, we all knew that whomever was on the way was coming not to collect a man but a body. That collection would result, much as we labored to put it off, in the irreversible transference of tense. An unalterable deviation from present to past. As if coming to the understanding all at once, we became endowed with an urgency to work against the stemming of that flow.

Thea was the first to speak up. "I smelled him this morning."

A dozen or so eyes turned in her direction, seeking clarification, begging her on.

"That smell, you know? That sour smell from his mouth, from the thrush. It woke me up not more than a minute before you called." She looked straight at me. "It pulled me out of a sound sleep, and I could swear it was like he was hovering right above me. I'd know that smell anywhere." In fact, we'd all come to know that particular tang over the last few days, when the responsibility for Dad's oral hygiene had fallen onto us. "And then, the phone rang."

"It must have been just as he went." Mom spoke through the hand-held to her mouth. "He was visiting you, Thea. He came to say 'goodbye.'"

A fluke, perhaps, but the idea that my father hadn't died but simply stepped out for a few social calls was a comfort. Mostly because it wasn't at all a departure for him.

Soon after, calls from overseas began to pour in—my mother's extended family responding to word-of-mouth. Each echoed the last: a somber, choked-up testimony to the man who had adored their darling girl and who had taken in each one of them as if they were his pack. In turn, they had adopted him as son, nephew, brother. The gracious declarations followed one after the next, beautiful words from pained voices. All melting together but cut short by abrupt exclamation. Each of our backs stiffened as the report came in. My father had, once again, been spotted.

"Era un sogno!" My mother translated the frantic Italian of her distant cousin just as quickly as it poured through the receiver. "It was a dream. Last night, Alina, I am walking along the street and I see you crying. I try to hug you, to comfort you. But you are inconsolable. Suddenly, on the opposite sidewalk I see Joe. There he is! He is following a crowd of people all dressed in black. He is smiling, happy. So, I call to him. 'Giuseppe! Giuseppe!' And I point to you. 'Can't you see? Alina is in pain. Please help her!' But he cannot. He turns to me, grinning from ear to ear, and says 'I have to go, cugina. I have to go.' So, he turns and marches to catch up with the crowd. And you cry. And I cry with you. And then...I wake up."

Somehow both there in the room with us and on the other side of the world, Dad had found a way to exceed the limitations of his own biology. In that way, he felt more alive than the living. Perennial patron of festivities large and small, my father had capitalized on the opportunity to turn his journey toward the next plane into some international farewell tour. It was rather marvelous in its believability. That, just as he had ever been to us, so now did he go on to become some sort of spectral headliner. Rabid in our reverence, each ensuing trill of the phone sent fire through the swollen-eyed devotees hoping for news of an extension, added stops on a growing list of appearances.

Perhaps it was easier to think of things that way. Perhaps that was the only method, at the time, I could employ in order to survive the treacherous movements I felt I'd hastened. If I could elevate him high enough, my father wouldn't die. He would ascend, body and soul.

So, when the sallow man and woman arrived in their boxy suits and ashen complexions, they were not undertakers but rather the security detail for a celebrated figure. When we lifted Dad from the bed and laid him on the ground, tucked his arms and legs, watched them draw up the zipper as if he were boxed lunch, it was not a body bag but a cloak to disguise him from the hungry crowds. When we carried the bag out the back door and down the patio steps, it was not because the front stairs were too narrow for the stretcher but because the secret exit might provide him with an unencumbered retreat. When the stretcher's wheels crunched and dragged across the loose pebbles of the landscaped yard, it was not the collision of kicked-up stones, but the clinking of flashbulbs from the press anticipating our concerted evasion.

"What was his name?" called a woman from the other side of the fence. The onlooker had seen the commotion from at the throng's edge, aware of the celebrity in her presence but unable to call up his name. Through the screened window, she bore a resemblance to the elderly lady who lived next door.

"Joseph," my mother croaked.

"I'm so sorry. I never knew him." The woman's words were gurgled, lapped up by a mounting tide of cries and shudders. Neighbors joined the fray, the rabble having drawn them to their doors, into the street, and onto our driveway. Tears in their eyes, they wrapped themselves around my mother or whichever pillar of sobs was nearest. Hardly anyone knew each other but shared adoration makes fast friends out of strangers.

A hand squeezes my shoulder from behind, but I cannot turn to see whose it is. Not until I complete my task. Not until I help slide Dad into the back of the vehicle. Not until he is strapped in and secure. Not until the car pulls off can I allow myself to look away, and even then I do not. Because I can't abide mourning with morning stretching on. When love and illusion and a jot of guilt have revealed the elasticity of time. If I can turn hours into days and days into weeks, then the space between the tenses can be flattened and pulled. If I can run our street out to where the earth bends then the car will never turn off, never pass away. So I keep my eyes trained ahead. I hold him in sight. As long as my eyes remained fixed, he won't ever be gone. Only going.

Going.

Part Three
Paroxysm

Margherita

Mom orders a Margherita.
"We don't serve alcohol," says the waitress,
and I know this won't end well.

Dad had asked for it
by name, not pizza, an echo;
eight slices of a former life.

One bite to wash away sin,
to paint his veins with nightshade
his white blood, *fior di latte,*

to let the devil have his skin
that he might grow epicarp,
olive, dance in the ash spittle

of the grove hearth, where
a boy of fifty—*Was he ever
that young?*—plucks him from

I'M NEVER FINE

a branch to make himself
a banquet before the cancer
can. Before it slides

across the table, a heap,
a red, rutted, tumble-down
onto a single splotch of cheese.

His immune system on thin crust,
made from dust and to dust
it returns in his mouth,

where there is no taste, only victory
in gnashing before the surrender,
if just to take flesh off the foe

who lays waste to the grove,
who leaves him shivering in June,
in our heat-stung eyes

where shivers may be dancing,
flour may be ash,
and olives may be cured.

Losing My Religion

Every whisper
Of every waking hour
I'm choosing my confessions
Trying to keep an eye on you
Like a hurt lost and blinded fool, fool

I haven't spoken to God in six years. Well, that's not true. Perhaps "called upon" is the more applicable term. I have not called upon God in six years though, to be fair, I have certainly called Him; called Him out, called Him names. I've taken His name in vain so many times that, should I find myself answering for those flagrancies in the hereafter, I've no doubt the heavenly arbiter should throw the book at me. *The* book. Like, Exodus. This is not hyperbole put forth to convince or to convert. I wax merely so that you, reader, might understand the state of affairs. See, to say I haven't spoken to God does not negate His presence. On the contrary, to disregard something is to affirm its existence, to concede there is something there to ignore. This could be read as dogmatic. On the other hand, to acknowledge a force simply so one might rebuke it would seem counterintuitive, if not outright obscene. Between obscenity and blind faith are a thousand levels with a thousand variants and a myriad of questions from those of us who no can longer bow our heads, those of us who choose to shout at the sky.

Before the shouting there was a miracle of sorts. In 1986 my mother gave birth to a baby boy after a hard-fought pregnancy rife with complications so incalculable they would have even the greatest statisticians scratching their heads. On a trip to Puerto Rico, she slipped in a puddle of water in her hotel lobby, crashing facedown onto the tile floor and flying home in a white-hot panic when she could no longer feel her baby move. Late in her third trimester, my father would wake early one morning to surprise her with breakfast in bed only to spill a steaming pot of coffee all over her lap. In tears, he'd carry her to the emergency room where layers of burnt, black skin would need to be flayed from her legs, pelvis, and lower stomach. These were all secondary to a host of inexplicable and increasingly debilitating symptoms that would later be diagnosed as a rare autoimmune disorder, one that shorted her nervous system, nearly stole her ability to walk, and whose recovery would require two years of intense physical therapy. When doctors warned that another pregnancy would be gravely misguided, she heeded their advice and clung to her only child who, by all accounts, should not have survived.

As that unlikely survivor and the only son of Italian immigrants, I was given to the Catholic Church, body and soul—a living, breathing tithe to the God who, despite the odds, saw fit to deliver me into the world. His very grace and salvation washed across my forehead with baptismal water. At St. Mary's School, my days began and ended between clasped fingers as I learned to pray the rosary, walked the Stations of the Cross, memorized the proper sit, stand, kneel choreography of Catholic Mass, and swallowed the divinity of Christ once old enough to receive Communion. Our parish, a large, suburban congregation scant miles east of the Belford fisheries, had outgrown the tiny farm church that long predated the town that grew up around it. Most Sunday Masses occurred in the school auditorium where the stage doubled as an altar. Each week, we'd attend the show where priests delivered their homilies under a darkened scoreboards and a banner emblazoned with the words "Go Cherubs!" in blue felt. My mother or father would hand me a crisp five-dollar bill to place in the collection basket. I'd follow the readings, sing the hymns, and pray for penance after offering my confessions to men in long, purple robes. Before long, I joined the cast, carrying the sacred gifts and assisting those holy men as an altar boy. It was a gesture mostly pious in aim, to be sure, though not without its fringe benefits. No student thumbed their nose at the opportunity to be pulled out of class at a moment's notice to make an easy five bucks working a funeral.

   The practice of religion is, by and large, ceremonial; whether it's the Catholic blessing of throats on the Feast of St. Blaise or the latihankejiwaan of the Subud, a spiritual renewal of contact with the divine force of life. This was evident even to us moderately perceptive adolescents. But ceremony is not without its function. On an elemental level, these customs bring together individuals to form a community. Schedule and ritual provide structure and ways to compartmentalize and allocate our lives. Routine provides comfort, and numbers beget a sense of safety and belonging. As long as traditions are built upon a foundation of teachings and principles that resonate, people willingly indulge the formalities for the sake of a higher purpose. For me, that purpose was to live up to the miracle, to legitimize everything my parents endured and went without in order to provide me with a life filled with everything I ever could have needed. To do this, I would model myself after the most human tenets of Christianity: live a good life, be a good man, and spread kindness to others through good works. Simple and pure enough. And so, thirteen and willing, I presented myself to the bishop who, with a stroke of oil across my forehead, sealed my covenant with God.

For the next chunk of my existence I set out to hold up my end of the bargain. I worked through four years of Catholic high school and prayed. I sang in the liturgical choir, played an apostle in the Passion Play, volunteered for outreach programs, sang badly in the common rooms of a hundred nursing homes, and prayed. Even in college, when my Mass attendance record took a notable hit, I got there when it mattered and prayed. Every night before bed I uttered my missives, calling to every angel and saint, deceased relative, and bygone pet by name—a list that grew longer every year. I repeated that same litany on airplanes, not even omitting the traditional bedtime prayer. True, "Now I lay me down to sleep" may not have been relevant to the situation, but how could it hurt?

Time went by, and my prayers got more and more specific. I prayed for my mother when my grandpa died, for my father when he lost his job, and again through his six-hour emergency bypass surgery. Although we continued to find our way to the other side of tragedy or near-tragedy intact, the result for me was an ideology not based in faith but in fear. We understand our parents are human and vulnerable and mortal. That is logical. However, it's just as human to respond to logic in illogical ways. For me, my prayers became all-consuming petitions for the health and safety of my loved ones. I prayed in the same way, with the same inflection and the same exact words because that was the proven method that had gotten results. But when this happens, prayer devolves into nothing more than wearing your New York Giants jersey inside out to help the team win the game. That's when superstition gets confused for belief. That's when the concern becomes not what might happen if you do pray, but what might happen if you don't.

> *Consider this*
> *Consider this*
> *The hint of the century*
> *Consider this*
> *The slip that brought me*
> *To my knees failed*
> *What if all these fantasies*
> *Come flailing around*
> *Now I've said too much*

I said my last prayer on the night of July 27th, 2013. Mom and I had tucked Dad into the hospice bed that sat by the living room window, the bed he'd occupied for the last ten days. At that point, we knew the fight was long over and our main concern had become keeping him comfortable and hydrated. The nurses who visited each day had told us that as long as he was taking fluids—and he was—he still had a few weeks.

I'M NEVER FINE

We'd taken to sleeping in the living room so we could be nearby, Mom on the recliner and I on the couch. Though the choice was practical in the sense that it made it easier to rush to his aid should he need it, the real reason was that we simply couldn't bear the idea of him being alone. In the silence, as I had done every night, I pulled my hands from under the blanket, pressed them to my lips, and prayed. Even then, even at the end of the line, I found myself begging for a miracle. Our family had been brushed by the miraculous before. It had happened once; I was proof of it. To be fair, I didn't quite know the rules. Perhaps each family is only allotted one miracle per lifetime. But if that were the case, if it couldn't be a new, then I begged to turn my miracle over to him.

The following morning I'd come to learn that miracles were nontransferable. The light had left my father's still-open eyes, and with it, any residual hope for divine integrity. That evening, after the calls were made and mourners mourned and officials officiated and dates were set, I climbed into an actual bed for the first time in weeks. Only this time, my hands stayed at my side. They've remained there ever since.

I want to be quite clear that this break in communication was not vanity, nor was it retribution. I'm not arrogant enough to think that God should care whether or not I recite a few "Our Fathers" or "Hail Marys." No, this was the reflex reaction of someone forced to the table with the object of his own dread. For as far back as I could remember, the mortality of my parents had been a particle in the eye of my consciousness that no amount of blinking could wash away. It was an ever-present part of the landscape, sliding into and out of focus with each doctor's appointment card pinned to our calendar. Despite the fact that Mom's illness hadn't reared its head since 1988 and Dad's heart condition was under control, every cough or headache sent me down Google rabbit holes that only served to augment my paranoia. Perhaps it's the crippling sense of ancestral responsibility endemic to the only child, hackneyed though it may be. Perhaps it's simpler than that. Perhaps the real object of my fear was the world I was fated to one day face alone and unprepared. Whatever the theory, in the midsummer of my twenty-seventh year, a scenario I'd spent my life bargaining with the Almighty to delay came into focus in 4K Ultra High-Definition. And amidst the scream and static of stereo feedback rang a deafening suspicion: somewhere along the line God had stopped listening.

The naïveté of my assertions is not lost on me here. I understand how self-righteous it sounds to expect something from the creator of the heavens and the earth in exchange for some good words and good deeds. But, in the grand scheme of things, my paramount appeal had always been the well-being of my parents. Setting aside all other worldly and material requests, prayer was my means of preservation, by protecting the only thing that really mattered. This was, I felt, a sacred accord between my maker and me. Then when the alternate party severed that covenant, my allegiance was irreparably damaged. With the blinders of blind faith removed and the dial on my celestial scanner finding crackles on every blessed station became all business. Taking account of every minute I'd ever spent in silent veneration, all of the sudden it began to look like I'd been scammed. When a stock fails to pay dividends, it's considered a bad investment. I couldn't see how this was any different. If my reliance on prediction is the fallacy of this conclusion, if one offers that the divine cannot be mapped or forecasted, then faith reads as no more than a gamble. Still then, if I was to accept this, it meant choosing between feeding my existential coins into some theistic slot machine or cutting my losses when the coins rattled at the bottom of my cup. Some people surely would have considered this questioning blasphemy. Yet, to me, operating solely on blind faith and muted prayer seemed more and more like a quick way to go spiritually bankrupt.

Above all else—the uncertainty and the suspicion—bone-shattering anger hindered threading the tear in my conviction. In the preparation for the funeral, I parsed through photo albums, lifting the rounded edges of sepia-toned snapshots away from their glue. Laying them out by month and year, I chronicled my father in 4x3 increments—a life in rectangles. Each image a memory and story that I wrung out of my hands and onto paper. When the *Gazette* needed an obituary, I filled out the form until it asked for the names of survivors. For the life of me I couldn't think of any. When the church asked me to deliver a eulogy, the priest placed his hand over mine and suggested I "keep it to five minutes" as if that were a reasonable request. Five minutes to capture sixty-seven years. I suppose God had better things to do. Or maybe, just maybe, some small part of Him couldn't stomach the grief.

After all the redlining and page crumpling and glossing over I could muster, what followed read more as a prosecutor's closing argument when the moment came. There, before a jury of my peers and with my back to the assailant,

I recounted the details of the case. Gripping the edge of the podium so as not to betray my shaking hands, I reflected on each exhibit: the soldier who answered the call of his country when it demanded he go to war, the work horse who balanced a day job and night school so he could build a life for the girl he loved, the husband who gave decades to a passionless career for the security of his wife and child, the bulldog who rode out the layoffs and took pay decreases because it meant putting food on the table, the craftsman who taught himself how to cut and lay tile and fix water pipes and build a deck and change his own oil so that he might save money and build a safety net for his family, the architect who constructed scale models of his father's barbershop, turned the living room into a model train village, sculpted a block of wood into a pinewood-derby car, duct taped liter soda bottles together to teach his son to shake up tornadoes and to find the art in life. I painted a picture of the future he'd planned to share with his other half: the house by the bay, his little slice of the world where he could watch the water, the dock slip where he would keep his modest little boat for modest little boat rides, the flat in Italy where he could split his time, visiting with family, smoking his cigars, and strolling through the cittàvecchia with a demitasse cup dangling from an ample finger. This vision, I told the tribunal, these well-earned proceeds for a well-lived life would, instead, get ripped from his outstretched fingers the very moment he gave himself license to reach for them. My father would, indeed, come to own that house by the bay; a house he'd occupy for fifteen short months as cancer robbed him of his hunger, his humor, his memory, and eventually, the rest of him.

Presenting the facts as they were, I drew a solid line between the evidence and my conclusion. This was no cosmic happenstance, no tragically beautiful illustration of life's inexplicability. This was an act of aggression, a targeted and premeditated attack. In tucking the pages into my breast pocket, I asked that the jury consider the promise of God's unconditional love and ask themselves one question: Is there reasonable doubt?

> *That's me in the corner*
> *That's me in the spotlight*
> *Losing my religion*
> *Trying to keep up with you*
> *And I don't know if I can do it*
> *Oh no, I've said too much*
> *I haven't said enough*

In the years that followed, I attended church only on the rarest of occasions and only as the product of maternal haranguing. Though I'd skipped a few Christmas and Easter Masses—a mortal sin in and of itself—the liturgies offered in Dad's name were far less easy to weasel my way out of. This self-imposed abstention was not one of protest but, perhaps selfishly, an active attempt to avoid discomfort. In the shadow of a crucifix I felt like the ultimate hypocrite, like I was filling the seat of someone more devout, more deserving. Keeping my head down, I followed the steps and did all I could to melt into the crowd. I dipped into fonts and sprinkled myself with holy water that rolled across my skin as if with oil. The body of Christ ate like the wafer that it was and nothing more. When prompted, I'd nod my signs of peace to fellow churchgoers then return to staring at my shoes and wondering just how many verses of "Here I Am, Lord" the choir was required to sing. Following the Mass was no longer instinctive. Since my school days the church had enacted sweeping changes to age-old blessings and their associated responses—an attempt to closer link the English and Latin Masses that doubled as an effective measure in exposing us outsiders. Time and again, the father would offer to the crowd *"The Lord be with you."* Time and again, the collective swallowed my now-defunct *"And also with you"* with *"And with your spirit,"* only reinforcing the fact that God and I no longer spoke the same language.

Here's where I might feel inclined to demonstrate how this disconnect was not some sought- after permit for malefaction. Even now, residual guilt compels me to disclose the preservation of my good nature by listing every door I've held open, every hour I've volunteered, and every bag of clothing I've dropped off at Goodwill. But I promised at the start not to engage in persuasion, nor do I believe the cataloguing of my merit badges would win me much favor. Moreover, I learned from experience that my scout sash proved only a mildly effective testament to skeptics, and before long, I found my character under scrutiny by family, friends, and even people I barely knew. As self-sufficient as I sought to be, there are those unavoidable moments of vulnerability in which, for one reason or another, we seek the counsel of those we trust. Although the intent was well-meaning, I'd find that most would seize on these opportunities to suggest that I seek strength in the church. Any rebuttals to these instructions only led to crooked frowns and words like "atheist" and "agnostic;" labels that were also incorrect. Try as I might, though, efforts to define my perspective morphed frowns into quizzical stares that remained until I gave up and changed the subject.

One can only explain themselves for so long, however, before the exercise proves just as hopeless as it is exhausting. With every set of eyes seemingly picking you apart, with every tongue twisting to fix you with a definition there's little room left to breathe. Suddenly your house, your city, even your country seems small. And so the time comes when you begin to look elsewhere, when the only way to correct the misunderstanding is to go somewhere they don't understand you. Because at least that's right, at least that makes sense.

So, I flew to Oslo. I flew to Oslo during winter because it was cheap and it was cold, and I thought I might become a snowman. My growing frustrations having rendered me combustible, I felt a blast of polar air might be the only force strong enough to knock them back. Right there, on the cobbles of Kristian IVs gate, I rendered myself that this new world might split my ribs and pour itself in. And that, it did. Norway fed me fish pie and sleeper trains, powdered pines and pelt-lined chairs, roosters, wood carvings, sugared butter bread, purple crocus, bacon in a tube, Ibsen, Munch, and bronze sculptures that blushed verdigris as they met the atmosphere. I slid down narrow corners and wove through crowded markets full of people who paid me no mind, who asked only that I step aside so as not to block the view of the lutefisk freshly crammed into their bed of crushed ice. The country gave silence and distance and meaningless street signs that told me where I was but not where I should go. It was in that quiet anonymity on a random night's walk that I fell into the open doors of a boxy brick building bleeding light onto the sidewalk. Inside stood a circle filled with pews all facing a wall upon which hung one simple crucifix—the only emblem preventing the otherwise unadorned space from being confused for a lecture hall. Enjoying the warmth, I kept to the back, following the curve of the wall so as not to disrupt the handful of solemn worshipers strewn about the place. Above my head, the ceiling dipped downward on a curve, a smooth stone lung holding its breath. For the first time, the church seemed more anxious than I was.

Just before me stood an iron votive stand from which I pulled a taper stick. Rolling it between my thumb and index finger I pressed the tip against my top lip and shoved two kroner in the donation slot. Maybe it was the fairness of the transaction, the equal exchange of goods, or perhaps the spartan design of the room feeling less oppressive, but as I torched the end of the taper and carried the flame to an unsullied wick, I lit a candle for my father without guilt or distortion. While I could not quite bring myself to pray, I did listen and watch. Looking around the rotunda, devotees straggled in and out, making a point in their day to commune with their Lord, to give their thanks, to make their petitions, and even to find some peace. I admired their devoutness and envied their conviction. I marveled at the architecture, the bare-knuckled work of men so certain in their faith that they had hewn stones and melted metal in its exultation. There was magic in the world; I had seen it, was seeing it. There were things so miraculous in design that they went beyond the scientific. It took Norway to remind me. It took Norway to tear a hole in the shroud of anger. While it was not a sweeping revelation, it freed me enough to rip off a shred and burn it on the flame.

I'M NEVER FINE

    Burning that first bit was the hardest, maybe because I felt some righteous claim to it or maybe because I confused it for an act of surrender. But color and light called from between the broken fibers until I was soon looking to give another piece to the fire. Every few months, I burned a little more. I burned on a midnight run along the lungomare, tracing the steps of my ancestors between the Duomo di San Corrado and the Basilica della Madonna Dei Martiri. I burned in Dublin at John's Lane Church, sleepy-eyed and whiskey-breathed. At Westminster Abbey, I pressed my hand to Dickens' headstone and asked for words, burned for words. The sun shining through the rose-tinted glass of Cathédrale Notre-Dame de Paris burned me right into the floor. I burned at Stein am Rhein, at Skalholt Church, at Agios Nikolakis, at Iglesia de la Nuestra Señora de la Merced, and at Chiesa di San Pietro Caveoso. Again and again I beheld the frescoes, watched moss sprout from lava, choked down unfiltered coffee, and dangled my legs over cliffs. There, at each pass, I saw more of what my father had always seen, what he'd always taught me to look for: the art in life. Yes, there remains anger, and no, the rift between God and myself is not yet mended. But that shroud of anger grows narrower at the flame, where the two of us meet from time to time, where my father is never more human; solid, liquid, gas...then soot in the air.

In Defense of the Apple

GOD never damned the apple. That's not what launched Eve from the garden. It was fruit from a tree, nondescript fruit from the tree of life, the tree of knowledge of good and evil. "You shall not eat it, nor shall you touch it, lest you die," said God, wrote the Hebrews. *Peri*, wrote the Hebrews. "Fleshy fruit." Any fruit. No fruit. Pomegranate, apricot, wheat, wine, offspring. Fruit of the womb. As Michelangelo scrawled a fig on the Sistine, his Latin brothers chose malus. "Apple," yes. Also, "evil." Depends on how you read it.

GOD never damned the apple. Good thing, too, 'cause I love them. Eat 'em by the bushel, the barrel. Eat 'em whole, seeds and all. I like how they taste of licorice. "That's the cyanide," my mother warns.

Same thing they took at the People's Temple. Same thing some nine-hundred disciples drank at the Last Supper. Right before turning their backs to the garden they'd sewn under the Guyanese sky. "All is lost," said the father. "Die with dignity." I suppose only the morning sun could judge. The truth is: an apple can't poison you. Not on its own. I'd have to suck an orchard through a swizzle stick to get to

Jonestown. Still, my mother worries. I like the seeds. I like how they taste of licorice.

GOD never damned the apple. John Milton did, with his pen. "...with an apple, he thereat offended," wrote John, he "...hath giv'n up both his beloved man and all this world." *Paradise Lost. All is lost.* Conviction not by the father, but by the son, the son of sons, the great-great grandson some millennia down the tree. A poet, no less. If his words can sentence perhaps mine can commute. Or, at least, force a retrial.

The fact remains, no amount of verse will filter out the toxins, but an apple's poison does not beget a poison apple. So, I'll keep eating, seeds and all.

Not to offend the father.
Not to vex the mother.
Not to harm the self.
Not to leave the garden.

I will eat to keep one foot off the ground, to peek over the hedge wall.

To figure out

      which side

            we're on.

Little Murders

In the summer of 2002, I fell in love with a hundred-year-old Russian imperialist. In my defense, he looked no more than seventeen at the time. We'd been introduced a few months prior, in a rehearsal studio converted out of a shuttered Wawa convenience store, both of us clutching freshly Xeroxed copies of the libretto to *Fiddler on the Roof*. The two lone Christians cast to antagonize the peaceful Jewish denizens of Anatevka, our schedule kept us largely separated from the main players. Inside—where the air was conditioned—Yente would make her matches, and Tevye would pray for riches while the two gentiles baked out in the July heat, attempting to master the Hopak. Pale, blond, and lithe, a poster boy for Eastern Europe, the Russian sailed through each move as if it were nothing more than an afternoon stroll, whereas I, with my umber mop and the grace of a Super Mario Brother, clunked up the rear, fooling absolutely no one. Nevertheless, across the parking lot, we squatted and kicked, kicked and squatted day after day, drilling the steps for passing motorists until the pavement sizzled under our boots.

Forced camaraderie soon gave way to fast friendship, the solitude obliging a shared teenage egotism and all-around saltiness that we justified as "method acting." We were, after all, the villains. His confidence, like his gait, was without effort, no doubt due to the years he had on me (all two of them). Such confidence bred conversation, and with prolonged exposure, inevitable admiration. He detailed his obsession with *The Rocky Horror Picture Show* (to a theatre nerd, impossibly radical) recounting the times he'd skipped class so he could rush tickets in the City (to a sophomore, inarguably badass). A class, I should mention, at a school no less than an hour away (to a non-driver, remarkably exotic). Insight only compounded my infatuation, something I labored to mask by meeting each of his disclosures with a nod or one-word validation. He unnerved me with his openness, something my untested gut could not interpret, and fearing confusion, I sought to explain it away. It wasn't until opening night, on a ratty couch in the basement dressing room of New Jersey's most majorly minor non-profit theatre, that he rested his leg across my knee and killed me instantly.

Somewhere between harassing Chava and wrecking Tzeitel's wedding, my territory was annexed right out from under me. Just above, the stage creaked under the roll of set pieces, sending sawdust into the air. To my left, behind the door to the orchestra pit, strings plucked out the opening notes of "Sunrise, Sunset." I'm sure that's just how it happened. That's how it had happened at every rehearsal. At that moment, though, I heard nothing but the ringing in my ears and saw only the leather boot perched on my right thigh. I just stared at it, seized up, as if some sudden movement might scare it away. At some point, I knew I had to go back on stage and deliver one of my two lines. But unless it was "Boot!" I'd long forgotten it.

To the fevered, time becomes more theoretical. After however long it took to regain my faculties—second-long minutes or minute-long seconds—I allowed my eyes to travel. I meandered past the laces and cuffs of wool trousers, dotted along the hem of a military jacket, jumped a thick black belt cinched across the waist, and climbed a ladder of gold fasteners to meet a set of eyes. His eyes. Blue eyes. Deep blue eyes. Deep blue eyes trained on mine. The kind of blue I might compare to an ocean because I'm in high school and can't think of a better metaphor. The kind of blue I could drown in if he'd grant permission. And then, permission. The spread of two lips. A crooked smile and a pair of extra-long canines to which I wanted nothing more than to offer my neck. I loved him in that moment and for many moments after, the kind of love we're prone to cheapen later in life because it's raw and unbleached. Yet, that first hit on the tongue is rich, unprocessed, not subject to regulation or standards that will inevitably diminish its quality. It's the delicious flavor that starts it all and the toothache we live with the rest of our lives.

In the ensuing weeks, after the summer theatre staff decided against casting a dusky Italian with a permanent five o'clock shadow as a young Siamese prince, I did everything within my limited means to keep the connection on life support. Not having a car relegated communication with the Russian to the shared family computer. Every evening we'd pound out ineloquent declarations as we worked out a plan to come back together. Foolish and desperate, I stretched my fifteen-year-old wallet as far as it could go and bought two nosebleed seats for *Rocky Horror*. "You're the best," he wrote. "The absolute best." A beautiful boy thought I was the best. We planned a day in the City. He'd play tour guide, taking me to Bleecker Street, the Village, the galleries, and all of his favorite hidden spots. Back then, any land outside of Midtown Manhattan might as well have been another country, a nameless place whose existence was known to me only by its presence on the subway map. I envisioned smoke-filled cafés, drag queens walking tiny little dogs, and dark corners where he would run his fangs along my bottom lip. It was all very sweet, and it was all very set.

I marked the days flipping burgers for beachgoers at the Puffin's Nest Snack Shack, making a little extra change for my looming adventure. One evening, after my shift, my father showed up to drive me home, an uncommon occurrence as it would have meant his having to leave work early. From the passenger seat he felt a million miles away, peeling off as soon as the door clicked into place without as much as a nod in my direction. Something was undoubtedly amiss. There was no tousle of my hair, no squeeze on my shoulder, no classic oldies blasting from the radio. His mouth was flat and his eyes Krazy-Glued to the road in an unpeaceful quiet; my mind filled with all manner of possible catastrophes. Something so horrible my father couldn't bring himself to speak it out loud. And when he did find the words, they were anything but reassuring.

"Listen, you can't go into the City on Sunday anymore. Tell your friend it's an emergency."

He pulled into the driveway and barely came to a full stop before bolting into the house ahead of me. I made my way up the porch and through the front door, expecting to step into a crime scene. Instead, the kitchen seemed perfectly in order. There was no police tape, nothing shattered or smoldering. My mother and father sat at the table, backs to the wall, staring at me over a spread of neatly arranged sheets of paper. Taking a seat across from them, the first thing I noticed was red. Each page bled like the nameless victim of a knife-happy psychopath. But, on closer inspection, these stiffs were not so anonymous. Above each puncture wound, words came into focus. *You're the best.* Familiar words. *How could you not know how I felt?* Private affirmations. *I can't wait to see you.* Each innocent admission slashed with thick crimson as the chronology of my sweetheart correspondence blanketed the tabletop. It was a crime scene, indeed. And I'd been called in to identify the bodies.

"You're spying on me?" I lifted my eyes to my parents while my stomach slowly began to devour itself.

"Absolutely not," my mother spat, arms folded tightly around her chest. "I was using the computer to send an email and...and hit some buttons by accident." Computer illiterate as she was, my mother was no idiot. Though it was clear she took me for one. "Besides, I have a right to know what's going on in my house."

"Nothing's going on in your house."

"Then what's your explanation?" She lowered her hand to the table and violently tapped the nearest page with her index finger.

Trouble was I didn't have one. Not only because I knew so little myself but also because it never dawned on me that this was something that begged justification. In that moment, I knew nothing I could offer would satisfy them. This wasn't an interview; it was a forced confession. They wanted a fast guilty plea and a rush to judgment. But doing so would be asking me to criminalize my own name. I could admit no wrongdoing where I saw none. Where I declined to respond, Mom met my silence with harsh accusations. Page by page, she poured through each line, framing the object of my affection as some manipulative deviant, assembling a timeline of my supposed indoctrination. I sunk into the chair as the mischaracterizations, each more absurd than the last, piled up until the words lost all meaning and her voice hit my ears like a mix of shrills and bellows. Dad sat to her left, muted, gazing down at the pages, defeated.

    The rest of that summer was spent under house arrest. Work release allowed me to return to the snack shack, where I'd bury my rage in overcooked fries. Car rides became captive ministries, the driver's seat a pulpit from which my mother bemoaned the pains and perversions of anal sex: "You really want a man to do *that*...to *you*?" After being perp-walked to the rehearsal studio to leave the *Rocky Horror* tickets for the Russian, I was instructed to cut off all connection with him. To my surprise, however, computer access remained unrestricted, and as such, easily exploited. This would later reveal itself to be a well-placed trap upon the discovery of a binder atop my father's armoire containing a spyware CD-ROM and printouts chronicling all of my covert transmissions to the boy. With the computer compromised, there wasn't an inch of the facility that wasn't under surveillance. Under those conditions, I submitted myself to a self-imposed solitary confinement. I kept my head down at meals and avoided eye contact to side step provocation, chewing in the close-mouthed stalemate forged between two parties unwilling to yield.

The bubble burst one afternoon as August waned. A creak at the bottom of the steps signaled the approach of one of the guards, neither of which had set foot on the second floor in weeks. Tucking my knees to my chest, I braced against the headboard of the bed as my father appeared in the doorframe.

"Can we talk?" His tone was meeker than I remembered, and his hulking silhouette somehow diminished.

Nodding, I admitted him. Taking a seat at the edge of the bed, he hunched over, locking his gaze on the carpet. In his lap, big, meaty fingers wrapped themselves around the fist he ground into his palm. For a time, he just sat there, filling and emptying his lungs, expanding and contracting. Each breath grew more intent, as if steeling himself for an attack. In my corner, I readied to thrash, calling up every verbal defense I'd spent weeks sharpening. But just as I prepared to strike, his latest exhale erupted into a fit of hisses and spurts. Suddenly, the impressive figure before me curled into himself, releasing quiet sobs into the hands that now enveloped his face. Having no way to predict or prepare for this left me impotent, left to watch the display carry out over knees tucked under my chin. Grabbing the bedpost, he righted himself and twisted to meet my eyes out of glasses that dripped with his own tears. And between heaves, he was short and to the point.

"I don't think you are...I don't think you are..."

Over and over, he repeated it as if wishing it away, wishing me away, but far more damning than the words was the weeping. That this man, the man who had not cried at his own father's funeral, was shattered by the discovery of who his son really was. That what I'd done to him was worse than death.

I'M NEVER FINE

For the accidental offender, distance is often a logical next step after time served. Though home looks almost normal through eyes readjusting to the light, punishing clarity is inescapable. Days become governed by tiptoeing around chalk outlines of your former self, by scraping residue off the walls; gunk from police tape gets under your nails. Eventually, it becomes necessary to leave before you rip up the floorboards and grind your thumbs down to the knuckle. It's a fast and unpleasant realization, after a trial, that association is not washed away by decree. The stench lingers long after conviction or exoneration, soaking into the follicles and fibers of our existence. At times, it is all we can do to outrun it, hoping that the wind to our front will keep the vapor at our backs.

I went to Washington at eighteen to exchange ideas and bodily fluids. College provided. The activist was handsome—a bit older, a bit shorter. He waited for our date outside my dorm in a gray hoodie, jeans, and a pair of Chucks: the picture of uncomplicated self-possession. I arrived in loose-fitting green cargo pants and a billowy orange Oxford unbuttoned so as not to obscure my blue t-shirt, the one emblazoned with "JOE" in bold, white lettering—just in case my identity crisis wasn't visible from space. At the Sunoco station, he handled the nozzle at the self-serve pump like a gunslinger, waving to me through the rear window. I spent most of dinner pushing a Caesar salad around its plate, unable to eat, unable to speak when he asked if I was okay; the memory of what had happened the last time I spoke my truth too fresh in mind. We went to the movies. *In Good Company*. There was a love scene.

Scarlett Johansson brought a boy to her room and draped a sheer red scarf over her lamp. It was incomparably slick. I brought the boy to my room and showed him my lofted bed. It was incomparably not. His lips were cold. He came back a few weeks later to borrow some DVDs.

Florida. Four years later. The heir to some grocery-store empire. "You should see their house at Christmas," his friend told me. "A tree in every room." This coming in the very same breath in which she'd uttered, "Stay away from him. He's doesn't do relationships." I pretended I didn't want one. We went to the piano bar, the Baron of Broccoli, him in a camel sport coat and me in a fog of tuna fish from the sandwich I'd eaten a few hours prior. He pretended to be drunk.

"How drunk are you?" I asked.

"Drunk enough to make out with you," he sloshed. They were the nicest words a boy had said to me yet. He took me back to his apartment. I was shivering. He gave me a sweatshirt and asked me to stay the night. I thought it was romantic. He'd wake up every hour or so to use my mouth. I kept the sweatshirt on. The next morning, through swollen lips, I told him how I felt. He responded by moving across the country. I do not regret the tuna fish.

Florida, still. Another two years. A cattleman asked me to sit and have lunch. He ate carrot sticks and had beautiful hands. I wanted him to feed me. Instead, he took me to the park and we talked about things I don't remember. At night, I watched the fireworks burnish his eyes as we lay in the bed of his truck. It took me three hours to touch his knee. It took him another hour to kiss me. On Halloween, I found him at a party and he found an empty bedroom.

Someone walked in to find Jack Sparrow straddling Elliot from *E.T.* By the end of the party, everyone knew. "I can't do this." By the next day, he picked another lunch table. "I can't stay here." By the next month, he'd gone back to the ranch in Colorado. Better to be herd than seen.

New York. The Belgian. He sold waffles in the park. "Don't make jokes." He brought leftovers to our first date, and I asked him to marry me. "Don't make jokes." We slid ice cream between them and split a cider. He taught me about chocolate—pralines and truffles, the proper portion of cocoa powder, and why the Swiss are pansies. I went to work the next day wearing the same clothes. "I want to spend a day with you," he said. "A whole day to learn about *you*." Saturday morning, first train to Harlem. He answered the door half-asleep and made me omelets. "You like manchego?" We went to the Met, the Anna Wintour Costume Center. *Death Becomes Her: A Century of Mourning Attire.* I held his hand at the museum. I'd always wanted to hold someone's hand at the museum. We drank with his friends, drank more at the bar. I kept my coat on. No cash to tip the attendant. He went to the bathroom and didn't come back. On the dance floor, a stranger's tongue washed me out of his mouth. He made sure I was watching. Sunday, 4 am train with my coat still on. A portrait through a moving window: *Death Becomes Him: A Century of Mourning Attire.*

St. Patrick's Day. St. Patrick's Cathedral. "It's almost one, so it's either now or never." The young financier stood between the spires: tall, slight, a stalk of wheat bending in the night air. The church was the easiest meeting spot for two semi-stoned tourists. *Matured & Bottled in Ireland.* He was better looking than his photos, if that was possible.

He was better looking still when pressing me against the iron fence. "I just want to try something." An exchange of Jameson-laced breaths in the shadow of God's house. I was a nonbeliever of sorts. He wore Jesus around his neck and light blue underwear. I could believe in that. I could believe he liked my body when he said as much. I could believe he wanted to see me when we got back home. I could even believe his house in a neighboring town meant more than just coincidence. For the sake of having his tongue trace my collarbone once more, I did all of those things. I did them knowingly and with intent. So when he slipped out of bed the next morning and took the stairs two-at-a time, when he stepped out the door with clothes swinging from his bag, when he said, "See you soon" but couldn't meet my eyes as he backed away, it was not his nature held accountable but my own. Another self-inflicted wound. Another hit in a history of little murders.

Be on your knees when I arrive.
   It always began the same way, some dark order from some dark figure; a sick fantasy cooked up with some unfamiliar who'd answered an ad. He'd ask for my stats: age, height, weight, length, body type, body hair, preferences, positions, kinks, limits. I'd regurgitate everything I'd already detailed in the post, holding back the urge to blast him for not taking the time to read it. There would be an exchange of photos. Anything with the face cut out was a non-starter, no matter how much they assured me I "wouldn't be disappointed." Even if most of it was faked— the names, the phone numbers, the email accounts—a certain level of honesty was expected and unavoidable since the naked truth would soon be on full display.

With the technical fat and gristle stripped away, we could get to the meat of the situation. What did he want? *To put me in my place.* Did he get verbal? *Hell yea, if you're into that.* When was he free? *Any time after ten.* At some point, I'd let him take the reins of the conversation, sitting back to watch the erotic novel write itself. He'd lay down the law, telling me how I would address him, how I would undress him, how, after tonight, I'd know what a real man was. In agreement, we'd choose a location, some public place halfway between here and there. In an empty lot or down a dingy side street, sex could be treated like the illicit act I'd learned it to be. The second to arrive would approach, squint through the window, and continue to the end of the road, pretending to be a lost driver should there be last-minute hesitations. There, they'd turn and cut their lights, sidling back, and rolling to a stop at the adjacent curb. A few seconds of nothing and then an outline, head down and hands buried in pockets, would make its way across the night and into my passenger seat.

"Hey, how's it going?" The illusion faded at the casual greeting that failed to mask the panic in his voice. Rubbing his legs, back and forth, with a hood pulled around his face, my accomplice looked more like a scared child than the dominant taskmaster he'd earlier proclaimed. He'd find something to talk about—usually my car—fiddling with the dashboard and knobs so as to place his hand in the vicinity of my leg, then on my leg. I'd follow suit, letting my palm travel in the hopes that it might awaken some dormant sadist in him. But the closer I came to his lap, the quieter he got. Inevitably he'd pull himself out, already erect. Between my fingers, he'd close his eyes and go somewhere else. And

I was left alone. The act itself was as carnal as starting a lawnmower; the stubborn, flooded engine grunted with every pull but refused to spring to life. After ten minutes or so—however long it took my hand to go numb—the only release I achieved was that of my grip as he angled away to finish himself off. With his forehead pressed to the window, he seized, emptying into a cupped hand and then licking his own essence from the creases, bringing the ceremony to its conclusion.

I drove home one-handed, and then hunched over the sink, running my filthy paw under boiling water.

You and me are gonna play a little Gag the Fag.
The seat of masochism sits where pleasure and pain become inextricably twisted. For some, the erogenous receptors fire at a swift back of the hand across the ass. For others, like myself, it wasn't so simple. Time and again, I searched for satisfaction in the twisted promises of nameless men. Coming up empty just meant pushing the water further down until it started bubbling up another pipe. It wasn't long before I became so entrenched in my own sense of worthlessness that I began to get off on it. And after years of validation through silence, I needed someone to say it out loud.

Every time I went looking I became more and more emboldened, taking greater risks to realize my reward. Public places became too safe, training grounds for big-talking cowards. Instead, I drifted through the cracked doorways of unlit residences with nothing more than a collapsible switchblade on my keychain. When that didn't work, I opened my own house to strangers, hiding knives in my sock drawer and wrapping anything of value in bath towels. But the change of location had no impact on gameplay. These so-called alpha males would beg me to prepare for domination, yet upon stepping through the threshold, barely uttered more than a few half-hearted grunts. Too soaked in beer and nicotine, they couldn't pick up the scent of my own discomfort. Too busy hating themselves, they couldn't bother to hate me. So, there I'd be, until my arm throbbed and my jaw ached, praying for it to be over.

Mornings after brought remorse and Listerine. I'd wake up extra early just to stand in the shower, hoping to burn off a layer of skin. Fingers pricked, I dripped blood into vials, mailing off test kits far too soon after exposure for conclusive results. For three months I was chaste as a cleric, flogging myself until it was time to go sit on tissue paper. More blood, swabbed cheeks, and the always-dignified rectal culture followed lectures and assurances that I was very low risk. "You're about the only gay man in New York who still uses protection." But I knew that karma could eat through latex. And that was the real issue. Not the disease itself or living with it, but rather, how it would verify everything my mother had said and my father had sobbed all those years ago. That was a diagnosis I could not live with.

When I received clemency, I'd vow that was the last time. Then a few more months went by.

When we lost Dad, everything shifted. Suddenly the shadows couldn't hide anything. Being thrust into the sun carried a sort of freedom with it. Not freedom from some malevolent force but instead a license to release myself from the belief that I was slowly killing him. Truth be told, not since that day in my room had my father shown me anything other than outright love. Though there'd always be a part of my life he'd have difficulty addressing with words, there were innumerable actions: care packages, voicemails, 3 am phone calls talking me through a panic attack, or the simple fact that he never once stopped saying "I love you"; things that should've told me everything I needed to know. Instead, I'd chosen to see his silence as some ill-conceived disgrace.

Now he was everywhere. The dirty laundry was aired. And as much as that might have made rolling around in the mud all the easier, I found myself no longer wanting any part of it. It had never been as fun as it looked nor had it been easy to wash off. I'd only gotten down there in the first place after allowing weaker men to dupe me into viewing my vulnerability as some crucial character flaw. But it is an incredibly difficult thing, to admit you want love. Even harder is accepting that you deserve it. While, for me, it wouldn't happen overnight, I'd slowly come to understand that there's nothing to be felt without feeling. So let the broken edges mend.

Eventually there would be a boy, a bit shaky and unsure. He'd find me at just the time I needed to be found. I'd be patient. He'd be open. I'd trust he wouldn't run. He'd call me "home." When he pressed into me, his eyes were open, and in them I could see that he was nowhere else but right there with me. Yes, he'd tell me he loved me. And no, maybe it wouldn't be forever. But the fact that it was at all meant more than I'd ever recognized.

Sometimes, the old thoughts do creep back in. Sometimes, I have to force myself to meet the mirror. The little murders are written in our reflections. Consider this my testimony.

Abide the Chirping

2011

At twenty-four I have convinced myself that I am dying of a progressive neurological disorder. At the time I live in Florida, I'm the privileged owner of an ever-elusive, if not slightly dust-worn, B.A. in Communications, I work at Disney World, and numbering among my most-apparent concerns of the day includes figuring out how many free popcorn coupons it will take to bribe a concessions worker for something useful, like a soft pretzel.

Somewhere herein, well into the third year of a four-month internship I conveniently use as a filibuster against making any solid (or, for that matter, even mildly-viscous) decisions about my future, a cut on the tip of my left ring finger develops into a numbness that persists for weeks after the external injury heals. Despite my best efforts, no amount of fist clenching or wrist flicking will knock the feeling back above the topmost knuckle of that digit. Ever the gumshoe, sleuthing only compounds the issue. Wanting nothing more than to quickly ascribe the anomaly to some benign origin, medical message boards and the perilous lacework of WebMD gives way to an anthology of degenerative afflictions, a serial of killers that would have Stephen King sleeping with a night light. Listed under each, an assortment of symptoms elastic enough to stretch to fit my predicament. Those I don't have present soon thereafter until what started as a tingle explodes into intermittent neuropathies in the extremities, involuntary muscle twitches, insomnia, photosensitivity, and regular bouts of three am dry heaving.

Night after night, I yank my father from a peaceful sleep. Night unto morning, from nine hundred miles away, he sits on the phone convincing me that I'm not going to die until I sob myself limp. Too terrified for a confirmation of my self-diagnosis, the pattern continues until weeks become months and placations become threats. Dad, bedraggled by his own son, issues an ultimatum: "Either see a doctor, or I'm getting in a car right now and dragging you home." Being chided like a preschooler has a way of unleashing the militant in even the meekest of us. Even the damned will embrace their damnation for the sake of proving their own sanity.

I hopscotch from internist to internist, each one echoing a similar dismissal without so much as shining a penlight in my eye or tapping my knee with that plastic hammer thingy. "Anxiety," they blurt, scribbling a referral to some shrink in a neat pass of the buck.

"Anxiety about what?" I challenge, grinding my teeth to paste. "I drive safari trucks all day. I work in an adolescent's caramel-coated daydream. Each shift begins with a parade and ends with fireworks. What the hell is there to be anxious about?" They demur, of course, unconvinced.

My body, equally dubious of my grounds for debate, airs its counterargument a few nights later when I wake, paralyzed from the neck up. The feeling returns in as much time as it takes to tumble off the mattress, but the shock is enough to send me pawing that referral slip from the trash.

The man across from the couch reads from a questionnaire. "If you had a magic wand, what might you change about your life?" He's short of everything: height, time, concern. "What would it take to make you feel more content, happier, more satisfied?" I'm short of patience, bringing every answer back to the physical, recalling every terrifying manifestation, certain that one of them will draw his face from behind the clipboard. None of them does. The remaining queries serve only to bend my neck and my resolve, redirecting my last answers toward yellowing ceiling tiles. "Generalized Anxiety," he mumbles, tearing a sheet from his pad. Diagnosis by cootie catcher.

2013

I stop the meds shortly before moving home. Turns out that coming off the pills is an easy decision once an entire Archer Farms pizza and half a tub of Toll House Scoop & Bake start to seem like a sensible dinner and not a suicide note. While that may be a simplification, it's characteristic of a larger problem. Drugs killed the anxiety in all of its physical forms, but it had taken reason and accountability down with it. Like using a blanket to smother a fire. Yes, the flames were out, but there was something underneath that still needed to breathe. I needed to be wild. I needed to make better mistakes than just those on my grocery list.

Most of all, I needed one more shot at dominion over my own body before I surrendered my twenties to the bottom of a prescription bottle.

Dad gets sick before I even unpack, before I can even be sure my system has sobered itself. After that, it is impossible to tell if the quick and chronic anxiety is a product of his illness or just the return of some feral thing I'd let loose. The tension stays too high and the engines burn too long so that, when we lose him, there is nowhere to go but down. To fall out of the sky. Then, the highs and lows seem normal, the expected sensations of trying to course correct through a field of air pockets. When the symptoms don't return and my electricity doesn't short out—after a tussle with a namable stressor—I begin to wonder if I'd spent a year medicating the wrong problem. That the ten plagues upon my old house had not been born of malfunction but of rejection; an allergic reaction from having stayed too long at the fair.

But the lights have their way of calling us back. The smell of sugared almonds and gunpowder traces across a night's dome to trick up memories of the sweet bright. So I return, unparented, a week-long tourist in a past life, fooling myself into thinking brevity might allow me to plunder my childhood before materiality sniffs me out. I wear my shades in the dark, slug back milk tea, get lost in crowds, dance in Morocco. In France, I wonder at *impressions*. In Germany, there is a silent love affair with a clock seller. It is beautiful and fast by design, plotted precisely to allow for a daily marathon of people trying to outrun themselves. Keeping pace with me is Ellie, the one part that had made leaving hard and the one friend who, despite knowing everything, never looks at me like a half-orphan. Where her face lacks pity, it is generous with eye rolls. Where she picks apart what you want, it is only to address what you need. The kind of person who won't let you run away with a Bavarian glockenspiel player. One who'll walk seventy miles over five days to entertain your irrationality, who'll sooner burst your balloon than let it carry you away—not out of spite, but because you're headed for power lines. The person each person requires but who so few actually get. A seer.

The seer sees what no one else can, the quiet storm. Somewhere in the hubbub of stiff, custom-printed, color-matched T-shirts and glitter eye shadow melted from the Orange County sun, smack in the middle of the queue for *Maelstrom: A High-Seas Norwegian Adventure*, it starts as a suspicion. Willow flute cascading from unseen speakers and tongue tasting of caramel apple, it is a day dripping with delirium, the fatuous oblivion of an emotional fugitive. Nevertheless, my skin crawls over still bones, mobilized by the irreconcilable feeling of wrongness. Behind, happy legs swing over guardrails. Waiting out ahead, nothing but trolls and polar bears. Euphoria abounds, spirits leap, and with each passing step, my feet fall harsher, faster, deader. At once, it becomes less about stepping than about being pulled to the ground. Revelers around me walk above the floor, carried wholesale by manufactured whimsy, while I hard-knuckle the railings as every single one of the earth's thousand miles an hour lassoes me to the concrete. "Are you okay?" Ellie asks over eyes washed with skepticism. Unsure if the abrupt stoppage of my blathering has tipped her off or if my tumult has become apparent, I glance around. But, having drawn no stares, it's all too clear how invisible the struggle is to anyone but the acute observer. I roil, shaken, but only enough to keep the ravaging self-contained. To the crowd, I am unremarkable, another in a line of lighthearted patrons, albeit one more reserved. None can know that reservation comes only as the byproduct of a man working to quell his own unjustifiable agitation, a man taking deeper and deeper breaths into lungs that fill but never seem to get any air. "We can leave," Ellie nods toward the exit. "We're right there," the concern in her voice more pronounced than before. Again, I refuse, stepping toward the loading platform. The rigor of some unseen menace may have grabbed me, but more paralyzing is the thought of having to explain what I do not myself comprehend.

When the Viking longboat pulls up to dock, I tell myself everything is fine. When we slosh into the black waters, I assure myself I can ride it out. Though pitch-black passageways veil me for a time; it's only so they might carry me under the scrupulous eye of Odin himself. *Those who seek the spirit of Norway face peril and adventure...*

2014

As it turns out, generalized anxiety, like its viral and cancerous kinsmen, is equipped with its own arsenal of defense mechanisms against any measures employed to suppress it. For some, medication helps with containment, keeps the bear locked in a closet, and leaves the rest of the house livable as long as the owner agrees to never again open that particular door. External factors—therapy, hardship, general bad juju—can also cause an impact of varying positive and negative degrees. In some cases, removing a tumor is a cure-all. In others, it switches the malignancy into survival mode, sending cells to lay low in half a dozen outposts throughout the body. For me, the meds had done their job in weakening the GAD. But, in coming off them, I'd allowed the conditions for it to regroup just enough that, when the trauma came along, it wasn't destroyed entirely. Instead, it shattered into a wind that blew the pieces into piles along the spread between me and Saint Peter. Panic disorder: a mutation. In the previous iteration (let's call him "Joe Classic"), the GAD would've meant contending with life on a perpetual low boil. This new prognosis (let's call him "Great New Taste, Better than Ever Joe") will mean spending extended stretches of time in states of something resembling composure. The catch being that mixed into the formula are intermittent onsets of intense fear and dread, with no warning and for no reason.

One of the more natural approaches to coping and managing with panic disorder is a breathing exercise. Diaphragmatic breathing—or deep breathing—requires a concentrated effort in order to access and utilize the necessary muscles involved. The idea behind the practice is drawing the focus away from a presenting episode, thereby instilling a sense of calm and hopefully expediting the body's leveling out. Meditation is often recommended, due to its principal involvement of deep breathing. This would work if not for the one crippling fear most anxious people harbor: the prospect of being locked in a quiet room with their own thoughts. In lieu of this poison pill, I take to hiking, an equally breathing-dependent activity with the added bonus of visual and auditory stimuli to distract the mind from itself. Down the road from my apartment, in the Buttermilk

Valley, is a convenient county park with trails that sprawl the entirety of its seven-hundred-and-ninety-four acres. A former WWII artillery site, landing strips and bunkers once thought to be bomb-proof litter the hilly expanse, all given back to nature and all of which I have come to know with more familiarity than the freckles on my own nose. Weekly jaunts turn daily, first trudging then walking then running, each time learning the feel of a new root under my feet or the degree of the bend as the Rocky Point trail meets the Grand Tour. It isn't long before my legs begin to anticipate the curves and inclines before I even reached them, shifting weight and adjusting breathing pace without conscious intervention.

There's a power that comes with that, a sense of invincibility. Commanding the terrain and learning and outmaneuvering the obstacles bring renewed confidence in what my body can do, what it is capable of adapting to. Overcoming, even. That exercise-induced arrogance has an addictive effect as the fall tips its hat over the East Coast. With dusk coming quicker each day, I rush home from work with the sole purpose of getting in a trek, my mastery of the map fooling me into believing I can beat the sun before it drips out of the sky. Knowing the route home, however, has never stopped anyone from making a mindless error. After second-guessing a fork in the path, the sun goes down on me faster than on Elton John. In a flash, my shoes forget everything they'd known. Skinny stumps confused for trail markers lead me further into unknown ground where I snag my toes in thickets, nose-diving into downslopes and pinballing against every rock and crag along the descent. Before long, the prospect of triggering one more God-deposited booby trap makes the thought of taking another step stomach-churning. Smelling of dirt and blood, I glom onto a rusted gate I can feel out of the darkness and hurl my curses down the throat of an old cannonry dugout. When I run out of epithets, I call Ellie, crying, as if there's anything she can do from a thousand miles away. I call a friend in the neighboring town, who jumps in her car as if I'm not lost amidst fourteen miles of trails under the cover of night. I call my mother who tells me to call the police, as if that won't make a precious headline in the morning paper.

> Sept. 28—Highlands Township—Police rescue 27-year-old man lost in woods. Mother unavailable for comment. Father deceased, presumably from shame.

Once I prove able to work through the laughable reflexes of impulsivity, there remains little to do in the dark but breathe in everything I cannot see. The soil, the sweat, and salt on my skin, the wet clay that folds around the mountain creek. In that quiet exhaustion, it becomes inevitable to recount the narrative. Without color or distraction, the cynic in me can't help but appreciate how the transcript reads. For so long, I'd labored to describe to others how a panic attack feels to someone inside of it. Yet, here I was, sitting in the middle of a rendering more perfect than I could ever write. I had waltzed onto accustomed grounds only to misplace myself. In the ensuing hysteria, rather than focus on the reality, I had allowed impetuousness to trip me up, dragging me even further into the maw. Even with help available, with friends quite literally at hand, I could tell them where I was but I couldn't tell them how to get to me. I was right there, on the other side of the trees, but perfectly inaccessible. That cold reality ushers swiftly to light two possible options. Either I can give fear the run of my faculties until it elects to leave or I can simply decide to exit first. So I pull myself from the ground. I step, deliberate and unsexy, feeling for the arc in the trail, trusting that anything downward will spill me onto the road, one way or another.

2016

"Okay, plank position. One minute."

I am down, but not really. Elbows, forearms, and toes to the floor, I am to hold the rest of my body rigid, suspended at a forty-five-degree angle above the matted floor. At this point, it's not clear what exactly holds me aloft, my own will or my revulsion at the scent of perspiration and sneaker grime that coats the rubber tiles beneath me. Either way, I'm where I need to be, rigid to the point where a stiff wind and some string could see me flown around the neighborhood. I'm not sure how much time has passed because counting somehow manages to make everything seem longer. Let it remain a mystery, concealed by the orange plastic backing of the stopwatch he glances at when not assessing my form. Him, with the boyish red cheeks he tries to hide behind a neatly trimmed beard, the *Vogue Hommes* hair that I know just fucking grows that way, the mouthful of teeth so white and straight they'd vote down-ballot Republican, and the frame that inexplicably wears the hell out of clothes two sizes too big. The man I've paid to break me.

"Hips lower. Breathe."

The attraction is irksome. But it'll pass. Why he couldn't have turned out to be another rotund juicehead, I don't know. But it'll pass. That's not what this is about. This is about the mind finding a way to feel unsafe in an otherwise safe environment. It doesn't matter if it's just him and me in his basement. One set of eyes may as well be a thousand. And fine. I came here to get uncomfortable. I came here to sweat and molt and bend my bones, to let tresses stick to my forehead. I came to address the softness, an exercise most unflattering in execution. Much as I'd like to hide the ugly bits, much as I contract the muscles in my abdomen, that which is not taut will go the way of gravity. Nothing to do but hang, be still, push through the minute. Be strong until I'm weak, then push through the weakness. This is an experiment to see how much the body can withstand and for how long. This is trauma, controlled, measured, annotated. Then repeated, again and again, at slightly greater intensity. There's pain, self-inflicted. Just about the only kind that won't result in a psych eval. The goal is not to create feeling where there is none but to manage feeling where there is too much.

"Thirty seconds. Remember to breathe."

Halfway there, and only now my legs begin to tremble. A new record. Whether the cause is overexertion or under oxygenation is up for debate. Just two weeks prior, it only took half that length to send me shaking. So, heads or tails, I chalk it up as a win. He wants me to breathe; he's made that much clear. Endeavor to please him though I do, my body compensates for faltering thighs by constricting my stomach even tighter. In turn, the fire works its way past my waist and into my lower abdomen. It's the muscles' way of reporting damage, that burn. The more strain I inflict, the more the microscopic fibers tear. The more the fibers tear, the fiercer the ache. The fiercer the ache, the more I fight to compress everything down to my cell walls. And round and round it goes. It's sick, and it's gorgeous. But it's endurable once one appreciates the process. How some masochistic demigod designed the system to thrive on punishment. How each fiber severed will increase upon itself, weaving together and forming new strands of protein as a protective shell. It grows, hardens, fortifies to bear up against the next attack. If something as simple as sinew can be so intuitive, surely the brain is of equal measure.

"Fifteen seconds. You're not breathing!"

I could cry battery acid, the way my nerves are scorching. But I still won't count. And I still can't breathe. And if I still can't breathe, I can't look at him. But I can't look down because the floor still reeks. So I turn my gaze forward and meet the stare of the quivering little lump in the mirror. *Quiver, lump,* I wish to say. *Don't think about how long a minute feels. Think, instead, of how you will renew when it passes. Think of a mind no stranger to pain, yet one that can rebound hardier than before. Think of the body, how it reacts, how it grows, how it can be reshaped, but also how the bones remain unaltered. Accept your bones. Move with them, even when they resist. They will carry you to the other side, where you can rest and rebuild. It all passes, this minute and the next, whatever it may hold. Everything passes. It just takes a little—*

"Time!"

2019

There is a cricket that lives in my house. I can't say where exactly, as I've never seen him. Though, if I were to guess, I'd say he's set up a nice little enclave for himself in the kitchen. I venture this simply because that's where his chirps reverberate the loudest. The word "chirps," in this case, is merely a point of reference and does not quite capture his true enterprise. The plurality of the term would imply a sequence of sounds broken up by blips of silence. In reality, this particular insect chooses to voice his presence through the belt of a single, sustained, seemingly ceaseless note. He does not relent. He does not come up for air. Not even long enough for the ear to recalibrate so that it might pinpoint his direction. When he sounds, he sounds everywhere at once. He is a cricket on amphetamines, a one-bug *Rigoletto*. So incessant is he that, when his tune first pricked my lobes some months back, I confused it for the peal of my carbon monoxide alarm.

Upon my realization of the intruder's occupancy, his racket swells to a pitch that had me longing for toxic gas. Hammer, anvil, and stirrups thrash with his soliloquy, I become an unwilling patron, increasingly unable to focus on work or even the simplest of household tasks until there's no other choice but to relinquish my residence in order to get anything done. Taking repose in coffee shops is a temporary fix, of course, and one that ends in my returns to unwelcome encores. It's not long before the eviction of the pest becomes my primary occupation. No expert in vermin, I first invoke methods aimed to terrorize. I summon my human might, stomping up and down the stairs, slamming doors, performing *Riverdance* across the hardwood; anything to make him believe the walls could come crashing down at any moment. But he is unflagging. So, I resort to annihilation. I lay glue traps in the corners and flood every crevice with enough Hot Shot to warrant an EPA tribunal. Still, he chirps.

It comes to be something larger than man vs. insect. It comes to be a matter of possession, of my outrage at the gall of some squatter who creeps in and takes up tenancy despite my objection, not to mention my authority as landlord. Try as I may to smoke him out, in the end it's only me who winds up with sore feet and lungs full of pesticide. He just goes on about his business. The choice then becomes to either demolish my house or to abide the chirping. I will not lose more of myself in some effort to curtail an invisible nuisance. I will not burn it all down just to hear him sing in the ashes. What I will do is move about my space, move about my day, for he will have his say whether I am aggrieved or not. Only then can I push him to the background, to that vague composition of refrigerator fans and circulated air, those sounds whose absence is indicated by the silence that speaks louder.

The house is so silent today. I opened a window to air out the place. Maybe that's how he left. Maybe that's how he'll come back. If not, there are countless other ways. In the meantime, I think I'll leave it open. I enjoy the breeze.

There is No Butter in Italy

Continue for five kilometers on Vianastrovurd. The bionic woman barked directions from her perch on the windshield, pronouncing street names about as well as someone ordering at Olive Garden.

Hands on the wheel, I tilted towards the screen of our GPS, Magdalena, in an attempt to decode whatever it was she'd just failed to communicate. "What the hell?"

"Keep watching the road!" Palms shaking, Ellie shoved my face back toward the rush of asphalt, doing her best to read off the screen from the passenger seat. "Stay straight on Via Nastro Vurdi...Verde? Oh, like it even matters."

My co-pilot had lost all faith in our digital navigator, and she wasn't without cause. Fluctuating between confidence and indecision, Magdalena had proven that her international expansion chip was about as functional as a Dorito. Having confused at least a dozen Vias for Vicolos along the way, her only success had been at doubling the length of our supposed three-hour drive from Rome toward the Amalfi Coast. We'd reached the area just in time to watch the remaining hints of light empty out of the sky. As I watched the blushed incandescence of Sorrento disappear in the rearview mirror, familiar passages called out from the recesses to kick dirt in my eyes.

> The 1962 Oldsmobile Jetfire, a high-tech model few people remember, boasted technical specifications many modern sportscars could envy. A turbo-charged, fluid-injected, small-displacement aluminum V-8 provided the heart and soul of this junior road rocket. Our test car is owner Joe Lezza's second Jetfire. His bought his first one as a used car in 1967 while dating the woman who would eventually become his wife.

Bending upwards with the road, the tiny sedan blew raspberries along the cliffside while I white-knuckled the gearshift to manage its ascent. On my right, Ellie burrowed into the fibers of the bucket seat, bracing herself against anything sturdy as she worked on swallowing the bottom half of her face. A few months prior, I'd successfully lured my good friend along for the ride with promises of blue grottos, fancy boutiques, and every assurance that I'd mastered the art of driving stick— technically, I had.

Weeks before our departure, I'd yanked the dustcover from my father's antique coupe in the garage and began the process of reintroducing myself. I spent the initial days thumbing the metal spokes of the steering wheel and ping-ponging up and down the driveway. Curiosity getting the better of me, I found myself rifling through the glove compartment and under the seats where I fished out an April 1996 issue of *Special Interest Autos* still flat and pristine in its plastic sleeve. After taking great care to remove it, I lost myself in the aroma of ink and acetate before falling, head-first, into a memory. "Turbo Before Its Time," the title sat in bold serif along the page header, announcing itself. Over the course of four pages, my father spoke to me through an interview I'd since forgotten, one he'd given from the driver's seat nineteen years ago.

Revisiting the article every day, I pored over the words until I'd gathered up enough guts to take the car past the property line. It wasn't long before I was sailing the wide-open streets of suburban New Jersey. Windows down, the magazine flapped on the dash as I crisscrossed through four simple gears like a knife through warm butter. For the first time in two long spins around the sun, sitting in that driver's seat, I felt a connection, a current running directly to Dad that I was determined to chase wherever it led. But, upon climbing into my rental at Fiumicino Airport some weeks later, I came to discover that there is no butter in Italy.

> Fast forward to 1993: Lezza, now married and with a young son, started thinking it would be nice to have a car of his own to take to shows. His wife, remembering the car they courted in, suggested he get another Jetfire. Nine-year-old Joey has developed an interest in the car. Father and son are fanatical about keeping the Oldsmobile polished. For Lezza, the Jetfire's appeal is nostalgic. For Joey, the best part of the shows is "all the compliments we get on the car." He drops his chin and does a little-boy growl to imitate a typical car show spectator: "Ain't many of these around anymore!"

Facing a console that may as well have been ripped from the cockpit of a 787, I'd managed to exit the AUTONOLEGGIO garage only to find myself orbiting the airport in an attempt to lash the car into submission. But, with our time in Rome limited, there was no choice but to take a collective breath and lurch toward the USCITA. In the heart of the city, I negotiated the streets with an erratic pulse. If I wasn't clenching my sphincter through frenzied roundabouts, I was dodging the Vespas that flung themselves into traffic like bullets from a machine gun. Every stoplight was a fractional nervous breakdown as I fought to prove myself capable of shifting out of neutral without stalling. Parking was worse. By the time we'd sidled off of the Piazza del Colosseo, a complete absence of street signage made it impossible to comprehend a patchwork of parking spots whose color spectrum rivaled that of a freshly opened pack of Lifesavers. From wild cherry to green apple, eventually we just picked a flavor and hoped for the best.

Asses sufficiently handed to us, we meandered down the sidewalk and grabbed a couple pieces of focaccia, all the while keeping the car within eyesight. After a few shaky stabs at the commensurate Colosseum photo, the two of us found a spot on a rock wall that overlooked the courtyard. Outside the main entrance, horse carriages teeming with tourists rolled along the cobblestones and children hopped metal chains over patchy lawns dotted with signs that read NON CAMMINARE. Not twenty years ago I'd slid through those same patches, squishing the blades of grass between my toes as Mom chided and Dad laughed. They did their best to impress the significance of the location upon me, but back then, the grass seemed like more fun than some old building. This morning, however, despite all the false starts and narrowly avoided scratches in the stradastretta, despite the accidental turn down a one-way street and a severe tongue lashing from the polizia (in which the only word I recognized was "stronzo"), despite even the electricity that ran up my legs at the thought of returning to the deathmobile, I'd managed to somehow find my way back. Although he wasn't waiting in the crowd as I'd secretly hoped, I had finally come to look upon the place the way my father had always wanted me to.

"Want to go inside?" I turned to Ellie.

With a healthy hunk of ciabatta trembling between her teeth, she tore a shard and looked me square in the eye. "No."

The worst was surely behind us.

> Steering is as good as any early '60s automobile. There's some lean in corners, enough to remind you that this is a compact coupe and not a true sports car. Otherwise, the handling is tight.

Continue for three kilometers on Vianastrovurd.

"Oh, stuff it, Magdalena!" Ellie gripped the door handle and admonished the GPS. Eyes glued forward, she redirected her attention at me. "Have you seen any sign for the hotel?"

"I haven't even seen signs of multi-celled life, never mind the hotel." Two-handing the wheel, I pounded out Beethoven's "Fifth Symphony" on the foot pedals and squinted into the darkness.

Somewhere, on the side of a mountain, a road no wider than my forearm bent and twisted and carried us skyward. I held the car in fifth gear and somehow managed to avoid Thelma and Louise-ing off of the swervy band of pavement with no guardrail, despite the fact that opposing vehicles continued to dart out at us from unseen corners. At once I was sixteen, inexperienced and unpracticed, yet also convinced that motor oil ran through my veins. In that moment, a ringing in my right ear resolved itself into the terrified echo of fatherly instruction. *Your turns are too wide. Hug the curves. Hug the curves!*

Continue for two...RECALCULATING.

"What'd she say?" Ellie leaned forward, glaring at the screen as if she were about to smash a bottle and ask it to step outside.

"That can't be right. How could we be off course?" I shifted my gaze just in time to watch an unmarked road splinter off from our neon pink path, dragging our little buggy icon along with it.

At first opportunity, make legal U-turn. Magdalena cracked jokes, stifling what I'm certain was a laugh.

Not wanting to venture too far off the trail, I pushed a bit further hoping to find a patch of drive wide enough to allow for a U-turn. That's when the road dropped out from under us.

> The brakes are also more than adequate to the demands of in-town driving. I don't know how they would hold up under continuous high-speed use.

The street banked downward, shallow at first but steepening until we were in a full-on nosedive. The prospect of reverse too terrifying, I jammed the stick into neutral and eased on the brake to manage our descent into what had to be the ninth circle of hell. Pavement soon gave way to pebbles that kamikazed against the car's undercarriage, their suicidal clangs harmonized symphonic with the rumble of our shifting bags. It is said that your life flashes before your eyes right before you die. But, as Ellie tallied all the wonderful ways in which to kill me should she survive, all I saw was a sadistic slideshow of every lovely and welcoming hotel we'd passed back at sea level.

The backside of the car began to fishtail and I eased off the brakes in a last-ditch effort to recover some traction, holding tight to the wheel as if it made any difference. Like the pilot that lowers the landing gear right before a crash, we have tendencies to show spirit even in the most hopeless of situations. Sand and gravel flashed in the path of the headlamps, our only source of light. But, in the midst of the crunchy lull, just as our plummet entered Mach 5, the car began to right itself. Without thinking, I shot my braking foot forward the moment we leveled out. Skidding across the uneven terrain, we circled the drain to find rest at the bottom of the basin.

Loss of signal.

> The bucket seats are comfortable and the cockpit is easy to settle in. This is obviously a compact car, but the hardtop styling gives the cabin an airy feel. The speedometer is right in front of me and easy to read through the steering wheel.

I stared at the dash, the two of us stunned as the motor idled, enduring. In the vacuum there seemed nothing else to do but re-examine the misguided influences that had led to this Sorrentine folly. My mind's finger flailed, flicking through a portfolio of blamable subjects: the Hertz representative who heard my American accent and handed me the keys to a Ford (a car clearly inadaptable to the sensibilities of the Roman landscape), the mother who suggested a hotel at an elevation requiring access by Sherpa (the same hotel where she and Dad stayed on the trip no one knew would be his last), and of course, the dewy-eyed child who took that advice as a part of some sentimental scavenger hunt (as if dear Father sat sipping an espresso in the lobby waiting to welcome with open arms). Loss is a hustler that way. It dupes the reasonable into believing the absent are not absent but simply lost, that they slipped out for a cup of coffee and lost track of time, that death is a winnable game.

Too exhausted to accept the onus, I moved to cut the engine when a knock came from the passenger side. Unable to see any feasible ways to worsen the situation, Ellie rolled down her window without a second thought as two round, elderly faces crouched and peered in at the two of us.

"Haibisogno di aiuto?" A bespectacled woman smiled, unfazed by our sudden appearance.

Ellie looked at me and shrugged.

"Buona sera, signora." I stammered. "Siamo Americani."

"Ahhh, Americani!" She nodded to her silent husband as if she'd won a bet. "How we can help?"

Awash with slight relief, I called up as much middle-school Italian as I could muster. "Dov'è L'hotel Villa Fiorita?"

"Villa Fiorita?" The couple turned to each other, exchanging mumbles and shrugs. "Is what street?"

Snatching a wrinkled piece of paper from under the emergency brake, I scanned for the address. "Via Nastro Verde."

"Nastro Verde! Ho-kay!" Connection achieved, the woman reached in with a healthy sized arm and pointed out my window. "Vabene. Turn arownd and tay-ek road back to top." Not what I wanted to hear. "Capisce? All deh way." She motioned with her thumb towards the ceiling. "An, at eh-stop sign, you make right. Is Nastro Verde."

I mirrored the woman's smiling nods as my throat closed in on itself. The old man clapped twice on the roof as his wife removed herself, the two of them retreating to the porch of a house neither one of us had noticed until this very moment.

"Gratzi!" Ellie called out as she rolled up her window and turned to me. "What are the odds that the two people who live in Dante's seventh circle would speak even a word of English?"

"Better than the odds of us getting back up that hill." Sitting back in my seat, I took a deep breath and accepting my fate, threw the car into reverse.

> The small-displacement V-8 revs like a weed whacker and the rasping exhaust note is soon joined by the shrill whistle of the turbo. The turbo's whistle is an audible indicator of its operation. There is no flat spot in the acceleration; it feels like it will keep building until the engine spins apart.

The first few attempts went about as well as anticipated. We'd scale the foot of the hill fine enough, building up momentum. Yet, each time, right at the point where the road vaulted toward its steepest, the car would slow to a ceremonious stop that no amount of revving seemed able to combat. Persistence would then dissolve into an ultimate resignation that saw us rolling backwards to the start.

The Sisyphean task carried on. Try after try, I slammed my foot on the gas and churned through the first four gears. The shift was sluggish, as if being dragged through heavy cream. Try after try, the car would reach the same exact spot before offering up a squealing surrender. Somewhere around the eighth or ninth failed endeavor, it became impossible to tell which one of us was screaming louder.

I screamed all the way down the down the hill. I screamed at the tether of the earth. I screamed until I thought my throat would bleed. The membrane wouldn't break. Fat into water, the globules of my life continued to settle at the bottom. And as tears filled my eyes, I looked out at the world through a liquid frustration that could not be whipped into a solid understanding.

"It's okay." Ellie cooed from her seat, unsure of what to make of my sobbing. "Breathe. It's going to be ok."

"NO IT'S NOT!" I snapped. "JUST GRAB YOUR BAGS AND FIND THOSE OLD PEOPLE BECAUSE WE LIVE HERE NOW. THIS IS WHERE WE LIVE, AT THE BOTTOM OF THIS FUCKING DITCH. WE'RE DITCH PEOPLE NOW."

Lips pursed, she stiffened. Readying for her inevitable return volley, I ran my nose across my shoulder, smothering a snot bubble the likes of which only Viola Davis could rival. But as the color bled back into my co-pilot's face, I realized her constriction was intended only to mask the shock of laughter that worked her whole body into spasms.

Her eyes, two mirrors I could not avoid, reflected the visage of absolute lunacy. In a flash, I saw myself bellowing, feral, foaming at the mouth while a flank of white-coated men crept toward me with enough Thorazine to housebreak a Megalodon. It was inarguable, hysterical, a childish tirade from the mouth of a man who ought to know better. Short of FEMA stepping in, I was left to acknowledge that the responsibility for mitigating the slow-moving disaster that was me was *me*. So there, at literal rock bottom, I eased up on myself. Just a little. Just enough to laugh along with her.

It was a start.

"Oh man." I took my first unlabored breath in hours. "I'm sorry. I just don't know what the hell else to do."

"Maybe we're going about this wrong," she replied.

"You wanna get out and push?" I drummed on the steering wheel.

"Watch it, or I'll flag down Miracle Max and Valerie again."

"No, you're right." I leaned my head against the headrest and stared at the ceiling. "This isn't working. I think I'm giving the engine too much at once."

"Maybe you need a different approach."

> Lezza has never pushed the car to its limits.
> He encourages me to drive briskly but asks
> me not to "floor it."

Locking eyes, Ellie and I sucked up as much air as our lungs could take, held it, and turned towards the windshield. The well-worn gearshift fevered in my hand, and as we slid into first, the car booted ahead. I swung us in a slow circle, making sure the wheels had as much grip as possible. Nudging the gas, we entered the climb.

> Upshifts seem to take a half second or so and are accompanied by a smooth surge. It's not unpleasant...

A dozen or so feet up and no sign of slippage, I knocked into second gear without as much as a kickback. A little more pressure on the gas and the car leaned into the thrust. Ellie was a statue. I'm not sure she ever exhaled.

I felt the pedal for any signs of laboring, but the motor's pulse held steady. And if she was steady, I was steady. So, I pushed into third and we broke into a jog.

After a brief surge, the needle on the speedometer settled. Metrically challenged, my eyes couldn't make heads or tails of 48kph. My gut, however, knew it wouldn't be enough. Notch by notch our angle grew steeper, and with the distance closing between us and the sharp upswing, I nudged into fourth.

With fourth came the familiar clang of the underside rubble. Initially, the car hesitated, shallowing my breath, but it caught up to itself in haste. By the way it retained the road, I figured it wanted out of this as much as we did. Nevertheless, a subtle rattle from the pedal betrayed its uncertainty as the embankment came into view. Not knowing what else to do, I set into a pep talk.

"Come on, you got this, buddy." The knob trembled in my hand. "Don't wuss out on me. This hill will not be your kryptonite. You're Built Ford Tough!" The engine belched and roared. "Ford-fucking-Tough!"

The time was now. Ellie bleated through gnashing teeth. The pedal stabilized, I threw the lever into fifth, gassed it, and burned through every Italian curse word my father had ever uttered.

The mid-range and high end are where this car exults.

A click, a jolt, and the briefest moment of silence later, the car launched itself into the incline. The two of us went limp in the grasp of the beast as it clawed its way up the Empire State Building. Not an atom of oxygen was exchanged for fear of what altering the cabin pressure might do. But, as soon as rough ground relented into smooth concrete, I came alive and chucked us into sixth with my foot to the floor.

The rest of the drive was spent without words. At the top of the hill was the "eh-stop sign." A right put us back onto Nastro Verde, and minutes later, we sputtered over the finish line in front of the Villa Fiorita. Ellie and I made our way down a set of tile steps with a set of pronounced tremors rarely seen outside of a detox clinic. Past the wrought-iron scroll gate a man named Enzo greeted us and flew out to the car to grab our bags.

Unfortunately, the Jetfire was short-lived.

Ellie slumped into the closest easy chair as I took a look around the lobby. As suspected there was no espresso, no open arms, no dear old Dad. Logically, I'd acknowledged the impossibility of this prospect but accepted the fool's errand. We do absurd things willingly, us leftovers. We fly thousands of miles and scale a mountain in a Hot Wheels car just to check a box; to make sure what's gone is actually gone. It doesn't make sense. It doesn't have to. That's the one freeing part in all of this. After witnessing the inexplicable, explanation becomes optional, an accessory. Nothing more.

Enzo lumbered down the stairs and through the gate with our bags in tow. Stepping behind the desk, he motioned me over and asked for the reservation name.

"Lezza."

"Ah, yes. Meester Lezza. If you like, we can valet you car. We haff a free shuttle bus into town every teerty minutes."

I turned to Ellie.

"Don't."

To Gran, Six Years Later

I have no intention of sending you this letter, so beginning it should be the easiest thing in the world to do. There is no need for pleasantry, no vague salutation that offers my wishes for the continuation of your good health. This isn't to say that I don't wish for these things. I do. But I find it counterproductive—and perhaps, even a little cold—to solicit the endurance of your wellness when we both know you haven't been doing well. One would think that, with such freedom and lack of responsibility, I might feel emboldened. I might feel licensed to discount the rules and write unencumbered by the threat of consequence. Yet, the one-sidedness of this practice creates an imbalance. Within that imbalance lie inevitable questions of motive, and so, I go back and scrutinize every word with double the usual intensity because the absence of accountability to a person does not negate the accountability to truth. I will break one rule, however, in an effort to free this missive of undue dramatization. To avoid any misinterpretation that this is, in some way, a character assassination in print; let me undercut that theory by scooping myself at the very outset: I, dear grandmother, don't hate you.

This might come as a surprise. Or maybe it doesn't. Everything I came to learn about you throughout my childhood and early-adult life has been so thoroughly undermined that, frankly, I no longer trust what instinct leads me to believe either about your person or about the way your mind works. Even as I sit here next to you on the sofa, thumbing through old photo albums and pointing to faces I don't recognize that you might identify them, the easygoing tone in which you couch your answers suggests that my presence in your house is unremarkable. Expected, even. Somehow, I cannot believe that you fail to perceive what is miraculous about that which takes place before you. In most cases, the death of a father doesn't absolve one from the love for their grandmother. If not love, at least the sense of obligation. Though, after what I witnessed, an arbiter might say this case met the standard for exception. But here I sit, underneath your roof, all in spite of a mother who toils day after day in an effort to brainwash me into believing you are the enemy. I believe that was how you worded it. *Brainwashed.*

Surely, this must register somewhere on your Richter scale. While your face might not betray you, something in the tightness of your bones indicates the needles have jumped. If only you knew what got me here, what put me behind the wheel of my car and did everything for me but turn the key. Could you, maybe? Is there some small statistician in some remote corner of your brain working out the probability that your grandson may be paying you a visit not as an act of rebellion against the woman you malign, but rather, in obedience of her implicit directive? Does any voice whisper from the recesses, "He may not have wanted to come?"

Seeing as you are furnished with no portal through which to issue a counterpoint, it would be unfair to expect an answer to these questions or to any others. In that light, I can promise you this: the interrogation ends here. Truthfully, I'm in no place to hold you accountable for your words or actions, much less demand that you defend them. I learned a while back that most answers are immaterial and rarely soothe the burn. What's more, it would be hypocrisy to put forth such a request, thereby insinuating that, between the both of us, I hold the moral high ground. No, as I am the one who takes offense, it is my responsibility alone to determine the cause, the effect, and the carefully lined path of dominoes that connect the two. Even if said path is illogical, even if it swerves, spirals, splits off and intersects with itself on the journey from A to B, as long as the map can be drawn and the geography abets, the "why" of it won't stop the tiles from falling. But it might help me to understand why someone might want to knock them down.

It starts early on, when everyone is a little more forgiving. At your granddaughter's engagement party, we gather on the patio and watch as you, always the matriarch, usher the groom's mother to our table and make quick work of introductions. You move around the circle, pointing to faces and pinning on names. It's all very polite. Until you stop at Dad, only a few months into his first round of chemo, so fresh from surgery the smell of sporicide lingers. The clothes on his back already showing signs of bagging where his frame has thinned, it is detectable only to us, those that circle him. Everyone outside of that, including the stranger on your arm, could simply take him in as he is. That is, right up to the moment when you open your mouth.

"This is my son. He has cancer."

More stunning than the fact that you say it is the flippancy with which you deliver the report. *He has cancer.* As nonchalantly as if you've said it a thousand times, to neighbors, friends, your mail carrier. *Cancer.* As if it was his name. You actually don't say his name at all. Do you know that? There, as he sits in the late-summer shade trying to enjoy a patch of air that isn't antiseptic, you slap the hospital bracelet around his wrist and admit him. After that, the world around you liquefies. I wipe the diffusion on my shoulder only to watch everything return to watercolor. Outside the specter of you, nothing registers, save for a momentary spasm that runs through the woman in your clutches, one she hastily fights to quash. The rest of the party drowns in the wails and shrieks of diesel engines and steam whistles that battle in my brain to see which is more deafening. Somewhere around my seventh lap through the den, past the kitchen, around the dining table and across the living room carpet, just before the rubber in my soles has melted clean off, my own mother has to twist my arm and plead with me not to make a scene. "She doesn't know," she hushes. "She doesn't know what she's saying."

I didn't buy that rationale. I still don't. It was nothing more than a melodramatic performance from an actress for once playing to a full house. But those are the rushed judgments of someone mired in ceaseless tension, making it impossible for me to observe anything with proper clarity. For my original interpretation to be correct, it would mean cancelling out any genuine sentiment that you held for your son. And I know this not to be true. Instead, I now wonder if the silence was slowly killing you. For someone not tracking his meals, not holding his hand in the treatment facility as toxins dripped into his veins, not on an unending search for a flavor of sports drink that didn't sit on his tongue like detergent, there's an intense need to call out the malignant elephant in the room. There's a want for conversation, for intel that might help to make one feel less kept in the dark or for reassurance that everything is going to be okay; even if that placation is based on nothing more than unfounded positivity. Maybe that's what you were looking for. Or maybe you simply hoped to siphon sympathy from an outsider. Either way, it's important to make the distinction.

Any silence on our part was no tactic employed to keep you uninformed, as much as it might have felt that way. The cold truth is that Dad was staring down the barrel of a disease that would never factor out of his life. Even if he made his way into that single-digit percentile to survive five years, even if he were to achieve remission, his future would be riddled with blood work and PET scans and doctors' visits all searching for the first sign that his body had decided to pull another kamikaze. Knowing this, the decision not to call up his illness in public was a single cog in a larger operation to provide the man little moments in which he might forget that he was a patient. He couldn't have a beer. He couldn't enjoy the food. He couldn't do much of anything that reminded him of who he was. At the very least, we could let him have his name.

At the time, I blamed you for taking that from him. Now, it makes about as much sense as blaming you for not being able to read minds.

Reconciling what you couldn't possibly have known was easy. To strike some kind of harmony with what you chose to ignore was much trickier. While there is much to be said about the idea of common sense and how it informs everything from the simplest of actions to the most elaborate maneuvers, sense is often the first system corrupted by a nonsensical pathogen. It mutates like a cell and confuses the host, making them believe that poison can be medicine and radiation can be restorative. Maybe they can be. But when I put it on paper, it doesn't read that way. So let's remove sense from the equation and not measure each other against it. It can't be trusted. Not as much as, say, the gut.

What does your gut tell you, I wonder, in the early to mid-months of his treatment when you come to visit him? Where you sit in the armchair parallel to his, turn your head when you think he isn't looking, and fix him with a stony stare. You stay that way for hours, immovable; the tears constantly welling in the corner of your eyes the only evidence that you haven't been hewn out of limestone. The trance breaks only at the sound of your son's polite opposition, at once revealing just how overt your covert attempts come across. Inevitably, you fall back into it. Inevitably, he beseeches you again, only at a higher volume. From the bleachers, Mom and I follow the ball as the two of you volley back and forth, neither of us saying a word knowing full well it'll only add chum to waters already churning with sharks. So the game plays on until Dad explodes and the force from the blast severs all of your trip wires. "I can stare at you if I want," you shout. "It's a free country!"

Within a few minutes he executes an escape to the bathroom, something not all that uncommon thanks to a charming list of side effects that could be attributed to any one of the dozen pills he ingests every day. Whether a function of gastric necessity or a respite from the relentless fixation of his mother, it's difficult to tell. But without question, he comes to prefer whatever waits for him on the other side of that washroom door.

I'll admit, the difficulty in getting past this particular thorn was seeing how straightforward he was in voicing his objection, an act that evoked not compassion from you but retribution. This isn't to say that the rest of us handled him delicately. We all had our turn in the ring with him when it came to things like strong-arming him into finishing his food or chiding when we would find medication hidden between the seat cushions. The difference there being that the benefit outweighed the cost, that we were willing to brawl with him because it meant keeping him fed and treated. With you, it seemed to be frustration for its own sake, an interchange that only served to poke at the ocean during those few hours in which it was at its most tranquil. However, the gravest failure was in setting my own behavior as the standard to which I held you and everyone else.

In this weird negaverse, I confused myself for the father, believing I could comprehend, even distantly, what it was you were going through, what it was like to face the possibility of losing a child. That was never the case. You carried the ancestral burden. You alone suffered the disorientation of bearing witness to your child's battle with mortality—an event that defies the natural order of things. To that end, I certainly won't invite a discussion about the hierarchy of grief or even entertain the idea that one experience is more harrowing than the other. Not only would such an exercise be steeped in ignorance, it would torpedo the very real, very legitimate pain each of us had to endure.

I suppose I should say that my initial disappointment came as a reaction to what I perceived as premature mourning. I believed that your silent weeping had surrendered my father to his fate while the rest of us still railed against it. What I didn't stop to consider was what you might be seeing every time your eyes got lost on him: not a dying man, but a boy with tufted, black hair craning over his birthday cake so that he might hungrily blow out a candle. You saw the besuited young man with a Virgin Mary medallion—the one you gifted him—glinting in the September sun as he shouldered the statue of the Holy Mother through the streets of Hoboken. In that heat, you watched Mary melt into silver. Watched her become oblong and embossed with his name, the name announced on a grainy black-and-white television when he wins the lottery in all the wrong ways. But you kiss your hands and press them to those tags and send him off to war. And the war gives him back to you, unscuffed. And you think you're the lucky one. But the war comes for him again. Only, this time, you get to watch it. In Technicolor.

The most difficult step in this postmortem was not rationalizing what you may or may not have known. The true and awful act was the search for reason behind the lies. To an extent, cancer makes inventors out of us all. Sometimes it's necessary. To get creative with numbers. Thirty-nine hundred survivors doesn't sound like lot, but thirty-nine hundred seconds sounds like an eternity. To be your own mad scientist. In a game of buying time, three very-expired Xanax and a vodka soda can stop the earth for a couple of hours. To concoct any and all childish and irresponsible remedies so that we can forgive ourselves for later because the sabotage was isolated to the self. It's when the invention is designed to inflict harm on others that you lose all government over forgiveness, not only because the intent is deluded but also because its assemblage of faulty parts renders the design unstable and the damage illimitable.

When I woke up that January morning, just a few short days after Dad's birthday, the screaming was so loud I confused it for the television. Never in my recollection had your lips produced words laced with anything other than meek, songful grandmotherliness. So foreign, in fact, did the high octave howls register on my ears, that I actually remained in bed for a short spell, convinced that the bluster was the product of some choreographed row indigenous to the landscape of syndicated daytime trash TV. Only when the row didn't abate, when it remained unbroken by the expected commercial break, and my eyes met the early hour on the clock did I kick my feet from beneath the sheets and rush to the door. That's where I meet you, out in the hall.

You're so ugly. My God, look at what an ugly face you have. I don't know which is worse: having to stand by, ensconced, as my mother withstands punch after below-the-belt punch or the fact that I'm powerless to stop you from throwing them. *No one loves you. People tell me all the time. They come up to me and tell me how much they hate you.* My last ounce of adulthood is spent creeping to close the door to my parents' bedroom that I might save my ailing father from waking to this nightmare. Then it's gone. From there to the top of the steps, a three-foot journey is all it takes to regress twenty years, leaving me balled-up with my chin between my knees. Panic-stricken. Paralyzed. A child. I'm not sure how long it goes on. The lack of breath between the shouts eventually sees them melting into one sustained blare, the high-pitched, doleful wail of a tornado siren that hangs over a town long after it's been muzzled. Caught somewhere between wanting to defend my mother and to preserve the father, all I find myself able to do is to sit and watch the dust dance in the light.

So much more was said. It's not for me to share. You know what happened. I suppose the point, and what's important to make clear, is so do I. I heard it all. Firsthand. Please do not think I labor under the miseducation of some biased retelling. I was there. As much as I leave out because your bullet was not meant for me, I also include because I was nonetheless grazed by its ricochet. The next thing I can remember was being pulled out of my infancy.

Feigning grogginess, I answer my mother's echo up the stairwell. You shout something about leaving; threaten to hitchhike. She steals your purse until I can throw a hoodie over my shoulders and help your trembling frame into my car. We spend the drive in silence. Me, failing to pretend I don't know what happened. You, fisting the door handle, not a drop of blood in your face. The shock is almost convincing. Anyone else might've bought it. That you were the one who'd been ambushed. Victim of an unprovoked attack. To them, the fact that you were dressed, coifed, and fully made up at 8 am wouldn't raise an eyebrow. But they didn't spend an entire lifetime watching you stumble down the stairs, robe-cinched and sleep-crusted, and never a minute before ten.

I pull into the driveway of the only house I've ever known to be yours. The corner ranch where I'd spent afternoons helping the plastic toad in your birdbath catch flies on its tongue. The house where I'd turn the giant metal foot pedal of your old Singer sewing machine into a kid-sized rocking chair after a lunch of Swiss cheese sticks. The same house I'd leave with a fresh bar of soap tucked between my hands, more excited than a child should ever be about soap. As I hoist your limpness up the path and across the threshold, your feculent soliloquy hollers in the reaches of my own mind, and I catch myself longing for a brick of Lux so that I might wash your mouth out.

Downstream, I'll learn more about the outburst, how it was born from the realization of your niece's plans to visit that morning. That Mom had asked her to tend to Dad and administer his Filgrastim. A shot in the arm to help his bone marrow produce more white blood cells, to help counteract all that the chemotherapy had vaporized. This woman, with scant medical experience, had trained herself to give an injection in order to save her cousin a two-hour drive for a thirty-second transaction. This very same woman, who yielded four days a week to sit with the man, feed him, and medicate him so that my mother might keep her job and the health insurance that paid for his treatment, was pulling double duty as an ad-hoc nurse in order to spare your son one more minute of marinating in the sterile funk of another doctor's waiting room. To her, you took great offense, all because she happened to be the daughter of a sister with whom you'd had a falling-out decades ago. No one's ever told me what the fight was about, and honestly, I don't care to learn. It'd surprise me if you could even recall yourself. All I know is, when weighing your own pride against the health of your child, the grudge mattered more.

I was ready to wash my hands of you. This was not because like-minded victims of your ire fueled my inclinations. It was because I found myself unable to submit that the grandmother—the purveyor of cheeses, the woman who tied ice packs on skinned knees with pantyhose—was as cold-blooded as she'd revealed herself to be. So at odds were these two iterations of you that it became impossible to believe they could both exist within the same individual. You became a fiction, some creation plucked from the pages of Robert Louis Stevenson. When faced with the task of having to figure out which reflected the truest form of you, I didn't feel the work was worth it.

Please know I don't belabor this point for grand effect or to make some monster out of you. I think it's important for you to know all that I've seen. To know just how far it went and how fractured we became. Most of all, to know that what prevented a clean break was the very person who had every right to snap those few fragments that remained hitched. Mom. After we lost Dad it was his wife who hounded me to call you, to visit you, to check and make sure that you were doing okay. The "ugly" wife, the woman for whom you claim scads whispered aspersions into your waiting ears; it was she who would not let me forget my familial duty. And I relented. Because of her I returned to that corner ranch. Because of her I bent down to hug you. I angled my face away to deny your kiss, yes, because I knew what those lips were capable of. I sat with you on the couch, under the oil painting of the Sears Roebuck family where my twenty-some-year-old father towered, the weight of him tilting the frame to one side. We'd scan the eleven channels your antenna received, and I'd pray it provide something interesting to discuss. All the while, my eyes would dart to the kitchen clock, working to determine just how quickly I could leave without appearing disrespectful.

It didn't stay a chore, however. In the months and years that followed, our visits grew longer—first by centimeters, then inches. The photo albums I dug from musty cavities started as a tool of necessity, a distraction to foment conversation and help the minutes pass. Then they became something altogether different. You gave the strangers identities and histories, quirks and virtues. Stories sprung from wherever my finger landed, and page by page, Vito by Vita, bouffant by pompadour, I thumbed my way through the annals of half my ancestry with your narration as a guide. The pictures bringing you to life, for a moment, returning the woman I'd thought forever relegated to rectangles of semi-gloss. There was joy in your voice, genuine if only because any joy after loss is hard-forged. But there was also hurt, hurt tinged with something I can only describe as regret. Perhaps I'm wrong. It's not for me to define. I suppose one just knows it when they hear it. Either way, whatever it was made it no longer possible for me to let my own injury eclipse yours. And moving it aside, I was left to stare directly into the sun.

My immediate assessment of your actions, while not wholly inaccurate, neglected to take certain variables into consideration. You *were* looking to pick a fight that morning of your January outrage. You'd dressed for it. But your fury was not with my mother. Not entirely. I believe now that, like us all, you burned to lace a contagion between your fingers and wring the life out of it. You wanted to scream at the sickness and shame it into exile. You were searching for the manifestation of a cancer to beat until your skin cracked and knuckles bled. In its absence, desperation and a complete lack of reasoning led you to attack a most undeserving target. To that, I can relate. I've felt the madness that curdles in the veins and sparks a reaction before your conscience has time to smother it. The dividing line is my choice to shout at railroad signals or to bash my fist through a light switch's cover plate that cracks when I try to install it. By contrast, I'm no nobler and no less a fool.

That's why this letter isn't about forgiveness, not in the traditional sense. For one, you haven't asked for it. For another, we both know it's not for me to give. What it is about is release, of grievances, of antipathy. I don't want to spend the rest of my life unable to show love for you because of some malicious apparition that stands between us. I've seen what a grudge can do, watched it consume its host from the inside. To exorcise mine meant achieving a level of understanding. Grasping the motive even if I couldn't endorse it. Maybe the method was flawed and the conclusions inaccurate. But in the end, you learn that harboring bitterness means accepting sole responsibility for its upkeep. And you're left asking yourself: *Isn't there enough to do already?*

Allora/Adesso

I've been thinking a lot about time travel lately. (Don't put this down. There's a point, I promise). When I say "time travel," I don't mean the plutonium-powered, flux capacitor, "Roads? Where we're going we don't need roads" sort. Although, Dr. Emmett Brown wasn't at all wrong when he decided to modify a 1985 DeLorean into a time machine for the sole purpose of performing an already reality-defying task with the imperative ration of '80s style. The decadence of that image has transcended trends and generations, and to this day, thirty-four years later, it remains sexy as hell. Still, it takes nearly the entirety of my focus and wherewithal to navigate a manual-transmission vehicle across flat asphalt, much less the space-time continuum. Were I to attempt such a feat, I'd surely wind up turning off at the wrong wormhole and mowing down Alexander Graham Bell on his way to the patent office, thereby depriving humanity of one of the most essential exercises of communication and diplomacy: rolling unwanted calls directly to voicemail.

No, the kind of time roving I refer to is not vehicular in nature. Nor is it voluntary. In fact, the only element essential to the mechanism is my own overactive thought process. Rare is the day when the most menial of errands isn't subject to temporal disruption. I may be out to pick up eggs and bread when I find myself tugged seven years into the past all because of the blue Honda Civic that merges into the lane ahead of me. Without warning, I'm twenty-three, and from my vantage in the passenger's seat, I watch a boy pilot that same car through the humid night that's settled over Little Lake Bryan. Hands on the wheel, he clicks the volume up on the radio and sings along to some country song I've never heard. There's something about *moonlight* and *kissing in the sticks,* but by the time the cowpoke crooner brings the chorus 'round to *check you for ticks* I'm gone, elsewhere. I think about how sweet and vulnerable an act that is, to sing in front of someone. How it means I've made him comfortable. How I've never actually been sung to and how I should be gushing, but instead I'm mortified. Because all I'm reminded of is how I haven't felt that way about him for weeks and what a coward I've been for not telling him. All out of some fear of hurting one of the few men who has never done anything to hurt me. I'd sooner fling myself out the window and watch my body twist into a ribbon of pulp around the axle than have what has become an unavoidable conversation. But there's little choice and only one tack that'll allow me to take my leave with some measure of dignity. Over his croons about *the only thing allowed to crawl all over you,* I crawl out from the burrow I've dug into my own chest. By the time I've pieced together a well-balanced monologue of honeyed words and self-deprecation, I am thirty again, standing in the middle of my kitchen with an armful of pre-sliced multi-grain and a carton of Eggland's Best without a single recollection as to how I got there.

I could be at the theatre, for instance, snug like a pretzel and fully reclined on one of the few nights I'm able to overcome the crush of some looming deadline. After a little coercion, I've purchased my ticket for two hours of previews followed by some light distraction. The opening credits fade into some hero or heroine who cleanly illustrates their charming predicament and I've bought into the suspension of my own life until one of the screen dwellers utters some beautifully crafted line like: "Don't make me hate you. Loving you is painful enough." And I'm gone. Marveling at the thoughtful construction of a phrase I consider quite eloquent, I begin to pay similar consideration to my own prowess as a writer. I think about the blank document with the working title that waits on my desktop screen, daring me to fill it with equally profound sentiment. I think about the next morning, the coffee circles on my desk, the blinking cursor. I scribble thoughts on the inside of my skull and debate the logic of some metaphor—time travel, for instance—and whether it's legitimate or demented. *It's theatrics,* I say to myself. *Stick to the substance.* Then, another voice: *No, no.* Me, still, this time in my best Christopher Lloyd. *It's not theatre; it's illustrative! Plus, how many chances do you get to work in an Emmett Brown reference?* I go back and forth, contradicting myself, comparing myself endlessly to artists who are my betters. Just before I can determine if I'm out of my depth, something explodes across the 2D reality playing out in front of me. There I am, knocked back into my cushy $13 pre-selected seat, left to use whatever context I can glean to piece together the ten minutes I've missed.

Of all the unwanted consequences that come with such an ability—or rather, inevitability—it's the missing that hits hardest. On the regular, it amounts to seconds or maybe a handful of minutes that get frittered away. But sometimes it can be as much as days that get lost. That's when the discrepancy is too glaring to write off. In the winter of 2018, my best friend Ellie had flown up from Florida to celebrate the turn of the New Year with me. That particular calendric zoetrope had been particularly rough for the both of us. Ellie had spent the last twelve months surviving on acting gigs in a fairly slow market, supplementing her income by grinding out impressive Pop Art canvases that she flogged on the convention circuit. For me, the holiday marked the end of an exasperating year-long pursuit of a new full-time position. In particular, I had just completed the final step of what turned out to be a one-hundred-and-twenty-day interview cycle for a job I'd set my heart on. The process had involved a dozen phone calls, one-on-one's with hiring managers, vetting with ancillary team members, project work, spec writing, and the delivery of two completely separate multimedia presentations. After letting me know of their desire to extend an offer to the chosen candidate by late December/early January, I shook their hands, slipped them my references, and greeted the cold New York wind with pronounced relief.

For months, I'd been slipping and sliding into walls, unable to gain any traction. Now, it was like the air had amperage. I'd found my footing, and socks to carpet had been picking up enough electrons that one grasp of a subway pole could have supercharged the whole grid. The ensuing silence in the days that followed was expected, if not a little disconcerting. A sudden stop of motion had left too much space for critique; time to pore over my words, my inflections, to think of things I could have said but didn't. By the time Ellie arrived, I'd squandered most of my stockpile of good mojo and welcomed not only the friendship but the bonus distraction. It was always fun to see Manhattan through her eyes. She's the kind of girl who finds just as much magic in a glittery skyline as she does in a rat gnawing on moldy pizza in a back alley. "I'll call him Sprinkles," she exclaims, snapping a photo of the bulbous rodent and heading off to discover the wonder of some other queer fish. Normally, it's easy to catch a ride on her exuberance. The immediacy with which she greets the world has a way of cutting through my signature cynicism. This time, the drug is less potent and I find myself back in boardrooms, trying to interpret vague facial responses to my verbal cues, wondering if my mind hasn't exaggerated them. I analyze conversations, trying to weed out the nefarious connotation in emails that read "Nothing but positive feedback." I think about what life looks like in a week if I don't hear back, what it looks like in two weeks. With each trip I lose swaths of valuable, irretrievable time to the point where my recollections consists of pumpernickel rolls at the Central Park Boathouse, making a tourist laugh with my impression of Aunt Bethany from *Christmas Vacation*, snagging a killer, military-style knapsack from an Upper East Side thrift store, and not much else. It isn't until the last day, in the lobby of a Fairfield Inn, that I'm smacked with the reality of my gross mismanagement of what should have been a delightful respite. Even then, emptying my lamentations onto her shoulder, I allocate our remaining minutes to regrets and apologies until there's nothing left to do but hoist her into a Super Shuttle.

I wound up not getting that job in the end. Good thing, too. Imagine pumping out all that sweat in order to worry the worst outcome into existence and having nothing to show for it.

Much as I wish I could blame this knack for jumping dimensional rivulets on genetics, I am now and have always been the son of two very cool customers. My father, especially. For as long as I can remember, I shouldered a great admiration for the way he always seemed to have two heels firmly planted in the here and now. I never knew the man to dally on remorse over any past transgression. Nor was he ever consumed with some theoretical outcome. Though he served two years in the armed forces, the shrink-wrapped formal uniform at the back of his closet spoke more about that time than he ever did. To him, it was something that was said and done. On another New Year's Eve, midway through my sophomore year of high school, I recall Dad standing over the kitchen counter, shucking clams in preparation for our annual family gathering. In a few hours, aunts, cousins, and neighbors would be crammed into the dining room to celebrate another trip around the sun, for earth and for my father, respectively. But at the moment, the house was still, save for the *crunch* and *thunk* of mollusks being halved and dumped to the bottom of the sink. So dedicated to his task that when the phone rang, I remember him answering with a paring knife still gripped in his other hand.

"Yes, hello Katherine." Earlier that morning, I'd fielded a call from his office. Though a work-related call on a major holiday had struck me as odd, the caller, whose name I hadn't recognized, informed me that she'd try back later. By the tone with which he greeted her, I could tell she was equally unknown to my father. A considerable beat followed the introduction, yet despite the peculiarity, it wasn't until his next words that my concentration broke off from the living room *Twilight Zone* marathon. "You know I'm a year away from receiving my full pension benefit." I hadn't yet completed my conversion to the church of fatalism, but his rapid shift to defensiveness was jarring. From the armchair, I tiptoed to the half wall that divided the rooms and watched through wooden spindles as his shoulders began to droop. Each time he'd interject, only word fragments would escape before something on the other end cut him off. So it went on, the pauses growing longer, his resolve growing softer. He angled his face more and more towards the opposite wall, an act clearly meant to obscure the conversation but one that failed to deaden the gut punch of what next fell from his lips. "You're going to do this to me on my *birthday*?"

When the call ended, Dad stood staring at the handset for a few seconds, curling and uncurling the pigtail wire from around his fingers. Then, without flinching, he went back to the counter and lifted a fresh clam from the pile, picking up right where he'd left off moments ago. Pulling up alongside him, I hesitated, my fear of the answer holding me back, but the ambiguity quickly became too much to bear. "Is everything okay?" Dad continued his task, unmoved by my inquiry, slicing, twisting, and wrenching the top shell from each bivalve.

"Oh, that was work," he said, tossing another husk onto the mounting bone yard. "Looks like I just lost my job." Were I a thermometer in that very moment, I'd have had mercury spewing from my skull. Every inch of my body felt radioactive. The words didn't sound right, didn't sound real. For fifteen years, my father had gotten up every day, ate the same eggs and toast, read the same paper, and left for the same office in the same cloud of Pino Silvestre. It was the A, B, C, 1, 2, 3 that had kept a roof over our heads. It was rote. Suddenly, there he was, on the cusp of fifty-five, employed to unemployed in less time than it takes December to become January. Nonetheless, in the face of a crisis that would've had me churning through every calamitous possibility until I'd goopified, Dad just kept on shucking clams. As far as he was concerned, the future was tomorrow's affair. Today, there was a party.

It may well be that routine is exactly what kept my father so moored to the day, a defined itinerary in which he was well-practiced and concerns for which he already knew the solutions. Thus, nothing to question. Or it may be that what grounded him was the weighted responsibility that came with being a husband and a father. At present, I am neither of those things, and routine frightens me. Once I can perform the steps without thinking about them, it frees my mind up for other activities, like traveling. That's why I find myself drawn to project work. There's always a new assignment, with its own particularities and its own objective. The constant recalibration demands attention, presence. It's not unlike conversation. With sufficient interest applied, a rhythm is soon established; the inherent beauty being that the moment it begins to feel repetitive, one can just change the subject. Still, even to avowed disciples of novelty, there remain elements whose day-to-dayness is unavoidable: home, commute, even lunch. There are only so many ways a salad can be prepared. Short of pulling up stakes and joining the touring company of *Mamma Mia*, there remains the lack of a long-term solution for the permanencies. Sans-panacea, the intermittent banality is assured, opening portals through which I will fall into the thousand elsewheres and else-whens I'm fated to visit.

For a while, I labored under the belief that geography was a major contributing factor to my temporal shifts. As if the angle at which we hang off the planet might actually affect our orientation, our ability to weather its spin. A turntable on a slant, however negligible, will never play right. The needle jumps and the record skips, and I found myself constantly having to find where it was I'd left off. Endless trips back and forth made the listening interminable until such time that I went in search of a more even surface. Sure enough, the vinyl proved to play seamlessly just about anywhere but home. I slunk through the grooves of other nations, narrow passageways that amplified every gorgeous crackle and pop of their cities. I followed funky smells to noisy open-air markets, tinny plucks to chamber ensembles in gated gardens. I made my way through the guts of each metropolis purposely without a map, to make sure to disorient myself. Having to feel my way necessitated a heightened awareness. It meant memorizing landmarks and street curves to use as breadcrumbs to find my way back. It meant listening with intent, the only way to locate the beat. It meant letting my feet wander so fast that my mind had no choice but to be still.

Soundtrack of the city at full volume—it was the lyrics, the language which settled the equilibrium. To the extent that I tried to familiarize myself with essential terminology in order to blunt my reception as a dimwitted American, any non-coffee or bathroom-related exchanges always involved a few rounds of charades. Even still, it's a game that can only be won by two players who are fully engaged with each other. However long it took, in the end some strange new friend made their sale while I made off with a strange new word to add to my vocabulary. Those that rang in my ears louder than others I'd scribble down to look up whenever it was I returned to my hotel. Storefronts and street signs worked like anagrams to be decoded around letters I'd never seen before. In Scandinavia, the alphabet had physicality, each character's form dictating everything the speaker needed to know about how to pronounce it. Need to shorten an "a?" Jam an "e" on the end to stop it running on too long (æ). If an "o" looks like it's been outlawed (ø), start by speaking the letter and then act as if someone's begun to choke you. In Greece, consonants and vowels intermingled with hieroglyphs. Words were built from horseshoes and pyramids. It was a language that appeared to have tumbled from a box of Lucky Charms. In all of it, a gloriously steady confusion.

A few years after Dad passed, I delighted in the opportunity to visit Italy for the first time without a middle-school bowl cut. As a child, I'd listen to my father soliloquize about the place to the point where it didn't seem real. Lopsided towers and towns with rivers where roads should be sounded like something ripped from my Walt Disney Classic VHS collection. Nevertheless, it was difficult to deny the otherworldliness of a land that inspired such intense fervor from its foster son. Though full-blooded, Dad was a born and raised native of Hoboken, New Jersey who'd reluctantly agreed to visit his ancestral state at the behest of his wife, an immigrant. From the stories, it became clear that his metamorphosis from conflict to crusader took no more than the length of the jet bridge. Just past the gate he fell right into the arms of my mother's family, who welcomed him like a savior, the man who loved and protected the daughter that had been taken from them. It was no wonder then that, scarcely after "Dada" had fallen out of my milk-fed mouth, I was enrolled in private Italian lessons and on a Rome-bound plane before I'd lost the last of my baby teeth.

"They can't wait to meet you," Dad said, one of several times as we crossed the Atlantic. "You have so many cousins and aunts and uncles that you haven't met yet. A whole half of your family you don't even know." Sandwiched between my parents in some godforsaken middle row, I recall feeling more connected to my packet of pretzel sticks than I could imagine being to this group of celebrated strangers, this concept. What I could never imagine, however, was how naïve my nine-year old assertion was. No sooner had I yanked my duffle from the carousel at Bari-Karol Wojtyla than I was engulfed in a swarm of oxford shoes and capri pants. Jostled from person to person, I was hugged and kissed and passed around more times than a good case of mono. But, in that fugue of lips and cheeks, something happened. I fell in love with the lot of them. I fell in love with each and every one of the nameless freaks. I was given no option. It was something akin to being overrun by a litter of Golden Retrievers. It was wet and frantic and unconditional. What's more, they wouldn't let up until you loved them back.

Fortune allowed me to return in tow a few more times during my adolescence. Every visit brought about wholeness in my mother and vivacity in my father that just didn't exist stateside. For them, Italy was the right angle, where their records played clearer than anywhere else. There they spun with the earth fluidly, gravity so cinched around their ankles that every removal had to happen by force, required crawling out of their own skins, leaving layers behind. It came with pain and meant returning from whence we came, each time, with a little bit less of ourselves. That incompletion would never abate, not fully. It would pull my parents back, time and again, and often without me after college and early adulthood became their own preoccupations. But, when the occasion arose, as I was about to tie a ribbon on my twenties, the prospect was no longer an option. Rather, it was a responsibility, a homecoming for myself and for the fragments of my father I could carry there with me.

Following such a significant interlude meant stepping back into that world with my language proficiency sorely atrophied. A shameful thing to admit for someone raised by a native speaker. To me, never having achieved fluency was a deficit of character. In light of that, I'd existed for some time under a self-imposed gag order. But while such a mandate could shield me within my own jurisdiction, the international courts refused to uphold it. Pushing thirty, I could no longer rely on an adorable helplessness and wait for my mother to translate. I was old enough and I had been gone for nearly two decades. People had questions. Where there was a silence that Dad had left, I was expected to fill it. So, I did, slowly and brokenly, begin to communicate. I traded in makeshift sentences, poorly conjugated. Though I was lighting a fire with wet logs, I somehow managed to strike a discourse. The more I ventured, the more I found words returning, spoken out loud before I'd realized I'd said them. It was as if the language itself was a portal, opening me up to iterations of old selves, filling the gaps in the sequence.

The benefit of my own deficiency, the not knowing, manifested in a reflex to listen acutely. With new ears, I developed an infatuation with the vernacular as I had so many times prior. Here, though, it was not about the shapeliness or the physiology of the words. It was about the artistry of them. As before, I catalogued expressions for research, only this time finding portraits where definitions should be. My pages read more like a flipbook, overflowing with words like affogato—a dessert consisting of espresso poured over ice cream yet, at the same time, a word that concisely means "drowned." Because why bathe the ice cream when you can murder it? There was piangere, to cry, a word almost indistinct from pioggia, to rain. Because, truly, is there a difference? Then there were those that rivaled DaVinci in their sheer craftsmanship. Arrabbiata, a spicy red sauce to the layperson, literally translates as "angry." On the one hand, there is an unquestionable appreciation for the drama that comes with conflating vexation with seasoning. But the real wonder is in its construction. Packed with consonants, the word not only tells the receiver how the speaker feels, but its double Rs, double Bs and crowning T manage to growl, punch, and then spit in their face for good measure.

The delightfulness of these phonetic masterpieces no doubt had much to do with their impermanence and the distance from which I observed them. They passed before my eyes and ears like glass-housed canvases bolted to the wall. I stood and enjoyed and moved on, filing them away as colorful impressions for some later recollection. It comes to pass, though, that some images are less easily indexed. Long past the exhibition, I found myself encountering reproductions, reminiscent patterns on 4x6 postcards and plastered to the sides of bus stop shelters. Inside a salumeria, an elderly woman inspecting the curly mounds of prosciutto proffered by the hand of her butcher announced her approval with a nod and a blessing. Allora, signore. Allora. It was a mysterious locution, more savory than the cured meats that hung from the ceiling. I repeated it to myself, gratified by the mouthfeel of the double Ls that held my tongue against my upper palate. A pronunciation so pleasing it actually slowed you down, made you enjoy it. Later that day, a similarly agreeable peal bounded from a corner in the town square. Adesso, Mama. Adesso! With the end of his mother's skirt bunched up in his fist, a fresh-faced boy pointed toward the entrance of a candy store. From a few feet up, the matriarch, having none of it, waved him forward, dragging her son's stomping feet down the sidewalk at the hem of her train. Adesso! Adesso! The word was a controlled burst, tasty but fleeting. With very little to grab onto, it exploded off of its early consonant and hissed past the lips. To say it at all was to watch a word turn to steam.

Evaporations did not stop me from flipping both phrases between the gums until such time as I was able to learn their meanings. "Allora, Adesso." Over the gurgle of hot air into a tin of milk, my cousin repeated the words I'd offered her with an inquisitive bend. Emptying the contents of her espresso cup in one shot, she slid the vessel back to the barista along with a fiver and turned back to me. "Is mean 'then' and 'now.'" Then and now. A slightly broken delivery but a whole coincidence. It seemed quaint, the relation. And my attraction to the words. But, aside from serendipity, there was nothing overtly remarkable about their presentation. Until there was. Until the words, then heavy with definition, began to work their way into every mouth in proximity. In restaurants, they punctuated orders. Allora, signore. My uncle, on behest of the table, requisitioned an entire evening's fare from primi through dolci; a distinct tune his segue from course to course. *Allora. Allora. Allora.* At night, the rising generation, having filtered into the heart of the old town, stopped for their cigarettes on the water's edge, halfway between their last bar and the next one. On a bench, an olive-toned string bean blew smoke to the sky and threw his arm around the girl pressed against him. Running the tip of his nose down the perimeter of her ear, he whispered something unheard but which extracted a squeal and a playful fist to the square of his ribs. *Adesso. Adesso.*

The words were everywhere—the markets, the churches, in mouths both strange and unstrange. With my date of departure looming, they increased in frequency, their relentlessness having stripped away all manner of whimsy, replacing it with a fear that my record had, once again, begun to skip. That this flat surface, this earthly angle so sacrosanct, had shifted to a point where it was no longer a place I could set myself down. When it came time, on that last of the disquieted days, to turn my key over to the front desk, it felt heavier than it had a week prior. My arm strained not just with the commensurate despair that came with leaving, but also with the weight of the notion that I was handing in the key to my country. Plucked from between my fingers, the key went with the manager as he moved to collect the bill working its way out of some dusty, old printer. As if summoned by the device's caterwauling, a pushcart clattered across the lobby led by a housekeeper who parked by the edge of the desk and extended a withered mitt to the man behind it. The manager, one-handing the slip of paper, outstretched his hand to meet the woman, drawing a line beneath a poster that was plastered on the back wall. Just there, in the bottom right corner, right above where their two palms eclipsed, a figure came into focus. My father.

I'd seen the poster at least a dozen times since my arrival. It was an advertisement for the annual Festa della Madonna Dei Martiri, a week-long celebration of the Lady of Martyrs. No stranger to the event, I'd spent years watching my Dad take part in the sister festival carried over to the North Jersey Shore by generations of expats who'd come before him. Sure enough, in a show of bilateral unity, the local organization had farmed a photo from their American counterpart. Right there, beneath the pile of red and white roses adorning the feet of the Blessed Mother, was the tuxedoed visage of my Dressed Father. Adesso. My momentary trance snapped at the manager's brusque direction to the housekeeper. Accepting the key, she tossed it on her cart and rattled off to her duties just as clamorously as she'd come. The transaction was clean, formal, mundane; but one that facilitated a meeting of eras, all because I'd cared enough to show just the slightest interest in what was happening. I stood there for a time, long enough to make the manager flee to the back office in discomfort. I stood there, in the now, looking at then, wondering how many times I had missed this meeting because of my perverse relationship with the two, because I'd spent so much of my life caught between allora and adesso that I'd hardly been anywhere at all.

   Depending on the doctrine one subscribes to, the laws of time travel are either stringent or baseless. If we're to believe Doc Brown, the exercise is possible but should only be practiced observationally. Interfering with a past version of ourselves can result in a dangerous alteration to the existing timeline. The Time Lords of *Doctor Who* were said to abide by a similar law that forbade interacting with their own subjective past or future. In the *Terminator* series, it was made abundantly clear that the time loop is predestined and immune to any changes a traveler may attempt. And then there's *Endgame*, in which Bruce Banner reasons that journeying to the past becomes our new future, rendering the former present a past that cannot be affected, essentially laying waste to eons of pop-culture canon. As for myself, I'm less concerned with what should or shouldn't be done than I am with what can or cannot. I *can* go back in time to that night on Lake Bryan in that blue Honda Civic and I *can* watch myself seethe, and though I *cannot* do anything to alter the timeline, I *can* use what I've seen to avoid repeating history. I *can* lament over deadlines and my own perception of adequacy, but I *cannot* do anything to impact them other than to sit down and fill the white space.

   These truths are self-evident. They're not the product of some grand realization nor will they inalterably change me. Much as I understand them enough to put them on paper, I can predict with great certainty that I will remain subject to the push and pull of time. Now, though, written into that timeline are two words, tireless protestors who once shouted me out of my stupor. There they'll remain, part of a past I can't get past without a thorough haranguing, waiting to chase me back to the present. Some might argue that allora and adesso were not alterations but predestined revelations in a narrative already written. Others might suggest divine intervention, cosmic happenstance, or just purely fortunate coincidence. And while there's merit to all of these explanations, I'm loath to dismiss the possibility that some past or future self didn't plant them. Portkeys. Talismans to carry me back. After all, is that not what I'm doing right here?

I'm Never Fine

Ask me how I am. Go ahead. Ask. But only if you're interested. Trust me, I know what it's like to put forth that question with the expectation of a concise, if not ambiguous, response, which I would plan to use as a segue into the real reason behind any one conversation. Often, that's just what I'd get. After which, I'd springboard faster than an Olympic diver. It's gotten to be that our inquiries into the wellness of others result from good manners more than genuine curiosity. We regard the concept as if it were a basket of breadsticks, just something to chew on until the meat arrives. Let's say, for the sake of continuing the metaphor, we are to examine dialogue as if it were a meal. Inevitably, there will be a member of the dining party arriving at the table hungrier than the rest. Generally, the difference is marginal, so much so that it's barely noticeable when one takes a couple extra bites off their sesame rod. It's not uncommon, however, for the disparity to be far greater, resulting in a ravenous cohort who unwittingly devours the entire basket, leaving their partner to survive on whichever projectile driblets happen to land on the other end of the table. In this specific case, both parties wind up putting off their entrees. This isn't to say that we should dismiss with the practice. Rather, we could do with a reminder that what has come to be accepted as a convivial custom is, in actuality, a labyrinthine proposition. It should not be entered without a willingness to abandon some presupposed motive. It should be understood that what lies therein might be more than we're prepared to handle. Should the questioner be lacking a vested interest in the questioned and harbor a reluctance to assume some of their burden, it's best to avoid the topic in its entirety. Otherwise, one runs the risk of spoiling their dinner.

No stranger to misusing the application, I have found myself unexpectedly pancaked by the rolling stones of another's relative unsettlement. Though I endeavor to reserve the question for individuals with whom I share a closeness, I'd be lying if I said there weren't times that I hoped for some deferential response so that I might quickly center the exchange around some pressing issue in my own life. But that's only because, at the time, my understanding of what qualified as a serious matter was profoundly flawed. Most of what I brought to conference existed within the realm of affairs to which any person could relate, however distantly. School, work, family, a string of relationships that would have Tennessee Williams sniping "Buddy, you're harshing the vibe." Triviality, the lot of it. All of which I hoped my consorts would greet with placations or endorsement or, when necessary, harsh but tender counsel. All of which I recognized, one day, I'd have to return in kind. That's the agreement, that's the unvoiced cooperation.

My withdrawal from that cooperative was formally submitted immediately following the death of my father.

People tend not to ask how you are in the abruption, the days between bereavement and burial. Not, perhaps, for a few weeks. In that bubble, even the most imperceptive can draw the obvious conclusion. When it does begin, the inquiries are fewer than you might imagine. Some—always those you never expect—will find the circumstances too foreign and too treacherous to approach, choosing instead to retreat from your life until a period of indeterminable appropriateness has elapsed. Those who do reach out may be no better equipped to empathize than the previously mentioned grouping, only they make up for their deficiency with a surplus of courage. In either event, there exists a strong subset of the dispossessed that find themselves loath to air their true feelings. However sincere the design of the inquisitor, it does not facilitate the level of preparedness necessary to wade through a sewer system teeming with nipple-high emotional gunge. Anticipating this, the besought often opt for ambiguity, relying on responses gauzy enough to pacify while ushering in a swift change of subject. For some, the hollow, well-meaning sympathy proves too harsh to stomach. Other may just be plain tired of talking about it. Whatever the reason may be, a great comfort can be derived from adopting the passive position, allowing others to dominate the conversation, if only because of the supplemental schadenfreude that comes with learning that everyone's drawing the short stick of life in some capacity.

Essential to whitewashing discourse is the employment of a verbal accelerant, some turn of phrase just vague enough to respect the investigation while prompting no follow-up. Each individual has his or her own preference, a concerted interval of trial and error revealing the most successful, nondescript clapback that sits in their holster just so. In my case, market research and focus groups had narrowed the list down to a single, four-letter f-word: *fine*. Other candidates had seen themselves considered but quickly eliminated due to practical inefficiency. *Okay*, for instance, was a contender. But it lacked the acceptable ration of positivity. *Okay* was how you described yourself after face-planting off a curb and managing not to lose any teeth. *Okay* meant "alive, but not great." In essence, it begged further questions. Also in consideration, for a short spell, was the tried-and-true tagline of the dogged stalwart: *hanging in there*. Initially, I'd been drawn to it due to its innate suggestion of the fighter mentality. Yet, whereas the expression was intended to evoke the spirit of perseverance and conviction, in reality, it was received all too literally. Listeners alike found it impossible to picture me as anything but a helpless figure, dangling precipitously off some sharp edge, my blistered fingers the only things keeping me from being tenderized upon the craggy ravine below. The impression was all-wrong, prompting the crinkle of a nose bridge, the pout of a lip, or worst of all, the extension of a clammy hand. People are going to pity those *hanging in there*; they're going to want to help. Expecting anything less is like expecting indifference when one decides to roam the streets in cowboy boots and a Stetson with nothing but a guitar obscuring their privates. Outside of Times Square, that's an explicit cry for help.

Fine, though. That did the trick. Without fail, it injected the right amount of menthol and honey for someone to suck on, soothing their burning curiosity without coming on too strong. Its effectiveness, I've learned, is conditioned on its malleability. It's what I classify a beige term, words like "terrier," "potluck," or "economy plus." It's khaki, buff, sand, granola, fawn, shortbread; different shades of the same thing that no one really clamors for yet, at the same time, no one purposely tries to avoid. It's just enough. There's plenty to go around. So much so, in fact, that the more comfortable I became using it, the easier it was to give away. The sentiment was a lie, of course, no more sterling than a counterfeit bill. But, because of its illegitimacy, there was little remorse in spending it. Before long, I was papering the town like a seasoned money launderer.

It does buy things, the word. Time, privacy, distance, maybe even a little comfort. Though only short increments. The dollar never stretches quite as far as one might want. So, we pay and pay in greater quantities until we've fooled ourselves into believing it's some sort of luxury. To a degree, we are responsible for our own misperceptions. However, I can't help thinking some of the blame lies in how it's been sold to us. In 1964, the Beatles, arguably one of the most iconic bands of all time, had just solidified their standing as a worldwide sensation by owning the top five slots of the Billboard charts. On one of their more B-side tracks released that year, the foursome—then at the dawn of their reign—sang about Baby; Baby who was *good to me,* Baby who was *happy as can be,* Baby who so much said it out loud and, owing to Baby's darling admission, the boys from Liverpool were moved to croon—at the close of every verse—the same three words: *I feel fine.* Whether this much-junketed "Baby" was, in reality, a lover or an abstract term meant to represent the broader idea of music and newfound success is anyone's guess. Yet, there they were, declaring their irrefutable gaga for someone or something, equating the ideas of love and fineness in a solitary lyric. And that's how the world bought it. Not a single person questioned how antithetical it seemed for one to espouse their devotion, and in the same breath, feel just *fine* about it. While this is certainly not a defining example and I can only make inferences regarding each of the men's relationships, history is telling. At the time, John Lennon, occupied in marriage to a woman he believed had trapped him, was still two years away from meeting the avowed love of his life. Paul McCartney was nestled somewhere between girlfriend number two and wife number one. George Harrison was similarly on the cusp of meeting the woman whom he would marry and later divorce due to his rampant infidelity. And Ringo Starr was a year off from wedding a woman he'd admittedly cheat on, abuse, and perhaps accordingly, drive into the arms of one of his already married bandmates. Considering all this, there might be a reason why that particular single failed to earn gold, bronze, or even limestone.

Why, then, have we come to doubt *fine*? Why, after prolonged exposure, does the word lose its power to persuade? My running theory has to do with the lack of a clear identity. *Fine* tries to be too many things. Per Google Dictionary, the term has four separate variations, with an aggregate of twenty unique definitions. Most frequently it is used as an adjective, at other times a verb, adverb, even a noun in some instances. It is a thing on Monday, an action on Tuesday, a state of being on Wednesday, and on Thursday, it takes a day off to rest. It is an object "of high quality" or "(of a person) worthy of or soliciting admiration." Yet, by some magic, it is synchronously "good; satisfactory" and "used to express one's agreement with or acquiescence to something." It is remarkable yet it just scrapes by. It is a contradiction. Yesterday it was "of imposing and dignified appearance or size." Today it is "sharp, consisting of small particles." Still tomorrow, it is a discipline, a "sum of money exacted as a penalty by a court of law or other authority." It is great and small. It is a burden. *Fine* silverware can be found in your grandmother's hutch, *fine* powder in your grandson's sock drawer. *Fine* brandy is available at your local liquor store, but only if it's from France and only if it's made from distilled wine rather than pomace. You can eat with it, snort it, and get drunk on it. *Fine* is everything at once while nothing really at all. It is the Swiss Army knife of words; fun to hold, but really, what are you going to do with it? Think about the last time you were in a hotel; think about that tiny bottle of all-in-one shampoo and conditioner. Think about how convenient it was, how you reached for it, and how it did its job in the moment. Then remember how, in just an hour's time, you could have easily been mistaken for one of the Mötley Crüe front men. That's what *fine*'ll get you.

The question then remains: How did *fine* become indefinable? To understand this, one must trace the word back to its starting point. And for this peculiar specimen, things are tricky from the get-go. While each iteration of the modern-day *fine* has roots in ancient Latin, etymology reveals its multitudinous fate was preordained, having been born of not one but two independent terms: *finire* and *finis*. From the outset, records defined *finire* as an act—"to finish." Over the centuries of adoptions and adaptions—Old French, Middle English—some letters fell away and some were restored, but the meaning remained constant. That is, until contemporary English saw fit to separate the two, establishing *finish* as a word in its own right and leaving *fine* as an abstract term, open to interpretation. By a similar process, France likewise appropriated the Latin *finis* ("end"), holding on to its original meaning while confusing matters—in a way only the French could—through the interpolation of a second: "payment." Seeking to simplify, Middle English ditched the old and kept the new, leading to the "license and registration" precursor to the *fine* we abhor to this day. Overall, it was the Italians who managed to preserve the purest sense of the term, evolving *finis* to the *fine* whose black-and-white text would announce the close of every melodramatic art house feature and overambitious student film everyone's been dragged to at some point in their life.

Stripped to its studs, clutter cleaned away, the word can be seen the way it was meant from the first, the way the architects had outlined. With nothing left to trick the eye, epiphany comes as a realization that, despite my efforts to exploit *fine* for purposes of deflection, I had been unintentionally speaking the truth all along. From its germ, the expression has been emblematic of a conclusion. And true to form, its users apply it in order to hasten a finish. For me, I was finished talking about death, trying to answer questions about it, trying to explain it. I was done living in its contours, being defined by it. So, I sought to end the conversation in the most efficient way possible. But, like its present-day understanding, the privilege was not without its price. Each deferral was an ignorance, an act of self-sanction with penalties that only compounded with interest. Much as I'd like to take some helping of credit for my accidental honesty, it doesn't forgive the debt. For one, because the objective was always to lie. For another, because the receiver still wound up misled. Yes, by downright coincidence, I'd maintained the authenticity of the word, but not a soul read it that way. To claim any sort of victory would be delusion.

Fooling yourself is much more straightforward when you choose not to examine all the facts. That way, when things go belly-up, you weren't flagrant, just uneducated. I, on the other hand, have done the exploration, the fact-finding. I've exposed my own verbal misappropriation, of which I was both the victim and the sole conspirator. Believing I was performing some service by not unloading upon my confidants, I swept past the topic, having dismissed their attentiveness as the child of formality and not of good faith. Not only did that reveal me as an individual short of trust, it left me as one heavy with discomfort. To continue then, with everything I knew, would make me a flat-out hypocrite. As a proponent of transparency, especially one who stands in opposition to the demonization of feeling, I can't—I won't—use the word anymore. Not until everyone agrees on what it means. Until that day arrives, let me tell you how I am.

I'm not over it. I won't ever be. I won't sanction the fact that my father got a raw deal. I can't stomach the likelihood that his own country killed him. I don't understand how a government can send soldiers to a warzone dusted with pesticides knowing their own men would breathe them in. I fail to see how something meant to kill trees and expose snipers could be harmless to the boys making bathtubs out of its emptied barrels. I reject the excuse that no one could have known or that it was all some big cover-up; no admission of negligence or duplicity will undo the damage. I abhor that my father fulfilled his part of the bargain and got cancer for it. I'm sickened at the thought that, somewhere, in some broken-down government office, a nameless, faceless peon had to distill his worth down to a dollar amount. I hate that blood money is no longer a foreign concept. I want them to know that a monthly check is not an absolution. I need to come to terms with what is out of my control. I'm getting better. But I'm never fine. I'm acknowledging the fact that I'll never be done talking about this. I accept that anyone I allow close to me will eventually ask about my father, and I will have to tell them. I'm also fortunate that there's much more to discuss about his life than there is about his death. I choose to see it as a way of keeping him around. I'm astounded at what I've been through, body and mind. I'm equally shocked that, after it all, most of the days are good. I still hope for a way to conceal the path that no one else becomes its unwilling traveler. I grasp how naïve that sounds. I promise to never see a cure as "too late," and to celebrate every life it saves. I concede that it will still be painful. I'm making peace with that. But I'm never fine. I'm grateful for the weird little joys that make waking up exciting. I enthuse over a blue energy drink, a short run on a fall morning, and the fat, little beagles with their fat, little butts at the park more than is probably necessary. I recognize that, on the ride there, I probably flipped off someone's elder for driving too slow. I'm immediately remorseful if it helps. I'm working on separating criticism from ambition and maybe, just maybe, taking it easy on myself once or twice a century. I wish I could believe those who offer praise, but fear of conceit has me firmly by the haunches. I'd rather take the business end of a horsewhip than a compliment. I will say I want to connect with people, and then hide behind my couch when the doorbell rings. I'm sure whoever's out there is selling something and I can't bear to turn them down. I'd like to introduce my younger self who yearned for love to the cynic whose system handles affection like an organ transplant. I think there's a whole person somewhere in-between. I'm lonely one day and self-contained the next. But I'm never fine. I can't stand still, yet I wish everything would stop moving so fast. I keep my blinds closed and enjoy a dark room. I write by candlelight. I buy too many candles, yes, but my electric bills are twenty dollars and I'm definitely surviving the first few waves of zombies. I adore the way the skin buzzes after a day spent out in the sun. I'm cool as anything in a crowded city or a bar yet my chest starts to tighten if I'm in the grocery store for more than fifteen minutes. I begrudge the fact that I'll always be some level of anxious. I seize up whenever my mother so much as coughs. I check her calendar for doctor names I don't recognize, yet I'm somehow amazed when she resists if I ask about them. I accept the waves because I know how; with each one that passes, I get better at riding them. I miss piloting jungle boats down artificial rivers under a night sky of controlled explosions. The exhaustion, the simplicity of it all. I blame myself for frittering Dad's last good years by indulging some childish lark, even if there was no possible way to have foreseen. I called him every day. I felt his warmth and support. I realize the guilt is one-sided and entirely of my own making. I'm trying to ease up. But I'm never fine. I laugh again, more than I'd ever thought feasible. I laugh like him, big and high-pitched. I do a lot of things like him: eat his weird foods, listen to forties jazz. I even have his squared-off toes. I've begun to wonder if a piece of him didn't latch onto me before he left. I pray it was the adhesive piece, the piece that glued the family together by force of sheer existence. I aim to be glue, but I feel I'm more like Sticky Tack. I count on the good, no matter how much it makes me sound like a T.J. Maxx affirmation. I prepare for the bad because I have to cover all the angles. I eagerly anticipate a two o'clock coffee run because depending on work, it might be the one time a day I get to step outside. I drink so much coffee my moisturizer needs moisturizer. I used to drink more, but then friends started forwarding me articles about kidney failure. I meander between thoughts that are seemingly unrelated and take far too much pleasure in mapping the tangent back to its bewildering jump off. I debate my own brand of weirdness: intriguing or screwy. I'm going to leave that one alone. But I'm never fine. I'm a walking refutation. I turn down invites to barbecues because small talk is crippling but watch me Uber into some dingy corner of San Jose to split Pisco Sours in the living room of a Peruvian I met on Tinger the day prior. I'm unable to explain it. I suppose I prefer to do things that make me feel alive. I fancy the idea of being meaningful in a way that's noble and not contrived. I distrust those who fawn—them and their signature scent. I'm overly vigilant about the way I speak; meanwhile, my fear of ineloquence trips me up more than anything else. I play with humor when recollecting pain, not to mask it but because you either find the funny bits or lose yourself to the gloom. I'm rarely brief with a story. I dawdle on the details. I drive the point home, mostly because the point is drunk. I'm more honest with myself on the page than I am anywhere else. I'm indebted to the writing, for the collectedness that comes with a finished piece, for providing better therapy than any prescription or couch session ever could. But I'm never fine. I share work with my best friend, fight to trust her approval, fret when she says, "That was a punishing read." I'm uncertain as to what she refers, my prowess or my life. I'm only bothered by one of those options. I'm confident you can figure out which. I *am* certain that, by now, a good number of you figure I'm a basket case. I surmise that, if you've made it this far, it is by the grace of charm or dismay. I decline to get caught up in the particulars. I'm just trying to tell you how I am. I told you I would. I'm a man of my word. I could go on, but I'll leave it there. I'm good for now. But I'm never fine.

To be sure, I'm not lobbying for sticking a finger down the emotional gullet at the slightest provocation. That'd strip the crust off anyone's warm rolls. What I am suggesting is that we start suspecting this word *fine*. That we pay closer attention to the users among us, with a particular focus on those who deploy it at high frequency. This is not an invitation to pry or to prod. Do that and you'll find yourself headed home with a lifetime supply of less ambiguous four-letter words. This is an imperative to be present, to take extra care. Every *fine* is a trip wire. Step with intent. To circumvent the minefield is to neglect the person who somehow sleepwalked their way to its center. No one's asking to be carried out. Just stay nearby. Talk about anything. Anything else. Anything but the ground. The distraction could be lifesaving.

As for myself, I can't say for certain if I've managed my way free of hazardous terrain. The moment I stop minding my stride is the moment something blows up in my face. I like that. For once, I've painted myself into a corner and I'm in no rush to leave. By coming out so unapologetically against an expression, I'm bound by my own declaration of independence. Attention must always be paid. Dialogue deserves contemplation. Words have to mean something. It doesn't mean unloading my dirty laundry on those with a predilection for pressing. It means being conscientious about my word choice—choosing terms that do justice to my frame of mind without soliciting a symposium. For too long, I conflated honesty with an obligation to full disclosure, forgetting that to be succinct is not to be disrespectful. No one's ever faulted me for feeling shitty and not wanting to talk about it. At the very least, the admittance endorses anyone at the table struggling with their own sense of *fineness*. At most, it authorizes the dispensation of their grievances—grievances I'm happy to drown in.

It must sound like sadomasochism, this relief that can be extracted from the ordeals of others. But, let me be clear, my relief comes in recognizing that anyone willing to discuss it is actively attempting to work it out. To talk about pain, however briefly, is to acknowledge not only that things have been better, but also that we expect the pendulum to swing back that way. To that end, I hope no one I know is *fine*. I hope no one reading this is *fine*. Much as I wish you cotton candy clouds and a life written by Nancy Meyers, I understand that there will be heartache and how, if that is the way of things, this might come across as insensitive. Before you burn this, however, I ask you to remember the last time you felt truly happy. Remember what it was exactly that brought about such feeling, how lucky you were to have something wondrous to misplace, how the joy would be meaningless without the necessary pain. Now, remember the last time things felt as hopeless as they might in this very moment. Then remember how it only became a memory because, in order to do so, it must—in some way—come to an end.

The Simple Guide to Redefinition in Oslo, Norway

There are a thousand and one reasons why someone might find themselves sitting at the airport, alone, holding a round-trip plane ticket to Oslo in the dead of February. Perhaps the combination of an immediate need for vacation and the untimely lack of a summer body made the thought of a warm island and a sea of spray-tanned six-packs less than desirable. Perhaps you have a travel agent with a really sadistic sense of humor. Or, perhaps, you've spent the last eighteen months floundering in the wake of something lost; a loss so complete, its forcible punch knocked a singularity into millions of nano-sized rivulets that slip endlessly through your fingers.

Whatever your reasons may be, dear reader, fear not. This trusty guide will be all the company you need on your solo sojourn through the staggering, salient vistas of your existential crisis in the heart of Scandinavia.

Now before you lose your nerve, pop a Xanax, blow up that blue fleece neck pillow that you'll never use again, and let's get started!

JFK International Airport, Terminal 1
(Lat. 40.741895, Long. -73.989308)

When it comes to travel, I happen to be of a singular breed. While the prospect of international adventure is a fail-safe way to spur excitement within, it's the charmless fellow excursionists that I normally can do without. In fact, the idea of hurtling through the stratosphere in the company of hundreds of onerous, odorous strangers fills me with a zeal so melodic it makes a dial tone sound like Diplo.

Now if you find yourself a member of that same category—and you also happen to be a passenger on Nordic Air—my first suggestion is to pay the additional fee and spring for a seat selection prior to boarding. (Travel tip: an easy way to secure a little extra personal space is to pay close attention to the large swath of seats that stretches down the middle of the aircraft). Your best chance at a moderately comfortable bubble is to bookend an empty middle seat in a row where the opposite aisle has already been nabbed. Nobody wants to be marooned in the smellscape often found between two strangers of unknown hygienic disposition.

Once comfortably nestled and after your third in-flight serving of Great Britain All-British Cheddar Crackers, you may be tempted to break character and actually talk to someone. Let's be frank here. You've undoubtedly spent the last couple of hours staking out your row companion and have concluded that she's a pleasantly tolerable girl of about the same age. So go ahead, reach into your knapsack and offer her a handful of Luden's to help her fight off that persistent cough she insists is caused by the airplane's "dry air." Within minutes, you'll come to learn that her name is

Sofie and that she and her friend Andra (sitting just across from her) are embarking on a whirlwind spring-break tour that will take them through Oslo, Barcelona, and Mallorca.

Their initial impression being favorable, go against your proclivity towards introversion and make plans to meet up with them tomorrow, especially since it seems the three of you are booked on the same countryside train tour. While normally, a polite flight conversation would not turn into something tangible, you can take comfort in the fact that, should they later reveal themselves to be subpar travel companions, their three-day stay in Norway comes with its own built-in escape hatch.

**Scandic Holberg, Holbergs Plass 1
(Lat. 59.91960599999999, Long. 10.734424499999932)**

After making plans to meet up with Sofie and Andra at Central Station tomorrow morning, board a train that will whisk you away from Gardermoen Airport and into the hustle and bustle of the capital city.

Your hotel, the Scandic Holberg, sits in a four-way intersection just a stone's throw from the harbor promenade. Once checked in, you may wish to unwrap the stark white comforter on the bed that housekeeping has folded into something resembling a crêpe and spread yourself across like cloudberry preserves. This is the perfect location for you to lie, motionless, staring at the ceiling for thirty to forty-five minutes as you contemplate how you've possibly managed to make it here while simultaneously eluding death and/or serious injury.

Time spent here should be brief, however, as you'll soon notice that the weighted heft of your life in the States seems to have dissipated while a chorus of alien blips from the crossing signals at the corner wafts through your window and beckons you outdoors. And so, after scrubbing off your surface coating of airport grime in a translucent shower tube straight off the USS Enterprise, pull a wool-knit beanie around your wet locks and head out into the world.

**Akershus Fortress, 0150 Oslo
(Lat. 59.90758599999999, Long. 10.737084099999947)**

If it's perspective you seek, look no further than Akershus Fortress, located just adjacent to the marina at the very end of the headland. This medieval castle, built in the 1300s, was once a stronghold for protection and has since been modernized into a royal residence open to the public. Lucky for you, guided tours are only offered in the summer, so you'll find yourself free to roam the setts stone pathways and run your fingers over the red brick façade which time and nature have weathered into a smoothed-out shell.

As you wander the narrow, dimly lit corridors past dungeons and servants' quarters, a familiar sense of suffocation may begin to twirl its fingers around your collar but press on. Press on through the kitchens, where a delightful blonde woman in a ruffled, period folk costume will quickly stub out her cigarette and proceed to mime the scrubbing of pots in a basin with no water. Press on through the ornate bedrooms and the empty expanse of the main dining hall as the walls carry the echo of your footsteps across the Nordic pine. Press on, up the stairs and through the chapel. Press on, past the gargantuan tapestries that dance in the wind. Press on, climbing the winding steps of the watchtower, higher and higher feeling lighter and lighter, until you push through the wrought iron gate and come face to face with the Oslo fjord—thick, sheen, and spreading itself so far you'd swear it must spill over the edge of the earth.

It is here that you should find a restful spot and sit. Dangle your legs over the buttress, close your eyes, and crane your neck toward the sky. Take a breath, the deepest breath you've ever taken. Let the Arctic air fill your lungs until icicles form and then (and only then) release it, and with it, everything that's come before. Now, open your eyes and look out and watch as a sherbet sun is swallowed away, and the slate is wiped clean. And when you're ready, fill your pens with the inky, black Viking water and start writing a new story.

Oslo Sentralstasjon, Jernbanetorget 1 (Lat. 59.91109599999999, Long. 10.752457400000026)

On Day Two, you're on a journey toward clarity. But pack light because it waits for you just a train, another train, a boat, a bus, and yet another train ride away.

Foggy-eyed and short of sleep, you will wake up somehow invigorated and take the stairs two at a time as you stop at the hotel's free breakfast buffet. After quickly spreading a delicious brown mystery cheese across a thickly sliced cinderblock labeled "Fjellbrød," you're out the door and into the midnight blue morning.

Follow the signs for Oslo Sentralstasjon as they take you down the main drag, freshly glossed with harbor mist.

Upon entering the main terminal, you'll quickly find yourself lost in a sea of skis, cinched tightly to the backpacks of hundreds of mountain riders up before the dawn. It is at this point that, much like a meerkat peeking over the thick African bush, you must walk and jump until you spot Sofie and Andra waiting for you by the entrance of the Norway tourism office. Minutes later, after safely boarding your first train of the day, watch as the city melts into an indiscernible white wilderness punctuated by the intermittent chalet that sits just at the edge of the tracks.

While, for some, the lack of audible and visual stimulation may prove unnerving, for you the effect will be quite the opposite. In fact, the further you ride into the margins of civilization, the further you disconnect yourself from your former sense of self. Each densely packed snowbank is a fresh sheet of loose leaf just waiting to be marked up. But don't feel pressure to begin when you're not ready. Don't force a connection. Instead, step back and listen. Let the story reveal itself to you.

Think you know what it's like to teeter on the edge of existence? Well, in Myrdal, you'll board the Flåmsbana wooden railway and slowly descend as the train hugs the treacherous cliffsides, passing under the cascades of frozen waterfalls, and sliding through black holes that have been blown through mountains with persistence and dynamite. Use the short break in Flåm to grab lunch by the waterside before the next leg of the journey begins. (Author's note: The Toget Café, built in a defunct railway car, serves a sun-ripened salmon that'll melt on your tongue like a creamsicle, restoring a sense of taste you've since thought long dead).

Next, you'll board a ferry across the glassy Sognefjord where simple fishing villages of ten to eleven houses sit at the foot of the mountains and beckon you with unspoken promises of a simple, unburdened life. In an effort to share the moment, run into the boat's main cabin to find Sofie and Andra passed out on adjoining benches, still likely hungover from the night before. After a light attempt to jostle them awake elicits a groggy, "What, is it just more houses and shit?" it's best to return outside whilst appreciating the fact that one man's catharsis can be rather unremarkable in the eyes of a stranger.

In Voss, a bus will carry you and your cohorts through the green countryside and past stream after innumerable stream, each one flowing with water so crystal and pure the first sip requires a set of godparents. But your thirst will be quenched only as you arrive in stately Bergen, your final stop on this cross-country day tour. At the Pingvinen restaurant, you can cap a long day with your two new friends over fish pie and a round of ice-cold Hansa beer. And before you know it, you'll be clambering into the top bunk of your private sleeper cabin as an overnight train launches you expressly back toward Oslo.

It's at this point—as you slide under the covers—that fatigue will set in like a big bear hug. But, for the first time in what seems like forever, it's not the familiar, dense slog of stress, insecurity, and futility. Rather, this is a body burdened only with the tonnage of a day vigorously spent plugging into the undercurrent of life, and for once, not talking over it.

I'M NEVER FINE

Wayne's Coffee, Lille Stranden 4
(Lat. 59.9082454, Long. 10.723248799999965)

After yesterday's expedition, you may be looking for a quiet corner to decompress and soak up some local flavor. Well, look no further than Wayne's Coffee, a delightful regional chain with a beverage selection rivaling that of Starbucks, but with a noticeable lack of condescension.

As you bungle your way through an enthusiastic "Hallo!" and fail to convince the barista that you're a local, they'll answer with a polite nod and proceed to pour you a tea so hot it should require a good slather of SPF. Fortunately, the gorgeous, chunky blue mug that holds your drink (available to take home for 7kr) could easily transport molten lava without once registering the slightest hint of temperature on its outer core. Be sure to take great care when attempting your first sip, however, as its deceiving heft could easily leave the overzealous drinker with a black eye.

Around your third or fourth swig of Ridgeback Blend, you may notice that no one in the café is paying much mind to you...or any at all, really. There are no knowing glances, no flashes of side-eye. You will catch no one staring with pity before quickly darting their gaze in a new direction once they realize they've been caught. In fact, you could very likely mount the table on all fours and lap at your tea like a Labrador without a single patron even flinching. It's here that you realize how, in this glorious place, you are remarkably unwritten. To these fishers and swishers, you are not the sad creature still smarting from the sting of one of life's leg-hold traps. You are not a pitiful soul in need of an equally pitiful platitude.

You, dear reader, are the nameless American tourist of the day. And while the natives tolerate your presence, they couldn't possibly care less to know anything more about you.

So, bask in their cold, Scandinavian indifference. Flourish in their frigid disinterest. Place your past and present situation into the proper context, put the numbing agent back beneath its child-proof seal, and resist the urge to kiss each and every one of them on their thin, dispassionate lips.

Never once has meaning so little meant so much.

Nordmarka Forest, Skogbrynet (Lat. 59.9178235, Long. 10.644323799999938)

High atop the mountains, on the outskirts of the city, sits a magical wintry "reset" button known as Nordmarka Forest. A quick thirty-minute trip on the number 13 metro will pull you well above sea level before cutting through the clouds and dropping you off in a lush, powdery landscape that could've been painted by Bob Ross himself. (Author's note: There's a good chance you've been watching a little too much *Beauty is Everywhere*.)

As you step into the chasm of white and green splotches, a dozen arrowed signs will point the way to all manner of hiking trails varying in length and degree of difficulty. Though the color-coded path markers on the tree trunks serve as a delightful safety net for the more neurotic hikers, I suggest taking this golden opportunity to explore for exploration's sake. Don't worry about getting lost. It's already happened. You're on a remote mountain abutting a strange city in a foreign country, and even the slightest inkling that you have command of your surroundings is a work of pure comedy. No, today is the day that you can be adrift because you made it so, and not because of some uncontrollable cosmic disengagement.

So, slip into the woods like the raw nerve you are and walk, untethered; a chewed-up piece of food snaking through the piney bristles. Climb over boulders and fallen logs while following the delicate footprints local wildlife have left in the freshly fallen powder. Follow the earth as it curves upward beneath your feet and leads you further and further into the fraying thicket that blots out the sky until all that hangs above you is a web of spiny green needles. In that absence of light, the snow somehow glows. Brighter, youthful, and recently lain, it gives way under your poorly insulated pair of Vans. The soft earth wraps its luscious lips around your ankles, and as soon as it gets a taste, it wants the rest.

Each step becomes a little more of a struggle than the one before as you sink into the ground. First it takes your calves, and then it goes for your knees. Your gait spreads and strides lengthen to maintain your pace, though it seems like it takes forever for your feet finally to land. You push through, though, as if toward some unseen finish line. But, after a short while, you'll find yourself waist-deep and breathless as sopping-wet canvas shoes render your feet numb and useless.

There's something in that numbness that's intriguing, however. For someone who's never known an unmagnified feeling, the chance to feel nothing is positively alluring. And so, with that, everything goes. Hat, gloves, shirt, jacket, and pants are in the wind and there you are, a mess of flesh and stretchy boxer briefs splayed on the snow as if it were a bearskin rug. Ball it up in your fists and run it through your hair. Wash your face with it. Let it seep into your pores and run through your veins until a familiar tingle overtakes you and your temperature finally matches your demeanor.

The static nothingness is almost pleasant, and for an instant, you might even feel as if you've got life all figured out. But, sooner or later, something always pierces through the white noise. And in this case, it's a searing burn that launches you up off the ground. It's as if, all at once, you've caught fire. Red, blotchy skin and swollen hands throb as you reach for your garments and strain through agony to pull them on. Piece by piece you put yourself back together, begin the thawing process, and start to work your way back. Much to your surprise, though, the return trip is not nearly as arduous since the deep prints you made on the way out provide for much firmer footing as you descend.

It's right about here where you'll begin to realize that no matter what unpredictably disastrous turn life has taken, you've figured out a way to traverse it. And more often than not, there's been some serious good that followed the bad.

It's an attractive notion, to no longer fall slave to feeling. But no partial freedom exists in it. It can only be accomplished completely. To give up anguish, you must also give up passion. To lose fear, you must also sacrifice confidence. To banish apathy you must also dismiss sympathy. And abiding by those terms, life would be nothing more than a fresh hell.

So what if you have to slip into the forest, skin-to-the-wind, to figure that out? There's no shame in the unconventional as long as the ends justify the process.

Remember, as the great Bob Ross once said: "Trees cover up a multitude of sins."

Hovedøya, Gressholmen
(Lat. 59.894189722105466, Long. 10.734672546386719)

If you've managed to regain all (or at least most) of the feeling in your extremities, I highly recommend beginning the last day of your Norwegian traipse on the island of Hovedøya. Located just off the coast of the mainland, this tiny floating lawn patch is easily accessible by boats that leave Aker Brygge on the half hour.

The island features some of the best locations for swimmers, not that you'll find any on this balmy twenty-seven-degree day. What you will find, however, is the chance to catch some sun (and maybe a little enlightenment) on the first bonafide clear day since you've been here. Stepping off of the water taxi, you'll notice most of the locals removing their shoes, and not wanting to seem like the outsider, it would be wise to follow suit. Be sure to build in a little extra time for your walk through the nature preserve as you'll soon catch yourself stopping every few minutes to wiggle the soft blades of grass between your toes.

On the North side of the island you can wander through the ruins of a twelfth-century Cistercian monastery that has since been turned into a picnic ground. Enjoy the euphonious crackle as city residents and their families gather in huddles and set up their portable griddles to get a good sear on their bacon-wrapped frankfurters. Legions of local fowl, some strange hybrid between a crow and a raven that you've decided to dub "cravens," gather in in the trees above and wait fervently for the chance to pounce on any morsel that hits the ground. Underneath their watchful eyes, you can meander down towards the shoreline and pop by the à la carte café, treating yourself to whatever the hell a kokosboller is. (Author's note: Literally meaning "coconut bun," the kokosboller is a rich, marshmallowy snack that is dipped in chocolate and rolled in shredded coconut).

Now as you begin to make quick wreckage of the ball of crunch and fluff in your hands, the combination of your sweet delicacy with the handholding couples and families romping wildly may start to feel just a bit too saccharine for you. But, before your typical cynicism begins to seep, take a moment. Take a moment to figure out where this is all coming from. Maybe—just maybe—your annoyance is not with those around you, but with yourself. Maybe, for some time now, you've been much like this island, listing at a safe distance just offshore but close enough where you can still keep an eye on things and dispense judgments. Maybe you've been a little too dismissive of those who can't comprehend something that's ultimately incomprehensible. Maybe you don't need them to comprehend it. Maybe just being there is enough.

Also, maybe you need to eat one of those bacon-wrapped hotdogs.

Restaurant Fauna, Solligata 2 (Lat. 59.9143494, Long. 10.72060650000003)

Well, here you are on your final night in Oslo! If you've managed to budget well and avoid purchasing your usual hoard of mementos—save for a couple of wooden Viking figures and one of those Wayne's Coffee mugs that'll surely send your luggage over the weight limit—then you should find yourself with a healthy surplus of kroner.

While the grown-up option would be to exchange your remainder for U.S. currency at the airport tomorrow and return home somewhat healthily in the black, I certainly don't see any grown-ups here, do you? Good. Now that we have that settled, abandon your packing and head to the hotel front desk to score a last-minute reservation at Oslo's Michelin-starred Restaurant Fauna. A hop, skip, and a sport coat later, you'll be greeted and seated, sipping chilled water farmed from the Arctic Circle and skimming the menu insert about Bjørn, Jo, and Anne and their mission to "highlight the relationship between raw nature, produce, and our cultural history."

The décor is simple Scandinavian, white brick walls with dark wooden accents and dim, recessed lighting to create a calm—if not slightly stiff—atmosphere. Your server Ingeborg (she didn't introduce herself but you've decided to call her Ingeborg) stops by now and again to deliver large dishes containing small morsels that she takes great pains to explain. White fish roe with rösti, caviar with blinis, paper-thin ribbons of venison over baby potatoes; they all swim elegantly in puddles of pastels at the bottom of the bowl, tiny galaxies of food that are gone in three bites. Each one bursting with a constellation of new ideas and possibilities.

In just a handful of days, you've managed to see yourself more clearly than you have in years. Maybe ever. Not just the you now or the you that came before, but the boundless versions of you that wait to exist. Whereas you once found yourself stuck in a never-ending loop on the same broken record, it never once occurred to you what could happen if you just tried another song. Yes, it might not repair the scratch, but it could very well change your tune. If the next track doesn't speak to you, then skip ahead once more. Or buy a whole new damn record.

Take a second. Think of all you've seen in such a short amount of time. Think of all you thought there was to see and how marvelously wrong you were. Think of what one tiny corner of the world revealed and how many hundreds of thousands of corners with hundreds of thousands of revelations remain unexplored. Think of Whitman when he wrote "I am large, I contain multitudes."

And as you sit there devouring the universe, let it fill you. Know that it's still expanding. Every day, making something new. Every hour, rewriting itself. Every minute, stretching the space between. Every second, moving you forward.

Endnotes

1. "How To Eat After a Whipple Procedure."Let's Win! Pancreatic Cancer, 1 May 2017, www.letswinpc.org/managing-pancreatic-cancer/2017/05/01/how-to-eat-after-whipple-procedure/. Accessed 20 May 2019.
2. Rashid, Lewis and Velanovich, Vic. "Symptomatic change and gastrointestinal quality of life after pancreatectomy."HPB Oxford, 14 Jan. 2012. www.ncbi.nlm.nih.gov/pmc/articles/PMC3252985/. Accessed 20 May 2019.
3. Ahmed, Kasim, Darzi, Ara, Penney, Nicholas and Purkayastha, Sanjay. "Taste Changes after Bariatric Surgery: a Systematic Review." Obesity Surgery, 31 Jul, 2018. www.ncbi.nlm.nih.gov/pmc/articles/PMC6153588/. Accessed 20 May 2019.
4. "FOLFIRINOX treatment for pancreatic cancer."Pancreatic Cancer Action.www.pancreaticcanceraction.org/about-pancreatic-cancer/treatment/chemotherapy/chemotherapy-drugs-for-pancreatic-cancer/folfirinox/. Accessed 3 June 2019.
5. Ahmed, Kasim, Darzi, Ara, Penney, Nicholas and Purkayastha, Sanjay.
6. "How To Eat After a Whipple Procedure."
7. "Taste Changes – Managing Side Effects."Chemocare.com. www.chemocare.com/chemotherapy/side-effects/taste-changes.aspx. Accessed 20 May 2019.
8. "Fluorouracil – Drug Information." Chemocare.com. www.chemocare.com/chemotherapy/drug-info/fluorouracil.aspx. Accessed 3 June 2019.
9. "Leucovorin – Chemotherapy Drugs." Chemocare.com. www.chemocare.com/chemotherapy/drug-info/Leucovorin.aspx. Accessed 3 June 2019.
10. "CPT-11 – Drug Information." Chemocare.com. www.chemocare.com/chemotherapy/drug-info/cpt-11.aspx. Accessed 3 June 2019.
11. "Oxaliplatin – Chemotherapy Drugs." Chemocare.com. www.chemocare.com/chemotherapy/drug-info/Oxaliplatin.aspx. Accessed 3 June 2019.
12. "Gemcitabine – Chemotherapy Drugs." Chemocare.com. www.chemocare.com/chemotherapy/drug-info/gemcitabine.aspx. Accessed 29 Aug. 2019.

Acknowledgments

"Death, the Moon,& Dry-Rubbed Steak" first appeared in *Still: The Journal* (Winter 2018).

"The Simple Guide to Redefinition in Oslo, Norway" first appeared in *Fearsome Critters* (Volume 1).

"Little Murders" first appeared in *Cleaning Up Glitter* (Volume 1, Issue 2).

The original version of "The Space Between the Tenses" appeared in the tenth anniversary issue of *Stoneboat Literary Journal* (January 2020).

"Wading Toward Willamette" first appeared in *The Hopper* (February 2020).

"Nice, Clean Margins" first appeared in *Occulum Journal* (November 2022).

The author wishes to thank these publications for their appreciation and concurrence for the

aforementioned pieces to be included in this collection.

In addition, the author wishes to express immense gratitude to any artists or individuals who influenced—directly or indirectly—this writing process, including: Cheryl, Joan, Phoebe, Bill, Michael, Peter, Mike, William, John, Lia, David, Eleni, Nora, and Alanis. Special thanks to my unofficial focus group: E.R., K.B., P.M., and J.G.Z. Intensely special thanks to Mom for providing access to her Pulitzer-caliber journals, for her generosity in resources, her belief when mine was lacking, her strength (whatever slight percentage I inherited), and chiefly, for giving me the space I needed to write this.

Sincerest appreciations are offered to the faculty and staff of the UTEP Creative Writing Department, and above all, my thesis committee. To Liz Scheid for uniting the words "lyric" and "essay" together in a manner most abrupt and life-altering. To Tim Hernandez, the exemplification of how to gather a story. And without question, to Dr. Nelson Cardenas, for indulging my calls and copious emails, for his thoughts and his challenges, and for demanding that I quit apologizing.

Finally, much love to the good people at Starbucks for keeping me in caffeine and napkins for the last two years.

Vine Leaves Press

Enjoyed this book?
Go to *vineleavespress.com* to find more.
Subscribe to our newsletter: